THE OUTLAW CHRIST

ALSO FROM JOHN F. DEANE

Achill: The Island, Currach Books, 2018

Give Dust a Tongue: A Faith & Poetry Memoir, Columba Books, 2015

The Works of Love: Incarnation, Ecology & Poetry, Columba Books, 2010

ALSO CONTRIBUTED ON:

Edge of Light, with photographs by Sean Cannon, Currach Books, 2019

Performing the Word: Festschrift for Ronan Drury, edited by Enda McDonagh, Columba Books, 2015

Beauty, Truth & Love, edited by Patrick Hannon & Eugene Duffy, Columba Books, 2009

THE OUTLAW CHRIST

THE RESPONSE, IN POETRY, TO THE QUESTION JESUS ASKED:
WHO DO YOU SAY THAT I AM?

JOHN F. DEANE

columba
BOOKS

First published in 2020 by

23 Merrion Square North
Dublin 2, Ireland
www.columba.ie

Copyright © 2020 John F. Deane
All rights reserved. Without limiting the rights under copyright reserved alone, no part of this publication may be reproduced, stored in or introduced into a retrieval system, or transmitted, in any form or by any means (electronic, mechanical, photocopying, recording or otherwise) without the prior written permission of both the copyright owner and the above publisher of the book.

ISBN: 978-1-78218-366-2

Set in Adobe Garamond Pro 11/15
Cover and book design by Alexis Sierra | Columba Books
Printed by Jellyfish Solutions

*To Michael P. Murphy
and the students of Loyola University, Chicago*

CONTENTS

ACKNOWLEDGMENTS 9

FOREWORD: The Teilhard de Chardin Fellowship in Catholic Studies, Loyola University, Chicago 11

1. The Outlaw Christ 19
2. Christ the Centre: Incarnation 23
3. The Dream of the Rood – *The Warrior Hero* 27
4. Woefully Arrayed – *John Skelton* 37
5. Priest and Outlaw – *Robert Southwell* 41
6. Who, Lord? Me, Lord? – *Phineas Fletcher* 47
7. East or West: Jack Donne or John Donne? – *John Donne* 51
8. To Win a Kiss – *Robert Herrick* 87
9. Guilty of Dust – *George Herbert* 89
10. Dressed, and on my Way – *Henry Vaughan* 105
11. Such Great Felicity – *Thomas Traherne* 115
12. The Scribe Evangelist – *Christopher Smart* 133
13. The Very Voice of God – *John Clare* 137
14. The Queen of Calvary – *Emily Dickinson* 153
15. Becoming Jesus – *Gerard Manley Hopkins* 173
16. The Cost of Discipleship – *Dietrich Bonhoeffer* 193

17. Art's Neurosis – *R.S. Thomas* 199
18. Late End of the Middle Ages – *Simone Weil* 207
19. Demented Wrestler – *David Gascoyne* 217
20. O Ever Greater Christ – *Teilhard de Chardin* 227
21. The Functional Ward of a Chest Hospital – *Patrick Kavanagh* 235
22. The Emergent Christ – *Ilia Delio* 251
23. Our Tattered Flags – *Pádraig J. Daly* 257
24. The Zone of Timelessness – *James Harpur* 275
25. That Body whereof I am a Member – *John Donne* 289

APPENDIX 299
SELECT BIBLIOGRAPHY 313

ACKNOWLEDGMENTS

I am grateful to the following for permission to reproduce some of the poems in this book:

R.S. Thomas: R.S. Thomas, *Selected Poems: 1946-1968* (Bloodaxe Books, 1986) (www.bloodaxebooks.com) and R.S. Thomas, *Collected Later Poems: 1988-2000* (Bloodaxe Books, 2004) (www.bloodaxebooks.com);

David Gascoyne: David Gascoyne's 'September Sun', 'The Three Stars', 'Lacrymae' and 'Ecce Homo' are reproduced from his *New Collected Poems* (Enitharmon Press, 2014) by permission of Stephen Stuart-Smith, Gascoyne's publisher and literary executor;

Patrick Kavanagh: The poems of Patrick Kavanagh are quoted from *Collected Poems*, edited by Antoinette Quinn (Allen Lane, 2004), by kind permission of the Trustees of the Estate of the late Katherine B. Kavanagh, through the Jonathan Williams Literary Agency;

To the poet and The Dedalus Press for poems by Pádraig J. Daly (www.dedaluspress.com);

To the poet and Carcanet Press, UK for 'The White Silhouette' by James Harpur. This exquisite poem is published in the 2018 collection of poems by James Harpur, that takes this poem as the title for the collection: *The White Silhouette*. (www.carcanet.co.uk).

FOREWORD

The Teilhard de Chardin Fellowship in Catholic Studies, Loyola University, Chicago

Colossians Chapter 1
The Son is the image of the invisible God, the firstborn over all creation. For in him all things were created: things in heaven and on earth, visible and invisible, whether thrones or powers or rulers or authorities; all things have been created through him and for him. He is before all things, and in him all things hold together. And he is the head of the body, the church; he is the beginning and the firstborn from among the dead, so that in everything he might have the supremacy. For God was pleased to have all his fullness dwell in him, and through him to reconcile to himself all things, whether things on earth or things in heaven, by making peace through his blood, shed on the cross.

Walter Kasper
Jesus sent his disciples and the Church out into the world. Consequently, with its message of mercy, the Church cannot restrict its activities to the individual, personal sphere or the intra-ecclesial sphere. The Church, so to speak, cannot retire to the sacristy. It must be yeast, salt and light for the world and it must be engaged on behalf of the world.

St Paul, in the epistle to the Colossians, talks of Christ as 'the firstborn over all creation'. The whole of creation was brought about with Christ 'in mind', Christ the source, the sustenance and the end of all of creation. With our knowledge of evolution and the awareness we now have of the developing cosmos, the limitations of our earlier and more naïve faith regarding who Christ really is and what our lives are to be, have to be dramatically changed. This must be so, not merely in the personal response to Christ, but in the response of every church and community. Cardinal Kasper, in his great book *Mercy*, is aware of this; the Church must be 'engaged on behalf of the world', not bound up in its own position, power and regard. Poetry, too, the poetry of faith, must be renewed, reviewed and responsive to the new Christianity. How is all of this to come about?

Alongside our hope and our being in Christ, there is today a much-needed emphasis on ecology, and our faith in Christ plays its part in this essential task. Sean Freyne, in *Jesus, a Jewish Galilean*, writes of Jesus that 'the source of his wisdom would appear to have been a deep appreciation of the natural world and its processes reflected on in the light of the Hebrew Scriptures and the creator God of which they spoke' (p.48). It has been too easy over the centuries to dismiss the Christ from any hold over and love in the wonders and beauty of creation. I have always held that poetry ought to be engaged in this area, questioning ecology and Christian faith. I was introduced to a book in French, in the year 1965, a small book, that transformed my instinctive love of this earth into a new faith; that book was called *La messe sur le monde (Mass on the World)*, written by a Jesuit priest called Pierre Teilhard de Chardin, whose work in the early twenty-first century has become central to Christian belief and Christian action. It began:

> Since, o Lord, once more and no longer in the forests of the Aisne, but in the steppes of Asia, I have neither bread, nor wine nor altar, I will raise myself above the symbols to the pure majesty of the Real and will offer you, I your priest, on the altar of the whole Earth, the labour and the suffering of the world.

That day, the work of Teilhard de Chardin entered my soul and I began to be aware that creation is an ongoing process, not a seven-day wonder once created in its polished perfection and gradually ruined by human egotism. There entered my consciousness a belief that the original

FOREWORD

seeds and resourcefulness of this created world are the power behind and within this evolution. Our earth, offered up to God with its joys and sorrows, movements of chance, surprise, collapse, decay – all of it creates a drama in which we live and move and have our being, and the final act is very far from being written.

> My chalice and my paten are the depths of a soul wide open to all the forces which, in a moment now, will rise from every point of the globe and converge towards the Spirit – let them come to me, the memory and the mystical presence of those whom the light awakens into a new day!

As a form of preface, I must outline the wholly providential role that Teilhard de Chardin has played in my life. In 1965, I was a seminarian in Dublin with the Holy Ghost Fathers (now known as the Spiritans). I had joined the novitiate in 1961, the same year that a young man from Mauritius, Maurice Piat, also joined. He spoke little English; I had done French in secondary school, and I was assigned the task of teaching him English, not in formal classes, of course, but during recreation times, walks, games, events. Eventually we were both sent to University College Dublin, to get our BA degrees so that we would be able to teach in Holy Ghost colleges. We studied French and English language and literature together, cycling in and out from seminary to college almost every day, side by side. (My older brother Declan had joined the Jesuits and was then in France, studying philosophy.) On one fateful day, our French teacher did not show up and Maurice and I spent the class obediently waiting until the time was up to leave. The other students left at least half an hour earlier. At length, Maurice produced a little book he had received from somewhere abroad and he opened it up. *La messe sur le monde*. We read it slowly together, Maurice clarifying the French where I did not understand it. I was smitten.

Later, I discovered that the work of Teilhard de Chardin was regarded with great suspicion by the Vatican and therefore held back by his Jesuit superiors. The notion of evolution appeared to contradict the book of Genesis, the notion of God's creating hand, the idea of the fall of one couple in Eden and our inheritance of sin and guilt. Teilhard de Chardin's work was suppressed and very difficult to find. When I left the Holy Ghost Fathers to return to 'the world', I forgot about that work. Maurice Piat continued in the order, was ordained and returned to Mauritius as priest. We stayed in touch.

Many years later I came upon Teilhard de Chardin again. My brother Declan and I were talking about Gerard Manley Hopkins, that great Jesuit poet; Declan was now an ordained Jesuit priest and he told me there were some negative feelings about Hopkins, the man, the Jesuit … not about the poems. Then I simply mentioned another Jesuit, de Chardin, and Declan became enthusiastic. So I searched the bookshops once more and came across a tattered copy of *The Phenomenon of Man* (now much better translated as *The Human Phenomenon*) and found I was only vaguely able to grasp the thinking behind the book. I persisted and grew more and more convinced that this work was remarkably important.

My brother died, much too young, in 2010, in Pleasant Hill, California, and I went out to the funeral. I met many of Declan's good friends out there. One of these, Michael Murphy, wrote to me some time later, asking me if I would give a talk on Flannery O'Connor at a conference being organised in Dublin. He reminded me that he had been a parishioner of Declan's but had now moved to Chicago and was teaching in a Jesuit university in that city. Hesitantly, I agreed to talk on O'Connor. When, eventually, it appeared that I had done well at the talk, Michael and I became closer and corresponded, a very little. I was utterly surprised, then, when he wrote in October of 2015, inviting me to take up the Teilhard de Chardin Research Fellowship in Catholic Studies for the Fall Semester of 2016. I could not turn it down! Declan, Teilhard de Chardin, and now this. (One of my favourites among the stories Flannery O'Connor had written is 'Everything that Rises Must Converge', the title being an

FOREWORD

exact quotation from Teilhard de Chardin.) I had actually begun to try and discover a poetry that might work on the thinking of de Chardin and saw this as a great opportunity to take that work further. While in Loyola University in Chicago, I received an email from the Spiritans in Dublin telling me that my old friend and fellow-seminarian, Maurice Piat, was being made a cardinal by Pope Francis. My faith in a working Providence has never been so strong.

> I wish that at this moment my being might resonate to the deep murmur of the agitated world, this human Ocean whose immensity terrifies us and brings trouble into the hearts of even the most fervent believers. All that will increase in the World, during this day, all that will diminish – all that will die – this, Lord, is what I gather up into myself to offer them to you; this is the matter of my sacrifice, the only one that you desire.

I had been given, through the work of Teilhard de Chardin, a firm ideological basis for understanding the ongoing evolution of humankind. I began to see the entire cosmos as one process of becoming, a whole, a unity, what Teilhard called 'cosmogenesis'. A new faith began to dawn in me, a faith that this wonderful, difficult world, in all its beauty and all its grieving, is where the human spirit takes root and grows. Without the strong and healthy health-giving soil of this earth, how could the spirit ever come to maturity and to a real awareness of the majesty, power and love of the Creator? The philosopher, Plotinus, wrote, in the *Enneads* – and this as far back as AD 270!:

> Now to understand how life is imparted to the universe and to each individual, the soul must rise to the contemplation of The Soul, the soul of the world. The individual soul, though different from The Soul, is itself no slight thing. Yet it must become worthy of this contemplation: freed of the errors and seductions

to which other souls are subject, it must be quiet. Let us assume that quiet too is the body that wraps it round – the quiet earth, quiet the air and the sea, quiet the high heavens. Then picture the soul flowing into this tranquil mass from all sides, streaming into it, spreading through it until it is luminous. As the rays of the sun lighten and gild the blackest cloud, so The Soul by entering the body of the universe gives it life and immortality, the abject it lifts up. The universe, moved eternally by an intelligent Soul, becomes blessed and alive. The Soul's presence gives value to a universe that before was no more than an inert corpse, water and earth.

In his book of essays, *New Seeds of Contemplation* (New Directions, 1962), Thomas Merton wrote:

For in Christ God is made Man. In Him God and man are no longer separate, remote from one another, but inseparably one, unconfused and yet indivisible. Hence in Christ everything that is divine and supernatural becomes accessible on the human level to every man born of woman, to every son of Adam. What is divine has now become non-natural to us in Christ's love so that if we receive Him and are united with Him in friendship, He Who is at the same time God and our brother, grants us the divine life that is now able to be ours on the human level. We become sons of God by adoption in so far as we are like Christ and His brothers.

The words that stand out in focusing on the personal response to the person of Christ are 'friendship', 'our brother' and 'sons of God by adoption'. Hence the utter importance of shifting our awareness of Christ from the vague and distant to our closest friend and best ally in our living.

My study has been Christ; my living has been love and poetry. In Loyola University I found the opportunity to share the study of both to-

FOREWORD

gether. The course I gave was on Christ as seen through poetry in English, through the centuries to the present. Several of the students commented as we went along; some of them wrote poems. I include some of the responses here. Gradually, slowly, we came to the conclusion that Christ was best seen, in the world of poetry, as an outsider – one who disturbed the status quo. Gradually, too, we saw how evolution fit into the pattern of development of our awareness of Christ, and began to search for a new poetry alongside what may be considered as a new Christianity. Christ the outsider then, Christ the outlaw.

1

THE OUTLAW CHRIST

Luke, Chapter 22: *'Then Jesus asked them, "When I sent you without purse, bag or sandals, did you lack anything?" "Nothing," they answered. He said to them, "But now if you have a purse, take it, and also a bag; and if you don't have a sword, sell your cloak and buy one. It is written: – And he was numbered among the lawless; and I tell you that this must be fulfilled in me. Yes, what is written about me is reaching its fulfilment."'* Here it is: Jesus saw himself as outlaw, as one of 'the lawless'.

Karen Armstrong begins her book on St Paul by reminding her readers how Roman rule during the time of Christ expected 'an explosive time in the Holy City' during the Passover celebrations, Roman rule being bitterly resented. The rulers would have noted, 'Jesus of Nazareth's provocative entrance into the city a week earlier, riding on a donkey', and the crowd shouting out for liberation by this Son of David. After which Jesus had 'charged into the temple and overturned the money changers' tables, accusing them of making this sacred place a den of thieves' (Armstrong, p.1). Pilate, the governor of Judea, and Caiaphas, the high priest, would have seen such actions as those of a dangerous upstart.

Why outlaw? An outlaw is one declared to be outside the protection of the law. Legal protection is withdrawn and others are empowered to apprehend the outlaw. In Roman times, as a further form of exile, the law forbade the offering of water and fire to an outlaw; outlaws were required to leave Roman territory and lose their property. If they returned, they could be killed. In English common law, a 'writ of outlawry' declared that an outlaw was one who 'bears a wolfish head', thus equating a criminal with a wolf in the eyes of the law, allowing others to kill him on sight as if he were a dangerous, wild animal. Christ found himself at odds with some of the Jewish laws of his time, laws that were inimical to the welfare of the ordinary people, or that promoted some sections of society at the expense of others. Down the centuries, Christ and his rule of love have so often been misrepresented, ignored or challenged in so many different ways, that he has been treated as outside the law, or the laws, of these times. Dietrich Bonhoeffer, in his great lectures in Germany after Hitler had set up the concentration camps and Goering instituted the Gestapo in March and April of 1933, said: 'Christ goes through the ages, questioned anew, misunderstood anew, and again and again put to death.'

In chapter 1 of John's Gospel there is this: 'The law was given through Moses; grace and truth came through Jesus Christ.' Grace and truth are not so easily accepted and understood as the tablets of the law; whenever human laws come into conflict with grace and truth then Jesus is Outlaw, and grace and truth will meet with great difficulties.

In Matthew's Gospel, when John the Baptist was arrested, Jesus knew he, too, would be soon in trouble and he 'withdrew to Galilee'. The 'Beatitudes', as gathered together by Matthew, subvert much of what had been the Jewish emphases up to then – the meek inheriting the earth, the poor in spirit etc. And in Matthew 9 the Pharisees object to Jesus dining and mingling with the pariahs of society, the tax collectors, the 'sinners' and the prostitutes. Jesus found he had to stay outside the cities and towns, lest he be arrested, and he had to warn those he cured not to blab too much about what he had done for them; he would be in danger of arrest. Christ's presence on earth, the Incarnation, offered an alternative view of justice, of truth and of love, alternatives that have proved unacceptable to dictators, oligarchs, the powerful, the self-centred and the wealthy, not just in their persecution of Christ himself, but in the persecution of all those Christians down the centuries who stood for 'mercy and not sacrifice', taking the side of the poor, the outcast, and the downtrodden against their self-styled masters. Christ, the outlaw, the one who stood against, and who still stands against oppression, injustice and untruth. And we who follow Christ must be prepared to be seen as outlaws alongside him.

2

CHRIST THE CENTRE: INCARNATION

Jesus the Christ came to the River Jordan to be baptised by John. He was clearly not in need of the cleansing that this sacrament embodies in its washing of the catechumen in water. Christ had no sins to be purged, nor did he need the sign of new life symbolised by the washing. His response to John was: 'Let it be done this way now, so that all due deference be done to the law and tradition.' Christ had come, not to do things in half measure, not to be superficially human, choosing and picking amongst the traits of our difficult living, but to be truly one of us, in everything save sin. So he went down into the water, mercifully and fully one of us. His life and death and resurrection thus became wholly sufficient for our rebirth, for our imitation and for our sharing. He became the firstborn of all humanity, and we all were invited to be, with him, born again into God. We, too, were born to share in the life, death and rebirth of Christ – all of us, without exception.

St Paul, in Galatians, speaks: 'I live, now not I, but Christ lives in me.' God the Creator is intimately implicated in all of 'Nature'; as Hopkins wrote: 'The world is charged with the grandeur of God'. The word 'charged' must be taken in both its senses. Julian of Norwich, in spite of pain and the bleak despair suffered before invading barbarians, says that, 'I was taught by the grace of God that I should steadfastly keep me in the faith … and that at the same time I should take my stand on and earnestly believe in what our Lord shewed in this time – that "all manner of things shall be well".' In Galatians 3, Paul writes: 'For as many of you as were baptised into Christ have put on Christ. There is neither Jew nor Greek, there is neither slave nor free, there is no male and female, for you are all one in Christ Jesus.'

THE OUTLAW CHRIST

Where, then, do we find hope in our own time? Hope that peace is possible after all, that care of the environment will be seen as an obvious necessity and that the history of humankind may advance towards a more loving consciousness? Hope remains in Christ; reason and intelligence slow to a dead halt before the mystery, where heart, aided and abetted by will, takes over. And poems? The poet-prophet may concede to the Spirit the writing of the poem when it is a very good one; when there is failure, as there so often is, then the fault is the writer's; perhaps he or she is not permeable enough to the inspiration to allow the material its own track, instead of imposing his or her own will or mind upon it. The whole of creation is God's own work of art, God's handiwork, and he has handed it over to humankind to read it, to direct and shepherd it with love towards its goal: the bringing of the whole of creation into unity with Christ, its origin. This is a powerful image, and has not yet been well treated in poetry. It touches, of course, on the work of Teilhard de Chardin, and on the sense of humanity, and cosmos, as evolving together towards consciousness and unity. John Donne puts it this way:

> No man is an island, entire of itself; every man is a piece of the continent, a part of the main. If a clod be washed away by the sea, Europe is the less, as well as if a promontory were, as well as if a manor of thy friend's or of thine own were: any man's death diminishes me, because I am involved in mankind, and therefore never send to know for whom the bell tolls; it tolls for thee.

In his book *Exploring Catholic Theology*, Robert Barron outlines Bernard Lonergan's method towards 'right thinking'; this is based, of course, on the work of St Ignatius. Firstly: be attentive; then, be intelligent, be reasonable; and, finally, be responsible. I am not convinced about the intelligent and reasonable bit; that does not leave much room for grace, for inspiration, for prayer and for the Holy Spirit.

So, there are the refugees. Here is a passage from St Paul (Colossians 1): 'For in him were all things created, that are in heaven, and that are on earth, visible and invisible, whether they be thrones, or dominions, or principalities, or powers: all things were created through him, and for him: He is before all things, and in him all things are held together.' My response was thus:

Refugee

This, then, is the Christ.
They named him Alan, Alan Kurdi.
He is three years old.

Red T-shirt, short-sleeved;
navy-blue shorts, shoes navy-blue.
He has been washed ashore.
He lies, face down, on the wet shingles.

He is helpless; he has been helpless
all his life. He was obedient
in everything.

He was lifted aboard a crowded dinghy.
He had few words.
He is the Word.

In him all things were created.
And in him
all things hold together.

The world was deeply moved by this child's fate, and by the images shown worldwide on TV. He touched, though only for a short time, the imagination rather than mere reason or intellect. People were moved by reasons of the heart. The paradigm was the self-emptying of one who was in the form of God, of one not indifferent to the sufferings of our world; Jesus, being amongst us, touches our hearts by his very existence. And this touching of our innermost being makes us know, beyond intellect, that suffering and death are not intended to be our end; by his sharing of our human problems, voluntarily for our sake, he gives us reason to hope, to be indignant, to act. Faith precedes belief systems, and may well travel on after belief systems are lost. Christ is the outlaw on whom we depend for a faith beyond faith. Imagination is the stirring spirit of poetry. The Christian imagination has dealt with Christ, quizzically, trustingly, but only sometimes offering a personal response to the very real person of Jesus the Christ.

3

THE DREAM OF THE ROOD: THE WARRIOR HERO

To begin, then, where the words of John's Gospel begin – where else but the Beginning.

> In the beginning was the Word, and the Word was with God, and the Word was God. He was with God in the beginning. Through him all things were made; without him nothing was made that has been made. In him was life, and that life was the light of all humankind. The light shines in the darkness, and the darkness has not overcome it. (1:1–5)

The Word was God, the Word came into the world; he was life, and life was light. The whole of creation was made through the Word, with Christ Jesus 'in mind', and all things were created through Christ. Christ the source, the sustenance and the end of an evolving cosmos. Yet, John says, 'He was in the world, and though the world was made through him, the world did not recognise him ... Yet to all who did receive him, to those who believed in his name, he gave the right to become children of God – children born not of natural descent, nor of human decision or a husband's will, but born of God.' So, in the first century of our era, the Word of God lived amongst humans and showed who God really was: 'The word became flesh and made his dwelling among us. We have seen his glory, the glory of the one and only Son, who came from the Father, full of grace and truth.'

Down all the centuries, the Christ has been known by many to be the source, the sustenance and the end of all of creation. Yet the awareness of Christ as being one of us, being a lover of humanity, showing us the great love and caring of our God, has often been lost through heresies, differing emphases, disputes, failings and, above all, I believe, a very superficial reading of the New Testament. Has the Christ been truly known as source, sustenance and end of all? In our own era, the discovery of evolution and the findings of science have tended to cast a mist over how we have seen the Christ. Yet 'the darkness has not overcome' the light. Perhaps the poets have clarified how the Christ has been viewed, known, or misrepresented down all these centuries? And has poetry in our time moved with the awareness of Christ as source of evolution, as the sustenance and aim of evolution? That is surely yet to be seen.

In the beginning … Well, there was 'The Dream of the Rood', written perhaps in the early eighth century in England, in Anglo-Saxon. The author is unknown, but the excellence of the writing has urged that the work be attributed to the poet Caedmon, or to Cynewulf. Of course we can be certain of nothing, of the reality of the 'true Cross' or the date or authorship, but we do know the value and excellence of the poem itself.

Christians have been 'glorying in the cross of Christ' for many ages and the unknown author of 'The Dream of the Rood' has taken this thought to its finest moment. In this poem, the crucifixion of Christ is retold from an unusual perspective, that of the cross itself. It is the cross, 'discovered and unearthed' by St Helena, the mother of Constantine, who seized power in 312. Constantine legalised the Christian faith around that time and Helena was a convert; she went to Palestine to search for the sites of Christ's presence and, while some of the old 'pagan' sites were being demolished, she came upon the place, she avers, of Christ's crucifixion. It appears that three crosses were discovered and Helena's followers brought a woman who had a terminal disease to see them; when she touched the third cross she was instantly cured. So goes the myth. St Ambrose wrote that when St Helena found the true cross, 'she worshipped not the wood, but the King, Him who hung on the wood. She burned with an earnest desire of touching the guarantee of immortality.' This is indeed the worth and purpose of relics and myths, to move beyond them to love of the source, of God. Devotion to the 'true cross' grew to a pitch in the Middle Ages and was particularly strong in England. Part of the poem was discovered on the eighth-century Ruthwell Cross, which appears to have served as a way of teaching people who had no other way of learning about their faith. The poem had, of course, that same purpose, but there is far more to it than that. So who is the Christ of 'The Dream of the Rood'?

We are reading a work that emerged from an age of heroes, when battle, service to one's lord and king, rewards for victories in battle, in fact all the traits and characteristics of a fearless and chivalrous and faithful hero, were greatly admired. We are introduced to a Christ who is preparing for a battle, who is stripping himself for war, who climbs willingly onto the tree of agony with the intention of suffering bravely and offering himself for the redemption of humankind. Christ, instead of being brought forcefully to his death, is shown as hastening to it, eager and prepared, ready for the battle to win humanity back for God.

In those years, the burial sites of heroes and kings were located in prominent places and honoured with ornamental offerings. The poem 'beautifies' the tree and in its burial sees the earth itself as being part of the redemption of humankind. The lines towards the end of the poem speak to the one who has carried the symbol of the cross about with him or her, or placed it on a wall or fixed it to the end of a rosary of beads:

> who have borne on your breast this dear, divine
> and best of symbols, have no fear, His blood
> has won you grace over the gravity of earth for ever.

The lines will surely recall the simple, yet questioning faith of youth, and suggest some consolation against our world of pain. Many years from then, the philosopher Simone Weil took up the notions of gravity and grace as the two great forces that command our human living.

In the poem, it is the cross that speaks in a dream; in this way, a created thing is made to be part of the work of redemption itself. The tree becomes a priest, a poet and a prophet, standing between the suffering Christ and the observing people. The tree bleeds for the dying hero, the creature suffers for the sufferings of Christ, refusing to bow down and yield though the earth around it 'shivers' in empathy. It reminds us of St Paul's telling of how the whole earth is in labour towards the coming of God's kingdom. Honour given to the tree is honour shown to the love of God. The poem is the first great hymn to Christ, and a hymn to the redemption of the whole of creation.

And so Christ on the cross is not a failure; he is the warrior hero who dies bravely and willingly. The jibes and humiliations offered to Christ are not part of this; the poem presents only the moment of heroism, the triumphant moment, the victory over sin. And it is the duty of the tree – as it was the duty of the lord's 'retainers' or servants – to support the hero to the bitter end. The poem, though it pertains to Christ's death, offers a bright and optimistic message, one of hope and belief in the future of the spirit. It tells of how in Christ there was life, and that life was the light of humankind, a light that shone in the darkness, and the darkness did not overcome it. I present the poem in my own translation, moving from the alliterative rhythms of the original to a more modern verse form, holding on to much of the alliteration but placing the poem in a loose copy of Dante's *terza rima*, and thus attempting to hold a sense of antiquity to the poem.

The Dream of the Rood

(A version of the seventh-/eighth-century Anglo-Saxon poem)

Pause with me while I tell the most precious and the best
of dreams, sent to me in the deep silence of night
when men, word mongers, were everywhere at rest.

THE DREAM OF THE ROOD: THE WARRIOR HERO

It seemed that I saw the most marvellous tree
lifted high on the air, all haloed in light,
most beautiful of all beams of wood; a beacon

bathed in gold. There were breathtaking gems that stood
all around the base, a further five were ablaze
high along the cross-beam. Holy angels of the Lord

looked always on its loveliness, enthralled.
This was no criminal's cross; there came to gaze
the saintliest of spirits, men everywhere and all

marvels of creation mused upon it where it stood.
How strange that tree of victory! And I – steeped in sin,
badly blemished all over – watched that glorious wood

adorned with banners, shining in all its beauty,
garlanded in gold, glorious gems worked in –
the wonderfully wreathed tree of the World's Ruler.

Yet straight through all that gold I could still see
the friend of once-wretched men, how it first began
to bleed on the right-hand side. Sorrow bore in on me,

and fear, before that vision; I saw the beacon change,
become clothed in colours; how at times the blood ran
drenching it in blood-dew, how it bloomed with a strange

beauty. I lay a long while, wretched at heart,
watching my Saviour's tree. Until suddenly, most
wondrously, the wood spoke, uttering these words:

THE OUTLAW CHRIST

'Long ago – distinctly I remember it! – one day
I was hewn down at the dark edge of the forest
and severed from my stem. Strong enemies seized me,

wrought me into a spectacle for the world to see,
commanding me to hoist their criminals on high;
men carried me on their shoulders and erected me

high on a hill – fixed there by many foes. I saw
the Ruler of mankind rush with real courage to climb
on me and I did not dare (my Lord had warned!)

bend down or break, though I saw the broad
surface of earth shiver. How simple – the Lord knows –
to smite His enemies! But firm and stout I stood,

unmoving. The hero stripped, though He was God Almighty!
robust and resolute, mounting onto the gallows
spirited, in the sight of many, to redeem mankind.

I wavered while the warrior embraced me, clasped me
and I did not dare bend down towards the ground,
fall on the earth's surface, I must stand fast.

I was raised up a Rood, carrying the powerful King,
high Lord of Heaven, and did not dare to bend.
They pierced me with bloody nails, the pain still stings!

the open wounds of malice. They made us fools
together. I was wholly wet with blood
streaming from His side when He gave up His soul

THE DREAM OF THE ROOD: THE WARRIOR HERO

and helpless on that hill I knew a fearful fate:
stretched out in agony the Almighty God
of hosts cruelly wracked, the heavens all in spate

above the body of our Ruler, that bright radiance;
shadows reigned supreme under a thickening cloud;
all of creation mourned, moaned this cruel chance:

and Christ was on the rood.

   'Now from afar came virtuous men, hastening
to that solitary Man. I saw it all, my many cares
grievously afflicting me, but I yielded to their chastening

humble and ardent hands. They held the God of Hosts,
took Him down from that dreadful torture; warriors
left me wet with moisture, wounded all over by arrows,

laid Him down, His limbs weary, stood watching at His head.
They looked on the Lord of heaven, resting for a time
weary from a woeful contest. A tomb was already made

in sight of those who slew Him, carved out of stone,
and they laid therein our Saviour, glorious, sublime.
They began to make their songs of sorrow, they mourned

until the fall of evening, then wearily wandered home
from that royal Throne, leaving Him there to rest.
We, however, a long while weeping, stood alone

on our foundations, fearing a dreadful destiny,
while that beautiful body chilled, that treasure chest
of life. Hastening then they hacked us cruelly

THE OUTLAW CHRIST

to the earth, planted us in a deep pit. Dark and cold.
But the Lord's retainers, His friends, freed us, and then
set me on high, enhanced with silver and with gold.

    'Now, dear friend, now it is time that the world knew
how I endured the wickedness of evil men
and grievous woes; it is time that the world show

honour to me through the whole earth and this broad
and marvellous creation, time they make their prayers
to me as a symbol. For on me did the Son of God

suffer agonies a while; so I won glory and was raised
high under the heavens, that I may heal the cares
of those who honour me and who offer praise.

Once, I became the most terrible of tortures, of pains
most odious to men, before I opened up for them,
for these word-mongers, life's true way.

See then how the prince of Heaven honoured me beyond
all the trees of the wood, true Keeper of the Kingdom,
as He honoured His mother Mary beyond all womankind.

    'Now I require you, dear friend, that you relate
what you have seen to others, reveal in words this vision:
the tree of glory on which God himself had to tolerate

suffering for the ways of men and Adam's ancient sin,
that He tasted death; that He rose truly in great
honour to give help to men, mounted high to heaven

and will come down on judgement day, angels at His side
to judge, each man and woman in whatsoever way

THE DREAM OF THE ROOD: THE WARRIOR HERO

they have measured out this transitory life. Nor let mankind
be unafraid of what the Ruler of the World will say!
Before the multitudes He will test, and try, to find
where is he who, for the Lord's sake, would taste

death's rancid savour as He did on the Rood!
They shall fear, for there are few who will discover
what to say to Christ that dreadfilled day. But you

who have borne on your breast this dear, divine
and best of symbols, have no fear, His blood
has won you grace over the gravity of earth for ever;

hope then always to dwell with Him in the highest Heaven.'

Oh I prayed then with courage to that happy Cross,
I was alone, no person by, knew powerful longing. My food
now is to love that tree of victory, all else is loss

and forfeiture, to honour it more often than any man yet has.
My will is directed wonderfully towards the rood,
I have no powerful friends in the world, they have passed

from the dreams of earth to the King's glory and dwell
in heaven now with the High Father. I long
for the day when the royal Rood of the Lord shall

fetch me finally from this transitory life and bring
me where is rapture and revelry in heaven, where all
the people of the Lord shall stand and sing

at the banquet where is bliss perpetual; and I pray
that our God who suffered on the gallows tree

THE OUTLAW CHRIST

be my friend, who has freed us to the light of day,
the Son and victor, stalwart, successful. He
who came with a glorious consort of spirits to stay
forever within God's kingdom; that I shall see

the Almighty Ruler, risen to where the angels stand,
with the holy company of saints at God's right hand,
the Hero, home with honour to His native land.

4

WOEFULLY ARRAYED

John Skelton (1460-1529)

John Skelton is a shadowy figure hovering at the door of English literature. Little is known about him apart from what his poems tell. He was clearly learned and a reader, quoting in his work from an impressive list of classical authors and mythic tales. He was of his time, secular, intelligent, rhetorical, and much of his writing aimed at getting him preferment at court. Perhaps another link with earlier literature is his awareness of the use of a persona, similar to the way 'The Dream of the Rood' uses the 'person' of the cross to speak. His language was also very much the daily language of the people and his rhyming skill made many of his verses hugely popular. But he is one of the first early-modern poets to touch seriously on questions of faith. His work is predictable and not very polished, but one poem stands out. In 'Woefully Arrayed' there is heard a personal honesty and commitment and a genuine pleading to his Christ. In this poem it is Christ who speaks.

Woefully Arrayed

> Woefully arrayed,
>   My blood, man,
>   For thee ran,
> It may not be nay'd;
>   My body blue and wan,
> Woefully arrayed.

THE OUTLAW CHRIST

Behold me, I pray thee, with thy whole reason,
And be not so hard-hearted, and for this encheason, *(reason)*
Sith I for thy soul sake was slain in good season, *(since)*
Beguiled and betrayed by Judas' false treason:
      Unkindly entreated,
      With sharp cord sore fretted,
      The Jewés me threated:
They mowéd, they grinned, they scornéd me, *(mouthed)*
Condemnéd me to death, as thou may'st see,
      Woefully arrayed.

Thus naked am I nailed, O man, for thy sake!
I love thee, then love me; why sleepest thou? awake!
Remember my tender heart-root for thee brake,
With painés my veinés constrained to crake: *(crack)*
      Thus tuggéd to and fro,
      Thus wrappéd all in woe,
      Whereas never man was so,
Entreated thus in most cruel wise,
Was like a lamb offered in sacrifice,
      Woefully arrayed.

Of sharp thorn I have worn a crown on my head,
So painéd, so strainéd, so ruefull, so read,
Thus bobbéd, thus robbéd, thus for thy love dead, *(beuten)*
Unfeignéd I deignéd my blood for to shed:
      My feet and handés sore
      The sturdy nailés bore:
      What might I suffer more
Than I have done, O man, for thee?
Come when thou list, welcome to me,
      Woefully arrayed.

WOEFULLY ARRAYED

Of record thy good Lord I have been and shall be:
I am thine, thou art mine, my brother I call thee.
Thee love I entirely – see what is befall'n me!
Sore beating, sore threating, to make thee, man, all free:
        Why art thou unkind?
        Why hast not me in mind?
        Come yet and thou shalt find
Mine endless mercie and grace –
See how a spear my heart did race,   *(wound)*
        Woefully arrayed.

Dear brother, no other thing I of thee desire
But give me thine heart free to reward mine hire:
I wrought thee, I bought thee from eternal fire:
I pray thee array thee toward my high empire
        Above the orient,
        Whereof I am regent,
        Lord God omnipotent,
With me to reign in endless wealth:
Remember, man, thy soul's health.

        Woefully arrayed,
        My blood, man,
        For thee ran,
        It may not be nay'd;
        My body blue and wan,
        Woefully arrayed.

There is that personal touch, new and fresh and moving, 'I love thee, then love me'; here already is George Herbert. This, in the context of the drama of the poem, is a teacher's exquisite point, a Skelton move, a preacher's trick. Yet its very immediacy and simplicity give it honour and truth.

THE OUTLAW CHRIST

In the rhyming power, in the swift onward movement of the verse, here is Hopkins already. In the deep sorrow and genuine urgings of the poem, R.S. Thomas can already be heard. The Christ of this poem is pleading with humankind for love, insisting that he himself is a great lover, willing to climb on the cross, to wear that crown of thorns, to die for the sake of love. In the late fifteenth and early sixteenth century, this awareness of the love of Christ was rare; the emphasis was more on human sin and divine punishment. With John Skelton, and with this real personal calling to the Christ, the dark door out of the forge has begun to open.

5

PRIEST AND OUTLAW

Robert Southwell (1561-1595)

(Chapter written by Mackenzie Hanlon: see Appendix)

Robert Southwell is a Jesuit priest and poet from the Shakespearian age and the time of the Reformation and religious wars in England. Southwell did most of his writing between the time of his return to England in 1586 and his execution in 1592. Critics have two theories as to the purpose of his writings. The first speculation is that his works were his defence of the faith and edification of Catholics. The second is that his pieces are versified doctrine, religious propaganda, and a substitute for preaching, even suggesting that his works are a direct attack on the Reformation movement.

Robert Southwell was the fifth child and youngest son of a family of eight born in 1561 in Norfolk, England. The Southwell family was part of a wealthy network of families. In 1576 Southwell, like many others, went overseas to study at the Jesuit School of Douai, where he was reported to be quite studious. His father, perhaps predicting his son's future path, affectionately referred to him as 'Father Robert'. Southwell became convinced he was destined for the religious life. He was admitted to the noviceship at Rome in 1578 and ordained as a Jesuit priest in 1584. Then, in 1586, at the age of twenty-five, he was sent on the English mission, where he worked secretly alongside a fellow Jesuit, Henry Garnet. According to Christopher Devlin, the survival rate of a Catholic priest in England was only one in three. Southwell led a hidden life as a priest for six years before he was captured by England's notorious priest hunter, Richard Topcliffe, in June 1592. After spending more than two years in the Tower of London, where he was subjected to severe torture, Southwell was brought to trial on 20 February 1595. The statute of 1585 made it treason to be a Catholic priest and give the sacraments; therefore, Southwell was sentenced to death by means of hanging, drawing and quartering. The sentence was carried out on 21 February 1595.

Southwell used his personal suffering as a common topic in his work. He felt that his life was a parallel to that of Christ. This theme is best portrayed in his poem, 'A Child My Choice'. In this piece Southwell explains how both he and Christ remained steadfastly loyal to God despite all of the suffering, torture and persecution they endured as a consequence of their loyalty. This loyalty is evidenced in the poem, which states, 'To love Him life, to leave Him death, To live in Him delight' (line 6). This line demonstrates Southwell's devotion to Christ by expressing the different positions that make up belief and their consequences. To love God is to live life, to leave God is death, the end of all things, while to live in God, to show loyalty, is the ultimate delight. Southwell, despite his suffering and persecution, still chose to maintain his steadfast loyalty. The second aspect of this piece is the paradox of both life and death being synonymous. To be born is to eventually die; therefore, life is death. Moreover, life, especially in the case of Robert Southwell and of Jesus Christ, is suffering.

One of the Southwell's best-known works is his poem, 'The Burning Babe'. This poem touches on the meaning of Christ's persecution and crucifixion. Jesus suffers for others. He was tortured and crucified for the remission of believers' sins and the promise of eternal life in heaven. 'The metal in this furnace wrought are men's defiled souls, / For which, as now on fire I am to work them to their good' (lines 12–13). Christ is in the throes of the fire's flames, suffering, for the purpose of working on the defiled souls of humankind to their own good. In other words, he is suffering so that they may be forgiven and live eternal life in heaven. Another element to this poem is a continuing theme in Southwell's works:

that life can be summed up as nothing more than birth, suffering and death. This trope was present in 'A Child My Choice' and can also be seen in 'The Burning Babe'. This is the parallel between the life of Christ and Southwell's own personal experiences of torture and execution. Southwell commonly drew on the mirroring of events between his life and Christ's, and this thread exists in most of his writings. He asserts that suffering is ever present in the lives of everyone. Due to the fact that followers of Christ experience suffering, they are living a Christ-like life since he also knew suffering. So followers of Christ are loved by God and therefore free of the devil's power. Birth, for Southwell, is the beginning of suffering and death is the end, the release from suffering. Christ is, then, not only exemplar and fellow-human, but his suffering and death give cause and merit to the sufferings of humankind.

A Child My Choice

Let folly praise that fancy loves, I praise and love that Child
Whose heart no thought, whose tongue no word, whose hand no deed defiled.

I praise Him most, I love Him best, all praise and love is His;
While Him I love, in Him I live, and cannot live amiss.

Love's sweetest mark, laud's highest theme, man's most desired light,
To love Him life, to leave Him death, to live in Him delight.

He mine by gift, I His by debt, thus each to other due;
First friend He was, best friend He is, all times will try Him true.

Though young, yet wise; though small, yet strong; though man, yet God He is:

THE OUTLAW CHRIST

As wise, He knows; as strong, He can; as God, He loves to bless.

His knowledge rules, His strength defends, His love doth cherish all;
His birth our joy, His life our light, His death our end of thrall.

Alas! He weeps, He sighs, He pants, yet do His angels sing;
Out of His tears, His sighs and throbs, doth bud a joyful spring.

Almighty Babe, whose tender arms can force all foes to fly,
Correct my faults, protect my life, direct me when I die!

The Burning Babe

As I in hoary winter's night stood shivering in the snow,
Surprised I was with sudden heat which made my heart to glow;
And lifting up a fearful eye to view what fire was near,
A pretty babe all burning bright did in the air appear;
Who, scorchèd with excessive heat, such floods of tears did shed
As though his floods should quench his flames which with his tears were fed.
Alas, quoth he, but newly born in fiery heats I fry,
Yet none approach to warm their hearts or feel my fire but I!
My faultless breast the furnace is, the fuel wounding thorns,
Love is the fire, and sighs the smoke, the ashes shame and scorns;
The fuel justice layeth on, and mercy blows the coals,
The metal in this furnace wrought are men's defilèd souls,
For which, as now on fire I am to work them to their good,
So will I melt into a bath to wash them in my blood.
With this he vanished out of sight and swiftly shrunk away,
And straight I callèd unto mind that it was Christmas day.

PRIEST AND OUTLAW

Christ's Childhood

Till twelve years' age, how Christ His childhood spent
        All earthly pens unworthy were to write;
Such acts to mortal eyes He did present,
        Whose worth not men but angels must recite:
No nature's blots, no childish faults defiled,
Where grace was guide, and God did play the child.

In springing locks lay crouchèd hoary wit,
        In semblant young, a grave and ancient port;
In lowly looks high majesty did sit,
        In tender tongue sound sense of sagest sort:
Nature imparted all that she could teach,
And God supplied where nature could not reach.

His mirth of modest mien a mirror was;
        His sadness temper'd with a mild aspect;
His eye to try each action was a glass,
        Whose looks did good approve and bad correct;
His nature's gifts, His grace, His word and deed,
Well show'd that all did from a God proceed.

The Virgin Mary to Christ on the Cross

What mist hath dimm'd that glorious face?
What seas of grief my sun doth toss?
The golden rays of heavenly grace
Lies now eclipsèd on the cross.

Jesus, my love, my Son, my God,
Behold Thy mother wash'd in tears:
Thy bloody wounds be made a rod
To chasten these my later years.

THE OUTLAW CHRIST

You cruel Jews, come work your ire
Upon this worthless flesh of mine,
And kindle not eternal fire
By wounding Him who is divine.

Thou messenger that didst impart
His first descent into my womb,
Come help me now to cleave my heart,
That there I may my Son entomb.

You angels, all that present were
To show His birth with harmony,
Why are you not now ready here,
To make a mourning symphony?

The cause I know you wail alone,
And shed your tears in secrecy,
Lest I should movèd be to moan,
By force of heavy company.

But wail, my soul, thy comfort dies,
My woeful womb, lament thy fruit;
My heart give tears unto mine eyes,
Let sorrow string my heavy lute.

Note from John F. Deane
In many ways, as Mackenzie Hanlon points out, the sufferings of Jesus Christ and those of Robert Southwell are close; both of them were persecuted and had to go into hiding. Southwell, then, mirrors Christ as outlaw, and here we see the priest, too, as outlaw, follower of the outlaw Christ.

6

WHO, LORD? ME, LORD?

Phineas Fletcher (1582-1650)

Phineas Fletcher was born in 1582 in Kent, England. He died in 1650 in Norfolk. His father, Giles Fletcher the Elder, and his brother, Giles Fletcher the Younger, were also poets and authors. Phineas was educated at Eton and King's College, Cambridge. He wrote the pastoral drama *Sicelides* for King James I in 1615 to be performed at King's College; however, the king had left before the play was performed. It was published in 1631. In 1627 he published *The Locusts or Apollyonists* in Latin (*Locustae, vel pietas Jesuitica*) and English, attacking the Jesuits. He also published two theological prose treatises in 1632, *The Way to Blessedness* and *Joy in Tribulation*. Furthermore, in 1633 he published *The Purple Island,* known for its religious and scientific significance. He married Elizabeth Vincent of Risley, Derbyshire, in August 1615. Fletcher became chaplain to Sir Henry Willoughby in 1621. 'Phineas Fletcher's poetry has not the sublimity sometimes reached by his brother Giles. The mannerisms are more pronounced, the conceits more far-fetched, but the verse is fluent and musical. His lyric poetry lacks neither colour nor ardour' *(Encyclopedia Britannica).*

(Note written by Mackenzie Hanlon)

The poem, 'The Divine Lover', however, is a very real personal response, a humble one, to the sense of Christ's love for the individual soul. The astonishment at the love offered by God to a sinner comes across as genuine; it is, of course, one of the very first such poems in the English language. How can the Christ call the sinner 'Love', or 'Friend'? Fletcher vacillates, then, between fear and hope, and is amazed by the thought of such a love, moving him to cry out. How sad it is that this emphasis on love, rather than on a God of vengeful watchfulness, did not remain among Christians down the centuries! The central part of the poem offers a dialogue between Christ and soul, a device taken up by many later poets, notably George Herbert. The images of light and darkness, of freedom and bondage, were also often used by later writers.

The Divine Lover

I
Me Lord? can'st thou mispend
One word, misplace one look on me?
Call'st me thy Love, thy Friend?
Can this poor soul the object be
Of these love-glances, those life-kindling eyes?
What? I the Centre of thy arms embraces?
Of all thy labour I the prize?
Love never mocks, Truth never lies.
Oh how I quake: Hope fear, fear hope displaces:
I would, but cannot hope: such wondrous love amazes.

II
See, I am black as night,
See I am darkness: dark as hell.
Lord thou more fair than light;
Heav'ns Sun thy Shadow; can Sunns dwell
With Shades? 'twixt light, and darkness what commerce?

WHO, LORD? ME, LORD?

True: thou art darkness, I thy Light: my ray
Thy mists, and hellish foggs shall pierce.
With me, black soul, with me converse.
I make the foul December flowry May,
Turn thou thy night to me: I'le turn thy night to day.

III
See Lord, see I am dead:
Tomb'd in my self: my self my grave
A drudge: so born, so bred:
My self even to my self a slave.
Thou Freedom, Life: can Life, and Liberty
Love bondage, death? Thy Freedom I: I tyed
To loose thy bonds: be bound to me:
My Yoke shall ease, my bonds shall free.
Dead soul, thy Spring of life, my dying side:
There dye with me to live: to live in thee I dyed.

A Litany

Drop, drop, slow tears,
        And bathe those beauteous feet
Which brought from Heaven
        The news and Prince of Peace:
Cease not, wet eyes,
        His mercy to entreat;
To cry for vengeance
        Sin doth never cease.
In your deep floods
        Drown all my faults and fears;
Nor let His eye
        See sin, but through my tears.

7

EAST OR WEST? JACK DONNE OR JOHN DONNE?

John Donne (1572-1631)

We are given a name at birth, and we have no control over what that name may be. Perhaps it imposes something on us we feel we must work to live up to, like Jesse James Duffy, or the names given to three sisters I met once, Faith, Hope and Charity. I was named John, innocent enough, after my grandfather; but then there were two characters with that name in the Christian canon. I was not too keen on imitating John the Baptist, with his locusts and wild honey. And there was John the Evangelist, purportedly the 'one whom Jesus loved'. That would do me. My grandfather, John Connors, was well known for being able to fix all sorts of things, from the workings of a carriage clock to a cartwheel. The other fixer we came to know on Achill Island, where I was born, was the local garage man, Ted Sweeney, who could understand and repair cars. So our grandfather, John, was always known to us as Ted. Never anything else: Ted. The fixer. Not even 'granddad'.

When I was a short-trouser, catapult boy, a little bold, a little wild, they called me Jackie. When I sent off my first poem to a magazine editor, many years later, he wrote back: 'Dear Jackie: I like the poem, but I don't know whether to call you Mr, Mrs or Miss Deane.' Decision time. I chose John, it seemed more weighty in the context of poetry. Then, John Deane: spondaic meter, a spondee, equal stresses on each of the two terms, sounded strict and unmusical. John Donne, also spondaic, sounds that bit softer, more amenable, more musical. I added the initial of my second name, F., for Francis. John F. Deane. Sounds possibly literary. But as I grew older, married, became a little paunchy, friends came to call me Jack. Jack

Deane, man about town, nice chap, good fellow. Jackie, John, Jack, John F. Confusing, isn't it?

Now there is our poet, John Donne. Or is it Jack Donne?

John Donne (1573–1631) rounded off the sixteenth century and opened up the seventeenth. It was an era of religious turmoil, an age when poetry had just settled into a worthy manse and provided its writers with weapons to acquire either preferment at court or a short and heady stay in the Tower of London. John Donne vacillated wonderfully between religious writing and secular, between God and his mistresses, between public service and hidden family, between east and west, his own life and loves, the greatest paradoxes of all. And for a time he was known, man about town, would-be and perhaps actual lover, courtier, writer of satirical verse: Jack Donne.

In 1530, England had broken with Rome and a convocation was forced to state that Henry VIII was the supreme head of the Church in England. In 1534 Parliament voted the king as head of the Church, and the break with Rome was complete. In 1549 Cranmer's Book of Common Prayer appeared and was quickly imposed on the nation. In 1588 Elizabeth came to the throne and in 1599 the Act of Supremacy forbade the authority of the pope. There were decades of persecution, beheadings and heresies, violence and despair, coupled with a great humanist lift in the excitement of the Renaissance, the arrival of the courtly lyric, a new grace in secular forms. Donne's age was a dangerous one; suspicion of being a 'Papist', a Roman Catholic, could mean loss of opportunity, dismissal, imprisonment and even death. Robert Southwell and the Jesuits offered a stinging example of what might occur.

John Donne's age was an age like ours, with its wars and fevers, the turning of a century, religious doubts and affirmations. Donne's progress as a poet and believer is exemplary of his time, and his self-questioning an example to everyman. He spends his life, both in his poetry and in his prose works, preaching a sermon to himself, eventually urging himself away from the arms of sensual pleasures and into the demanding arms of his God. A perennial struggle, sometimes lost, won, apparently, in the end.

EAST OR WEST? JACK DONNE OR JOHN DONNE?

John Donne was born to a mother who came from a prominent Roman Catholic family. Two of John's uncles became members of the Society of Jesus. In 1581 one of these uncles, Jasper Heywood, returned to England from his studies abroad as a Jesuit missionary, but he was quickly captured, imprisoned, tried and condemned to the Tower. In 1584 Donne matriculated from Oxford at a time when the law demanded that those pursuing university degrees acknowledge that the king was head of the Church, but Donne appears to have been young enough to avoid having to take that oath. Later he studied law at Lincoln's Inn. In 1593, his brother Henry was arrested for harbouring a Roman Catholic priest, William Harrington, in his rooms. The priest was executed and Henry died of the plague in Newgate prison. More salutary lessons; John (or rather Jack) Donne, needed to keep a watchful eye on his friends, his activities, his words.

His – Jack Donne's – poetry was secular, romping through witty love conceits, clever twists and turns of language, clear and mastered forms.

> My face in thine eye, thine in mine appears,
> And true plain hearts do in the faces rest;
> Where can we find two better hemispheres
> Without sharp north, without declining west?
> Whatever dies, was not mix'd equally;
> If our two loves be one, or thou and I
> Love so alike that none can slacken, none can die.

It was a life lived away from reality, a life of love and of lying abed, unwilling to have the light of everyday sunshine interrupt:

> Love, all alike, no season knows nor clime,
> Nor hours, days, months, which are the rags of time.
>   Busy old fool, unruly Sun,
>   Why dost thou thus,

> Through windows, and through curtains, call on us?
> Must to thy motions lovers' seasons run?
> > Saucy pedantic wretch, go chide
> > Late school-boys and sour prentices,
> > Go tell court-huntsmen that the king will ride,
> Call country ants to harvest offices;

His poems circulated in manuscript form; he thought publication of his work was unworthy of a serious man whose courtly ambitions were very great indeed. The vigour of his lines was new and profoundly memorable, yet all the time he was preening himself in public and haunting the centres of worldly comfort, he remained deeply sensitive and close to his mother, remembering always her lessons and example. He was already distancing himself from Roman Catholicism; over the centuries many critics have thought this was merely a ruse to escape punishment and to win court favour. While seeking high office, Donne spent some time as a soldier, stating that he wished to escape the consequences of his amours, and that he wanted to earn, in service to his king, some court advancement.

Elizabeth had died in 1603 and James VI of Scotland succeeded to the English throne. Donne was eventually appointed to high office under Thomas Egerton, the Lord Keeper, where he was highly favoured and given serious and important employment. While he was working for Egerton, he met and fell in love with a young girl, Ann More, who was just fifteen years old when they first met. Her mother had died and Egerton had become her guardian while she was in London, where her father, Sir George More, came to carry out his affairs. Donne knew that he would not be accepted into More's family so the meetings with Ann were clandestine and, when she was sixteen, he married her in secret. The marriage brushed aside several conventions, the most important being that Ann, at such a young age, needed parental approval. Sir George, when he was at last informed of the marriage, was furious and had Egerton sack Donne, then arrest him and imprison him in the deadly Fleet prison,

EAST OR WEST? JACK DONNE OR JOHN DONNE?

from which few escaped with their health intact, never mind their lives. The fact that Donne spoke of Ann as 'her whom I tender much more than my fortunes or life – else would I might neither joy in this life nor enjoy the next,' speaks to the seriousness and commitment of his love for his young bride. He was soon released and the marriage, though not accepted by George More or Thomas Egerton, was declared valid by the Established Church. In gaining the hand of his beloved Ann Donne had lost everything, prestige, a job, the possibility of serious advancement. His imprisonment had greatly shocked him. His health had suffered even during the short period of his detention, and he suffered intermittently for the rest of his life.

It may be salutary every now and again to remind ourselves of the possible inherent value of suffering. Our age has long been fiddling about at a crossroads; the largest and most glaring sign points west: to prosperity, self-aggrandisement, wealth and power. The lesser one, grimy from years of neglect and dust, points east: not back to where we have come from, but towards a new perspective on faith, charity and hope. Decisions, decisions! West, towards the glory and ease of a wonderfully setting sun (it is setting, however); or east, towards the demands of a chilly and rising sun (to be followed by a day of difficult labour)? West, towards the blandishments of reason, or east, towards the accommodation of a ridiculous faith, a yielding to heart and imagination? Does the world rest in a material adolescence forever, or see with clear eyes how we are destroying the world we live in with our focus on perishable things? Does the world learn from its errors and turn to lasting, spiritual truths? Donne, in life and work, offers the answer.

For some time after the marriage, Jack Donne was not to be found in the city. In 1605 the gunpowder plot set England on edge again, and Fr Henry Garnet, head of the Jesuit order in England, was charged with treason and executed. In 1604 James banished all priests. Donne and his young wife were given a damp and unhealthy cottage at Mitcham, not very far from London. Here Jack Donne began again to try and win preferment, but to no avail. He had no serious or influential backers now. For a time he lived by offering informal legal advice. He continued to keep quiet about his belief that all Christian faiths could lead to God; even this would have been seen as dangerous thinking, standing out now as much ahead of its time. Children were being born to the Donne family and Ann was often in poor health. Eventually, in 1607, Donne was offered a church benefice by the Dean of Gloucester, who asked him to take holy orders; Donne turned down the offer. But his mind had curved with great seriousness towards religious questions.

Donne wrote a poem to Ann shortly after their marriage: he was then our Jack Donne, the would-be man-about-town, but the poem offers an example of many of the traits of his poetry, of the impulses and thinking and language that will carry over into the later poetry of John Donne, the priest.

The Good-Morrow

I wonder by my troth, what thou and I
Did, till we loved? Were we not wean'd till then?
But suck'd on country pleasures, childishly?
Or snorted we in the seven sleepers' den?
'Twas so; but this, all pleasures fancies be;
If ever any beauty I did see,
Which I desired, and got, 'twas but a dream of thee.

And now good-morrow to our waking souls,
Which watch not one another out of fear;
For love all love of other sights controls,
And makes one little room an everywhere.
Let sea-discoverers to new worlds have gone;
Let maps to other, worlds on worlds have shown;
Let us possess one world; each hath one, and is one.

EAST OR WEST? JACK DONNE OR JOHN DONNE?

> My face in thine eye, thine in mine appears,
> And true plain hearts do in the faces rest;
> Where can we find two better hemispheres
> Without sharp North, without declining West?
> Whatever dies, was not mixt equally;
> If our two loves be one, or thou and I
> Love so alike that none can slacken, none can die.

Isaak Walton, Donne's first biographer, called his marriage to the young Ann 'the remarkable error of his life; an error which though he had a wit able and very apt to maintain Paradoxes, yet he was very far from justifying it'. What an error! To marry for love, and a clearly mutual love at that. It was, in fact, perhaps the most remarkable and best move of his life. He did come to regret much of his earlier poems, referring – as a later poem does – to his 'many profane mistresses'. Yet in another poem, written shortly before the judgment of the Established Church on whether his marriage was or was not legitimate was issued, he tells how he finds it hard to believe the fuss his marriage has caused. He goes on to seek solace in the prospect of being buried with his beloved Ann, both of them 'saints of love', if not in a mighty tomb, then at least in a well-wrought urn, as well as in well-wrought poetry:

> We can die by it, if not live by love,
> And if unfit for tombs and hearse
> Our legend be, it will be fit for verse;
> And if no piece of Chronicle we prove,
> We'll build in sonnets pretty rooms;
> As well a well-wrought urn becomes
> The greatest ashes, as half-acre tombs,
> And by these hymns, all shall approve
> Us Canonized for Love.
> ('The Canonization')

THE OUTLAW CHRIST

It has been too easy to read Donne's move from Roman Catholicism to the Anglican Church as a young man running scared; this love affair, the marriage and his ongoing commitment to the one he loved, as well as the poems he wrote to and for her, show he was not afraid of the consequences of his actions. Donne, raised a Catholic, was moved by natural disposition and by nationalistic fervour towards the English Church and away from Rome. He had joined the Earl of Essex in his raid on Cadiz, and was among Raleigh's forces in raids along the Portuguese ports, putting his life at risk for the sake of adventure, but also for his country. He had already railed against the laziness, illiteracy and loose living he had witnessed among Catholic priests. He spoke of 'England, to whom we owe, what we be, and have'. He worked for Thomas Egerton, who took part in the torture inflicted on many Roman Catholic priests, including Thomas Campion and Robert Southwell, though it is known that Donne did not condone such an approach. He believed in a natural, intelligent and free evolution of religious beliefs. He saw the Roman Catholic Church as an institution too hide-bound to move and change with the changes in the world around it. In our own era, many facts and events simply show how right he was, both in his notion of the evolution of beliefs alongside the changes in the world, and in the stick-in-the-mud stance of the Roman Curia.

When he himself looked back on the life of Jack Donne, Roman Catholic and would-be courtier, he felt he had been deeply sinful and untrue to his God, whether as a Catholic, or now as an Anglican. As his children were born (some of them died young, one at birth) and as he felt all hope of progress in secular life was hopeless, and knowing, too, that his health was compromised and he could die without much warning, he began to take his commitment to God more seriously. Conscious of sin and unworthiness, he turned to Christ and began to believe that as Christ had suffered and died for all of humanity, it would be necessary that he, Donne, would have to be purged, by suffering, of all his sins. He proclaimed himself ready to endure.

EAST OR WEST? JACK DONNE OR JOHN DONNE?

Having moved away from Catholicism, he also found that many of the encouragements offered by that religion had also been removed – the devotion to Mary, the aids of pictures, statues, sacraments and rituals – and that as an Anglican he found himself living in an unlovely universe, depending mostly on scripture. Calvinism was growing strong, too, and it attempted to remove any natural supports outside one's own strict adherence to doctrine. Predestination was a frightening doctrine to John Donne, who was haunted by the thought that he was doomed to hell.

Donne (John) developed a sonnet sequence that began his deep analysis, through a poetry technique and experience that he had mastered in his 'secular' poems, of the Christian faith. *La Corona*, a sequence of nine sonnets, uses the notion of a circular form: the last line of each sonnet forming the first line of the following one, the final line of the whole 'crown' repeating the first line of the sequence. The strongest and most obvious techniques, apart from the rhyme-pattern and sonnet formation, are his use of paradoxes and puns. The date of the sequence is somewhere around 1607, when Donne is beginning to focus his attention on faith, when Jack Donne is beginning to dress himself as a faithful, repentant John Donne.

The first sonnet in the sequence begins with the line, 'Deign at my hands this crown of prayer and praise', and the last line of the final sonnet repeats this. In this first poem the third line is: 'All changing unchang'd Ancient of days'; thus initiating a fugue of paradoxes that really help to hold the sequence together, alongside the repeated lines. The whole sequence remains on the level of prayer and praise and does not enter into the deep soul of the poet. Some of these poems are weaker than Donne's best, but some of them display his strong faith and his exploratory spirit. They work to admit Donne to God's benign presence, to prove, to himself at least, that he is putting the strong power of his will and intellect to work in an attempt to purge his sinful soul and prepare himself for heaven.

THE OUTLAW CHRIST

Annunciation

Salvation to all that will is nigh;
That All, which always is All every where,
Which cannot sin, and yet all sins must bear,
Which cannot die, yet cannot choose but die,
Lo, faithful Virgin, yields Himself to lie
In prison, in thy womb; and though He there
Can take no sin, nor thou give, yet he'll wear
Taken from thence, flesh, which death's force may try.
Ere by the spheres time was created, thou
Wast in His mind, who is thy Son, and Brother,
Whom thou conceiv'st, conceiv'd; yea thou art now
Thy Maker's maker, and thy Father's mother;
Thou hast light in dark; and shutt'st in little room,
Immensity cloister'd in thy dear womb.

Here, in this second sonnet of the sequence, the line 'That All, which always is All everywhere', refers to Christ, of course, the 'Wisdom' notion of Christ being there at the creation in the 'mind' of the Creator. Christ is the one who cannot sin but must bear all the sins of humanity. He who is immortal takes from Mary's flesh, and flesh is mortal. Mary herself, Donne says, was in the Creator's mind as Christ was; this gives the poet delight in the paradox of calling Christ 'thy Son, and Brother'; and that Mary now is 'Thy Maker's maker, and thy Father's mother.' All of which is rich in its paradoxical nature and touches on the great mysteries of the Christian faith; it leaves the reader amused, bemused, but still that distance from the actual love of Christ. It is interesting to note, given the climate of religious belief of the time, Donne's insistent approach to the Virgin Mary, a note certainly not welcomed by Puritans and Calvinists of the time. The new man, John Donne, was beginning to live on the edge of outlawry.

EAST OR WEST? JACK DONNE OR JOHN DONNE?

The third sonnet treats of the 'Nativity', taking the 'immensity' of the last line of the previous sonnet and showing how it has made itself 'weak enough' to come into our world. There is a joyful play on the notion of imprisonment in the womb, and the failure to find space in the inn. The central lines relish the paradox:

> See'st thou, my Soul, with thy faith's eyes, how He
> Which fills all place, yet none holds Him, doth lie?

Then Donne moves into the 'Temple', where Jesus, aged about twelve, was found sitting amongst the Doctors, and here Donne really pushes hard on paradox:

> The Word but lately could not speak, and lo,
> It suddenly speaks wonders, whence comes it,
> That all which was, and all which should be writ,
> A shallow seeming child, should deeply know?

The poems are self-indulgent to a point, the poet keeping a personal distance from the moments and events described.

Crucifying

> By miracles exceeding power of man,
> He faith in some, envy in some begat,
> For, what weak spirits admire, ambitious hate;
> In both affections many to Him ran,
> But Oh! the worst are most, they will and can,
> Alas, and do, unto the immaculate,
> Whose creature Fate is, now prescribe a Fate,
> Measuring self-life's infinity to a span,
> Nay to an inch. Lo, where condemned He
> Bears his own cross, with pain, yet by and by

When it bears Him, he must bear more and die.
Now Thou art lifted up, draw me to Thee,
And at Thy death giving such liberal dole,
Moist, with one drop of Thy blood, my dry soul.

This sequence of poems reads almost as if Donne were musing over the scriptures, finding the paradoxes, the puns, the points of focus, an intellectual but not a personal pursuit. In this poem, he approaches the Christ more nearly. Immensity has become limited 'to an inch' in humanity's dealings with Christ. The point Donne is making in dealing with Christ bearing 'his own cross, with pain' touches deeply on Donne's awareness of how much he needs to bear his own cross, and find his 'dry soul' moistened with even one drop of Christ's blood. We are witnessing, in these poems, Donne's gradual approach to a deeper faith in Christ.

Resurrection

Moist with one drop of thy blood, my dry soul
Shall (though she now be in extreme degree
Too stony hard, and yet too fleshly,) be
Freed by that drop, for being starv'd, hard or foul,
And life, by this death abled, shall control
Death, whom Thy death slew; nor shall to me
Fear of first or last death, bring misery,
If in Thy little book my name Thou enrol,
Flesh in that long sleep is not putrefied,
But made that there, of which, and for which 'twas;
Nor can by other means be glorified.
May then sin's sleep, and death's soon from me pass,
That waked from both, I again risen may
Salute the last, and everlasting day.

EAST OR WEST? JACK DONNE OR JOHN DONNE?

At last, if the poet's soul can find some life through the blood of Christ, then life can control death, and he can begin to hope in everlasting blessedness. The use of pun and paradox continues but they are being used with more serious intent already. The notion of death and re-awakening is central to the sequence and here brings power and a musical and rhythmic finality to the last line of this sonnet: 'Salute the last, and everlasting day'. These poems read like rehearsals for the real thing; they move like intellectual exercises, punctuated by a self-conscious wit; they are auditions to the self for the real thing. The final poem in the *La Corona* sequence is 'Ascension', taking up from the 'Resurrection' poem with 'Salute the last and everlasting day'; it then plays on the word 'uprising', with 'Sun' and 'Son', and the sequence ends with the first line of the first poem being the last line here:

> And if Thy holy Spirit, my Muse did raise,
> Deign at my hands this crown of prayer and praise.

During these years, Donne was participating in theological controversies and wrote a pamphlet, *Pseudo-Martyr*, in 1610, where he tried to persuade Roman Catholics to accept the Oath of Allegiance. He took holy orders in 1615, partly urged to do so as a result of the success of his pamphlet, though he hesitated for a long time, remembering his ambitions, his worldliness and his sins. It was during this time of semi-poverty, of vacillation, of living between bouts of good and ill health, that he wrote his great Good Friday poem, in 1613. He was aware of his advancing age and his own ill health, so he was aware that his opportunities for position and wealth and power were fast diminishing. He was unaware, of course, that Ann was shortly to die in childbirth. The poem opens his heart to his own doubts and difficulties, hopes and sufferings, longings and weaknesses. Decisions, decisions! This is a poem that arises from a particular moment, an event in his life, and is not just the result of an intellectual absorption in paradox or doctrine. As in most of his best poems, Donne becomes a watcher on the battlements of himself, an actor on a stage reasoning with his own soul. This is a method of self-analysis that takes place before his public and that, at its best here, satisfies the whole man, the artist, the cynic, the lover, the believer. It begins with the notion that a human is like a sphere, like a billiard ball, perhaps, that has within himself the principle of his own movement, 'devotion'; however, if such a sphere yields to the impulses of a foreign body – like devotion to wealth, or court, or advancement – then the soul is impelled in directions other than those in which it ought to travel. East or west? Good Friday, a day when the heart is impelled to examine itself, the urgencies that give it motive and motion, facing the paradoxes of Christian belief and the demands that belief makes. Decisions! What are the motives that set the soul towards its goals?

Good-Friday, 1613. Riding Westward

Let man's Soul be a Sphere, and then, in this,
The intelligence that moves, devotion is;
And as the other Spheres, by being grown
Subject to foreign motion, lose their own,
And being by others hurried every day,
Scarce in a year their natural form obey;
Pleasure or business, so, our Souls admit
For their first mover, and are whirl'd by it.
Hence is't, that I am carried towards the West,
This day, when my Soul's form bends to the East.
There I should see a Sun by rising set,
And by that setting endless day beget.
But that Christ on this cross did rise and fall,
Sin had eternally benighted all.
Yet dare I almost be glad, I do not see

EAST OR WEST? JACK DONNE OR JOHN DONNE?

That spectacle of too much weight for me.
Who sees God's face, that is self-life, must die;
What a death were it then to see God die?
It made His own Lieutenant Nature, shrink,
It made His footstool crack, and the Sun wink.
Could I behold those hands, which span the Poles
And tune all spheres at once, pierced with those holes?
Could I behold that endless height, which is
Zenith to us, and our Antipodes,
Humbled below us? or that blood, which is
The seat of all our soul's, if not of His,
Made dirt of dust, or that flesh which was worn
By God for His apparel, rag'd and torn?
If on these things I durst not look, durst I
Upon his miserable mother cast mine eye,
Who was God's partner here, and furnish'd thus
Half of that Sacrifice, which ransom'd us?
Though these things, as I ride, be from mine eye,
They're present yet unto my memory,
For that looks towards them; and Thou look'st towards me,
O Saviour, as Thou hang'st upon the tree.
I turn my back to Thee but to receive
Correction, till Thy mercies bid Thee leave.
O think me worth Thine anger, punish me,
Burn off my rust, and my deformity;
Restore Thine Image, so much, by Thy grace,
That Thou mayst know me, and I'll turn my face.

Donne was riding westwards on Good Friday, aware that true devotion is man's greatest task in this world. If devotion as motive is missing, then other impulses take over, as in his duty or object in riding west on this special day of devotion to Christ on the Cross. He knows in his soul he ought to be heading east, to celebrate that truly awesome event; but the man, the poet, cannot resist the pun and paradox: 'There I should see a Sun by rising set, / And by that setting endless day beget.' But he turns at once from this device to a favourite topic, sin and its redemption. He feels that to see the death of Christ might bear too much down upon him. Once again he presents the sights he might see in paradoxical ways, emphasising his topic of life and creation as a sphere. Donne, the former Catholic, also feels he could hardly cope with seeing the mother of Christ suffer, and he speaks of her as furnishing half of the sacrifice that redeemed our sins. Donne's theme again: he could only look on the face of Christ if he himself had been purged. Now Donne speaks directly to Christ, outlining how this purgation will make him give up all other impulses save that of devotion.

The poem is one of Donne's most direct and uncluttered pieces to treat his need for Christ. While he occasionally indulges in pun and paradox, they serve in this piece a more serious purpose and come from the heart more than the head. This is John Donne; Jack has slipped quietly from the stage. It is clear from the tone of the poem that the motives of 'pleasure or business' will soon give way to 'devotion'. He is seeking penance for his past misdemeanours, simple pardon not being sufficient.

Allied to this strong poem is the series of *Holy Sonnets*, perhaps Donne's finest achievement in verse. Ill health and the awareness of the fragility of life had sobered him, yet the poems retain the vigour of language and the mastery of paradox that had lifted his love lyrics to great heights. It is the glory of the best of the *Holy Sonnets* that they bring the ragamuffin Jack Donne before us, redeemed by his very real struggles to accept what religion requires: a total commitment. John Donne's poems plead to God to take the initiative and *force* Donne to be a saint! He had moved to Drury Lane in 1612, a more affluent area of London, still hoping against hope for a court appointment. His children were often ill, Ann had a miscarriage and by 1614 he had a great many financial troubles. By now three of his children had died. Both he and Ann were weakened by

EAST OR WEST? JACK DONNE OR JOHN DONNE?

illness. Entering holy orders seemed a last resort, but in early 1615, John Donne became a priest. Ann died; she was only thirty-three; she had brought twelve children into the world, losing five of them. In the same year Donne was appointed a royal chaplain to the king; he would give sermons in the king's presence. He gradually became admired for them and, through a system of patronage and some obsequious pleading, he was made dean of St Paul's Cathedral in 1621. It appeared that, at last, and after many years of suffering, some of his dreams had come true, but not in the way he had imagined.

His sermons were carefully listened to and monitored; he had to remain careful. He still missed the old ways of Roman Catholicism and its reassurances. His quarrel with Rome was basically not with doctrine but with its political interference and assumptions, and his belief that no subject could accept and acknowledge both king and pope; for this reason he found it easy to preach loyalty to the king and the Church of England.

The *Holy Sonnets* were published posthumously in 1633, part of *Songs and Sonnets*. The nineteen sonnets exhibit a new and powerful rhythmic movement; the imagery is always forceful and immediate; the sonnets are prayers that touch on personal doubts and hesitations, on his fears of sin and punishment and his deep and ongoing sense that he could never be worthy of the great Master, Christ. They are much stronger and closer to the heart and bone than the sonnets of *La Corona*, and by contrast greatly overshadow the earlier work.

Oh my black Soul ...

Oh my black Soul! now thou art summoned
By sickness, death's herald, and champion;
Thou art like a pilgrim, which abroad hath done
Treason, and durst not turn to whence he is fled,
Or like a thief, which till death's doom be read,
Wisheth himself delivered from prison;

> But damned and hal'd to execution,
> Wisheth that still he might be imprisoned.
> Yet grace, if thou repent, thou canst not lack;
> But who shall give thee that grace to begin?
> Oh make thyself with holy mourning black,
> And red with blushing, as thou art with sin;
> Or wash thee in Christ's blood, which hath this might
> That being red, it dyes red souls to white.

Colours figure strongly in this poem, from the blackness of the sin and unworthiness of the poet's soul to the red of Christ's blood that will wash that soul to white. Sickness brings the possibility of death and Donne knows that the evil that has discoloured his soul must be purged if he is to gain heaven. He lives, then, in a form of exile and is not able to return in case he be executed when he does. Echoes of Donne's early experience with the Jesuits he had known and who had suffered imprisonment and execution, shiver through the sonnet. Grace is needed, and grace can be given freely only by Christ; so, take on a different kind of black, that of mourning, and then Christ's blood, which had been shed for humankind, will wash him clean. The easy and hastening movement of the poem, its rhythms and rhymes, convey the urgency of the thought. The images of pilgrimage and exile deepen the colour metaphors, the idea of life as a journey towards death and then either victory or loss. The awareness that Christ is the source of all hope has grown instinctive to John Donne as was prefigured in the Good Friday poem. The temptation to pun and play around with paradox has lessened; this is more serious work than the *Corona* sonnets.

At the round earth's imagined corners ...

> At the round earth's imagin'd corners, blow
> Your trumpets, Angels, and arise, arise

EAST OR WEST? JACK DONNE OR JOHN DONNE?

> From death, you numberless infinities
> Of souls, and to your scattered bodies go;
> All whom the flood did, and fire shall o'erthrow,
> All whom war, dearth, age, agues, tyrannies,
> Despair, law, chance, hath slain, and you whose eyes,
> Shall behold God, and never taste death's woe.
> But let them sleep, Lord, and me mourn a space,
> For, if above all these, my sins abound,
> 'Tis late to ask abundance of thy grace,
> When we are there; here on this lowly ground,
> Teach me how to repent; for that's as good
> As if thou hadst sealed my pardon with Thy blood.

One of the major worries of Donne's life was the loss of his soul into eternal damnation. So the judgement day, that particular judgement of each individual after death, and the final judgement day, at the end of the world, were often in his thoughts. Following the Book of Revelation, he uses the imagery of the general rising from the dead at the final judgement, envisioning all the bodies reuniting themselves with their souls, as well as those who may be alive when that final day hits creation. Now he prays that day may yet be far enough off for him to repent his sins and be pardoned. Repenting, he adds, is as good 'as if' Christ had already sealed that pardon with his own death on the cross. He knows, of course, that that is the case, the pardon is sealed; so the poem is, in fact, one of his most optimistic. If he is anxious about predestination, as the Calvinists insisted loudly at that time that one should be, then Christ's death has already guaranteed repentance and pardon and that these have already been won. Donne has reached out in plea and prayer to the Christ who is the only one who can save him from his own sinful nature.

In chapter 15 of the first letter to the Corinthians, St Paul wrote: 'We shall not all die but we shall all be changed in a flash, in the twinkling of an eye, at the last trumpet call. For the trumpet will sound and the dead will rise immortal and we shall all be changed.' If the earth is thought of as a sphere, then it will have 'imagined corners'; this, too, is a favourite metaphorical device of Donne's. The poem reads dramatically, as, for the poet, the issue is a vitally important one. And, once again, it is Christ's suffering and death that give hope and, in this poem, certainty, that pardon is offered to all.

The *Holy Sonnets* move through many facets of Donne's beliefs and hopes, and touch often on his personal troubles. Illness, and he suffered a good deal, continues to force him to thoughts of death. Linked with 'At the round earth's imagined corners … ', is the next sonnet, touching once again on the thought of the final destruction of the earth.

What if this present …

What if this present were the world's last night?
Mark in my heart, O Soul, where thou dost dwell,
The picture of Christ crucified, and tell
Whether that countenance can thee affright,
Tears in His eyes quench the amazing light,
Blood fills His frowns, which from His pierc'd head fell.
And can that tongue adjudge thee unto hell,
Which pray'd forgiveness for His foes' fierce spite?
No, no; but as in my idolatry
I said to all my profane mistresses,
Beauty, of pity, foulness only is
A sign of rigour: so I say to thee,
To wicked spirits are horrid shapes assign'd,
This beauteous form assures a piteous mind.

Donne is reimagining the time just before his death, or before the final judgement. Soul and heart are here more or less equated, and this allows mind and affections to peruse the image of the crucified Christ.

EAST OR WEST? JACK DONNE OR JOHN DONNE?

Gazing on the face of this great lover, how is it possible to think that such a face could utter the words of condemnation to hell of any soul? There are tears in the eyes of Christ, the thorns have brought blood to his brow. And if Christ prayed to his Father, 'Father forgive them for they know not what they do', and this forgiveness is asked for those who have just driven nails into his hands and feet, then how can words from that same tongue condemn anyone to eternal suffering? Donne is remembering his past when, as Jack, he lived in 'idolatry', holding other things before Christ. He sounds a somewhat alien note here, alien to this poem, and perhaps with a little too much pride and self-adulation, when he speaks of 'all my profane mistresses', as if he had indeed succeeded in making many conquests of women before his meeting with Ann. He expects that beauty in a mistress is a sign she will take pity on him, and that foulness would be a sign of rigour, or hard-heartedness in a mistress, and here, in Christ. There is no sign of foulness in Christ; there can, therefore, be no hard-heartedness. Although it is a telling phrase and a memorable one, 'as I said to all my profane mistresses' is really something of an ego-booster and an intrusion into this poem. The word 'all', in particular, is a little over the top! Donne, in this poem, has, however, written another powerful piece to deepen his own faith and trust in Christ.

Has he, then, done sufficient penance for his past sins? Has he gained forgiveness and a sure and certain pathway to eternal life?

Batter my heart ...

Batter my heart, three-person'd God, for you
As yet but knock, breathe, shine, and seek to mend;
That I may rise and stand, o'erthrow me, and bend
Your force, to break, blow, burn and make me new.
I, like an usurp'd town to'another due,
Labour to admit you, but Oh, to no end,
Reason your viceroy in me, me should defend,

> But is captiv'd, and proves weak or untrue.
> Yet dearly I love you, and would be loved fain,
> But am betroth'd unto your enemy:
> Divorce me, untie, or break that knot again,
> Take me to you, imprison me, for I
> Except you enthrall me, never shall be free,
> Nor ever chaste, except you ravish me.

It appears that all the application of a searching spirit is not sufficient to give certainty of real repentance and therefore forgiveness. This sonnet may well be based on St Paul's lines in Romans, 'the things I want to do I do not do … ', and Donne is aware that this will apply to his own human efforts. Grace is not something to be dragged down out of God's hands; it is a gift to the soul and must be earned. And even the earning of the gift is a gift in itself. Donne therefore knows that he depends fully on God's unbreaking gift and this poem pleads for this, even violent, unbreaking. He makes rich use in this poem of his love of paradox. As well as paradox, he develops twin metaphors. The first is a fortified town that has to be broken into by the use of a battering ram, a town that has been usurped by an enemy and must be broken into from outside. This metaphor continues through the 'usurp'd town', 'viceroy'; the force must be used to overthrow the strength of reason and open up the heart. The second metaphor takes its lift from this one; wishing to 'love' God, he finds himself 'betroth'd', engaged, to the enemy. The last three lines link both metaphors quite delicately; he would wish to be imprisoned and enthralled and in this way achieve freedom; he wishes to be 'free' and 'chaste' so that God may ravish his soul. It is, perhaps, one of the best poems where paradox and cleverly threaded imagery work to great advantage. Behind the reasoned thought and the richness of the imagery, there is a strong sense of urgency and integrity, admitting that reason cannot help him to grace, and that he depends wholly on the good gift of God.

EAST OR WEST? JACK DONNE OR JOHN DONNE?

Since she whom I lov'd...

Since she whom I lov'd hath paid her last debt
To Nature, and to hers, and my good is dead,
And her Soul early into heaven ravished,
Wholly on heavenly things my mind is set.
Here the admiring her my mind did whet
To seek Thee God; so streams do show their head;
But though I have found Thee, and Thou my thirst hast fed,
A holy thirsty dropsy melts me yet.
But why should I beg more Love, when as Thou
Dost woo my soul for hers; off'ring all Thine:
And dost not only fear lest I allow
My Love to Saints and Angels, things divine,
But in Thy tender jealousy dost doubt
Lest the World, Flesh, yea Devil put Thee out.

The second line of this sonnet has caused some disturbance but it may be clear enough: Ann has died and, in becoming dust, has paid her last debt to Nature. She is now dead to her husband's good and to her own, therefore Donne can set his mind wholly on Christ. He does pay compliment to Ann in saying that she had set his mind already on things of God, and so she is like a stream that has shown him where the source may be. Now he seeks to find greater love and asks why this should be. Christ is wooing his soul, as he did Ann's, and offers all of his in exchange. Donne's somewhat humorous comment is that perhaps God is jealous of all of his creation, including the devil, lest anyone else sought to engage a human's love.

It still appears that Donne is far from the position of personal affection and love that Herbert displays in his poetry and his approach to Christ. Donne comes at it from a broader perspective, perhaps, seeing how the whole of the earth is linked in God's love into one sphere; it is a basic premise of his thinking and of his poetry that all of humanity in particular is linked together, and this more intellectual basis for his writing removes him somewhat from a more personal and affectionate awareness of Christ. It is nonetheless valid for that. It may, perhaps, be viewed from a more prosaic perspective, and clarified by an examination of some of Donne's famous sermons. These spring powerfully from his fears, fear of death, fear of damnation, fear of making mistakes, which might throw him back into a form of Roman Catholicism that could place him in danger of losing his position as dean of St Paul's. In this way, he may be said to be 'preaching a sermon to himself'.

In 1623, John Donne fell seriously ill. It was a form of what was called 'spotted fever'; it made him very weak and he was almost certain he would die. He was then aged fifty-one, he had lost his young and much-loved wife, he had tried, and was trying still, to come to terms with his sensual leanings. The fever, which left him thoroughly weakened, brought with it insomnia and prostration, as well as the usual pains associated with fever. And, of course, it was a fever into which there was every possibility he would 'relapse'. There were long periods of convalescence, giving him a good deal of time for the contemplation of our sorry human estate, something John Donne was always happy to examine, and remind himself of, in his attempts to curb the body's appetites. He would dwell more especially on humanity's more negative aspects, and most of all on death. He issued a series of what he called 'devotions', moving from an intellectual examination of how we stand and fall, towards a deeper understanding of spiritual things. The aim of these devotions was to urge the spirit towards the love of God rather than wasting life, as he told himself he had done, in transitory loves. Perhaps the most famous quotation from Donne comes, in fact, from one of these devotions. He reminds himself of how he had lain prostrate on his sickbed and heard a bell tolling from somewhere outside:

> Perchance he for whom this bell tolls may be so ill, as that he knows not it tolls for him; and perchance I may think myself so much

EAST OR WEST? JACK DONNE OR JOHN DONNE?

better than I am, as that they who are about me, and see my state, may have caused it to toll for me, and I know not that. The church is Catholic, universal, so are all her actions; all that she does belongs to all. When she baptizes a child, that action concerns me; for that child is thereby connected to that body which is my head, too, and ingrafted into that body whereof I am a member. And when she buries a man, that action concerns me: all mankind is of one author, and is one volume; when one man dies, one chapter is not torn out of the book, but translated into another language; and every chapter must be so translated; God employs several translators; some pieces are translated by age, some by sickness, some by war, some by injustice; but God's hand is in every translation, and his hand shall bind up all our scattered leaves again for that library where every book shall lie open to one another.

The word 'translation' here means, as he writes, 'translated into another language'; however, it also holds its original Latin meaning, to 'carry across', to 'bring over'. The imagery of 'one volume' is richly developed in this passage; 'every chapter must be translated'. Every poet addresses his work to somebody, most usually to himself, and Donne's work – even, I believe, his most fusty sermons – are directed to convince himself of the truths he needs to hold. There are so many poems beginning with a call to the self to take notice: 'I am two fools, I know … ', 'Good we must love, and must hate ill … ', 'O, my black soul, now thou art summoned … ', 'This is my play's last scene … ', 'What if this present were the world's last night?', 'Wilt thou love God as he thee? then digest, / My soul, this wholesome meditation'. It appears that Donne had to keep convincing himself of the truths he held close to him, perhaps mostly out of fear.

In our early years on this earth, the concept of time does not impinge that much. For Jack Donne, in his early, sensually occupied years, time was both a joy (when he was with his lover) and a trouble (when they had to part). Thus, even his early poems are alert to antinomy and paradox:

> Now thou hast loved me one whole day,
> To-morrow when thou leavest, what wilt thou say? …
>
> Love, all alike, no season knows nor clime,
> Nor hours, days, months, which are the rags of time …
>
> For every hour that thou wilt spare me now,
>   I will allow,
> Usurious god of love, twenty to thee,
> When with my brown my grey hairs equal be …

Having secretly married the under-age Ann More, Donne soon found himself in jail, thrown out of his job, rejected by the parents of his young bride. In an effort to get his lover to be more condescending to his wishes he wrote 'The Flea', one of his secular poems:

> O stay, three lives in one flea spare,
> Where we almost, yea more than married are.
> This flea is you and I, and this
> Our marriage bed, and marriage temple is.
> Though parents grudge, and you, we're met,
> And cloistered in these living walls of jet.

She goes on to 'purple her nail' with the blood of the flea, thus killing three at one go, because the flea had sucked his blood, and then hers:

> Just so much honour, when thou yield'st to me,
> Will waste, as this flea's death took life from thee.

The point of the writing is in the writing itself, the pleasure is in the argument, the humour, the serious fun. Donne wrote a great deal of wonderful poetry in similar vein, witty, reasonable, filled with paradox and

EAST OR WEST? JACK DONNE OR JOHN DONNE?

paradigm – until life hurt him, and death. His beloved Ann's death left him perplexed and stricken. When he eventually got the preferment that he had longed for and laboured towards, a high seriousness had taken over. As he still suffered regular bouts of serious illness, death was constantly before his mind, and two of his most perfect faith poems, 'Hymn to God the Father' and 'Hymn to God my God, in my Sickness', were written. And even here, in these late, great poems, Donne will not resist the temptation to a little bit of verbal trickery and fun. It is this dexterity with language that makes the poetry strike home to the rest of us, who tend to resent any high seriousness if it is not gently sauced with wit and humour. Indeed, the point of Donne's sermons and poems is that they are addressed to himself as well as, and as much as to an audience, and this sense of being a watcher and a hearer, rather than the one addressed, takes the reader unawares and wins assent the more readily.

> As therefore the bell that rings to a sermon calls not upon the preacher only, but upon the congregation to come, so this bell calls us all; but how much more me, who am brought so near the door by this sickness. There was a contention as far as a suit (in which both piety and dignity, religion and estimation, were mingled), as to which of the religious orders should ring to prayers first in the morning; and it was determined, that they should ring first that rose earliest. If we understand aright the dignity of this bell that tolls for our evening prayer, we should be glad to make it ours by rising early, in that application, that it might be ours as well as his, whose indeed it is.

In January 1631 Donne's mother died. He had been caring for her for some time, a fact that seems to show that she and Donne, in spite of his removal from her Roman Catholic faith, never really lost trust in one another. He died very soon after her, in March of the same year. The intensity of his seriousness in later life as he pursued his calling as a divine goes some way to dissolve the complaint that his dismissal of the Roman faith was done out of fear of imprisonment at that time. But he did not come to God all complete in his devotion, 'all saucered and blowed', all prepared for divine love.

Hymne to God my God, in My Sickness

Since I am coming to that Holy roome,
    Where, with thy Quire of Saints for evermore, *[choir]*
I shall be made thy Music; As I come
    I tune the Instrument at the door,
    And what I must do then, think here before.

Whilst my Physicians by their love are growne
    Cosmographers, and I their Map, who lie
Flat on this bed, that by them may be shown
    That this is my South-west discovery
    Per fretum febris, by these straits to die,

I joy, that in these straits, I see my West;
    For, though their currents yield return to none,
What shall my West hurt me? As West and East
    In all flat Maps (and I am one) are one,
    So death doth touch the Resurrection.

Is the Pacific Sea my home? Or are
    The Eastern riches? Is *Jerusalem*?
Anyan, and *Magellan*, and *Gibraltar*,
    All straits, and none but straits, are ways to them,
    Whether where *Japhet* dwelt, or *Cham*, or *Shem*.

We think that *Paradise* and *Calvary*,
    Christ's Cross, and *Adam's* tree, stood in one place;

EAST OR WEST? JACK DONNE OR JOHN DONNE?

Look Lord, and find both *Adams* met in me;
  As the first *Adam*'s sweat surrounds my face,
  May the last *Adam*'s blood my soul embrace.

So, in His purple wrapp'd receive me Lord,
  By these His thorns give me His other Crown;
  And as to others' souls I preached Thy word,
  Be this my Text, my Sermon to mine own,
Therefore that He may raise the Lord throws down.

Donne develops a hugely interesting and intriguing metaphor here, that even when he thought himself at death's threshold he could think out the image and develop it. He is not actually thinking of joining 'thy Choir of Saints', but that they shall be using him and his arrival in Paradise as their tune. Therefore he wishes to tune the instrument, himself, before he gets there. Here is the poet urging himself to prepare for imminent death: 'what I must do then, think here before'. This is high seriousness to begin with, high seriousness with a basso profundo of humour in the imagery. A second favourite metaphor is added, that of the person as a map, with his doctors as map-readers and then, since west meets east in all maps, death touches, in the same way, on resurrection. Both 'Adams', Adam in the garden and Christ on the Cross, he sees as having been in the one place; Adam's sweat of death is on Donne's face, he pleads again that Christ's blood might embrace his soul.

He sees the poem as a sermon directed to himself, a warning, a warning that moves on, however, through his delight in the play on the words 'strait' and 'straight', to develop his theme in playful seriousness. Lying on his back in bed he sees himself as a map of the world, laid out flat, the west therefore tipping the east, and (as in the great poem 'Good Friday, 1613. Riding Westward') death and resurrection are also seen to tip each other. This 'conceit', in its wit and accuracy, convinces Donne and the reader, during the time the poem is being absorbed, because of the strength and serious ongoing flow of the stanzas. It must be remembered that Donne was writing in a time when religious controversy was something new and intense, and did not bother too much about the accuracy of the statements he might make in the second last stanza. What matters here is Donne's effort, by using words and music and paradox, his beloved tools, to convince himself of what he wants to believe. And all of it moving inexorably to the final line, itself the ultimate paradox, which is here stated in simple terms, without strain or anxiety in the monosyllables, resulting in a resolution of his sorry state. As so often in the poetry of Donne, it is the wit and sharpness of the intellect that moves us; after reading the poem and relishing it, it is not easy to actually 'feel' what the poet must have felt in his deep heart's core.

In the poetry of John Donne, as he gradually moved from human, sexual love to the love of God, there is a delicate growth in trust and faith, indeed in joy, in spite of all his physical ailments. The shift to a poetry of faith is indeed so delicate that the sensual imagery that gave zest to the early poetry turns into the imagery of joy in the Lord. The shift towards a trust in the spiritual grows easily and organically out of his zeal for the natural man. Donne's religion is far from being that of a dour Anglican clergyman, or of a Calvinist disgusted with natural things, but is rich in awareness that the natural things of life are even more wonderful when underpinned by the grace of God. Yet Donne was conscious of sin and guilt, of how a sinner falls over and over again, and is forgiven over and over again. It is, in Donne, a constant cycle of falling, of repentance and forgiveness, of falling again. In God's continual willingness to forgive, Donne finds his joy; in his own continual willingness to fall, Donne finds he has to keep reminding himself of God's mercy, he has to keep preaching a sermon to himself. He has to come to terms with his sensual and sinful self in terms of his newfound faith in the love of God; as he would say to himself, I have not yet got John Donne settled: 'When I have done, I have not done … '. If his earlier poems were written with an eye to an audience of bright young things, both male and female, at court, the later

EAST OR WEST? JACK DONNE OR JOHN DONNE?

poems take on more of an awareness of an audience that he wants to lead through to eternal life – the main person in that audience being himself. Donne develops a spirituality that is deeply involved with the natural man, aware of lust and of sickness, of wars and natural disasters, and it is this down-to-earth spirituality that still touches us deeply today.

> Wilt thou forgive that sinne which I did shunne
> A yeare, or two: but wallow'd in, a score?

The bell doth toll for him that thinks it doth; and though it intermit again, yet from that minute that that occasion wrought upon him, he is united to God. Who casts not up his eye to the sun when it rises? But who takes off his eye from a comet when that breaks out? Who bends not his ear to any bell which upon any occasion rings? But who can remove it from that bell which is passing a piece of himself out of this world? No man is an island, entire of itself; every man is a piece of the continent, a part of the main. If a clod be washed away by the sea, Europe is the less, as well as if a promontory were, as well as if a manor of thy friend's or of thine own were: any man's death diminishes me, because I am involved in mankind, and therefore never send to know for whom the bell tolls; it tolls for thee ...

Donne, in his early poetry, used paradox to great effect, injecting the humour of his quiet but certain wit. Later he came to see that the God he was growing more and more to believe and trust in was a God of paradox. 'That He may raise, the Lord throws down'. Nor is it possible to resolve this paradox. 'To whom God gives more, of him He requires more'. In a sermon he called 'Christ the Light', preached at St Paul's Cathedral on Christmas Day 1621, he developed the light and darkness paradox. 'In all philosophy,' he told his riveted listeners, 'there is not so dark a thing as light'. Indeed, Donne had come to see living itself as paradoxical, 'in the midst of life we are in death'. In that sermon he said:

> He that should come to a heathen man, a mere natural man, uncatechized, uninstructed in the rudiments of the Christian religion, and should at first, without any preparation, present him first with this necessity: that thou shalt burn in fire and brimstone eternally except thou believe in a Trinity of persons, in an unity of one God, except thou believe that a virgin had a son and the same Son that God had, and that God was man too and being the immortal God yet died, he should be so far from working any spiritual cure upon this poor soul, as that he should rather bring Christian mysteries into scorn than him to a belief. For that man, if you proceed so (believe all or you burn in hell), would find an easy, an obvious way to escape all; that is, first not to believe in hell itself, and then nothing would bind him to believe the rest.

The paradoxes on which the foundations of the whole Christian faith rest brought John Donne face to face with his own excitement over language, and his own utter dread of death. His poetry, and his sermons, urged him on to an acceptance of the God of love, light and life, who brings us down into darkness and death so that that love can be fulfilled.

In his sermon preached at St Paul's in 1625 he said:

> All our life is a continual burden, yet we must not groan; a continual squeezing, yet we must not pant. And as in the tenderness of our childhood we suffer, and yet are whipped if we cry, so we are complained of if we complain, and made delinquents if we call the times ill. And that which adds weight to weight and multiplies the sadness of this consideration is this: that still the best men have had the most laid upon them.

EAST OR WEST? JACK DONNE OR JOHN DONNE?

And there is the great 'Death's Duell' sermon that was preached during Lent 1630 at Whitehall in the presence of King Charles I. Here, at last, there is resolution of enigma, there is melding of antinomies, a breathing away of paradox, all in the awareness of the unconditional love of God.

> ... it is in his power to give us an issue and deliverance, even then when we are brought to the jaws and teeth of death, and to the lips of that whirlpool, the grave.' This is the final paradox, that we shall find 'a deliverance in death. Not that God will deliver us from dying, but that he will have a care of us in the hour of death, of what kind soever our passage be ... ' 'We have a winding sheet in our mother's womb, which grows with us from our conception, and we come into the world, wound up in that winding sheet, for we come to seek a grave.' 'How much worse a death than death is this life, which so good men would so often change for death!' Contemplating our death he speaks with Job, 'Corruption thou art my father', and he says to the worm 'Thou art my mother and my sister'. And goes on, with great relish: 'Miserable riddle, when the same worm must be my mother and my sister and myself. Miserable incest, when I must be married to my mother and my sister, and be both father and mother to my own mother and sister, begat and bear that worm which is all that miserable penury.

These are the resolutions that lead him to his last great poem:

A Hymne to God the Father

I

Wilt Thou forgive that sin where I begun,
   Which is my sin, though it were done before?
Wilt Thou forgive that sin through which I run,
   And do run still: though still I do deplore?
      When Thou hast done, Thou hast not done,
         For I have more.

II
Wilt Thou forgive that sin by which I have won
   Others to sin? and, made my sin their door?
Wilt Thou forgive that sin which I did shun
   A year or two: but wallow'd in, a score?
      When Thou hast done, Thou hast not done,
         For I have more.
III
I have a sin of fear, that when I have spun
   My last thread, I shall perish on the shore;
But swear by Thyself, that at my death Thy son
   Shall shine as He shines now, and heretofore;
      And, having done that, Thou hast done,
         I have no more.

The poems lead up to this moment, 'I have a sin of fear, that when I have spun / My last thread, I shall perish on the shore'. The tone of this poem is playful and, given the theme, this playfulness underscores a trust and hope, an ease with his faith, a certainty that forgiveness will be there and he will be taken past the shore and into heaven. He has persuaded himself, through his poetry and his dealing with a difficult and painful life, that God is there, is loving, forgiving, and has overcome death. All of this has been achieved with the help of an understanding of paradox in that faith, and a joyful use of the paradoxes with which language is rich and rife. And of course the poem brings us back to the name of the poet, this is Jack Donne, this is also John Donne; when Donne is finally in death and forgiven his sins, then God has done … he has done everything to bring the poet to heaven, and he also has Jack and John Donne in his care forever.

> Neither can we call this a begging of misery, or a borrowing of misery, as though we were not miserable enough of ourselves, but must fetch in more from the next house, in taking upon us the

misery of our neighbours. Truly it were an excusable covetousness if we did, for affliction is a treasure, and scarce any man hath enough of it. No man hath affliction enough that is not matured and ripened by it, and made fit for God by that affliction. If a man carry treasure in bullion, or in a wedge of gold, and have none coined into current money, his treasure will not defray him as he travels. Tribulation is treasure in the nature of it, but it is not current money in the use of it, except we get nearer and nearer our home, heaven, by it. And another man may be sick too, and sick to death, and this affliction may lie in his bowels, as gold in a mine, and be of no use to him; but this bell, that tells me of his affliction, digs out and applies that gold to me: if by this consideration of another's danger I take mine own into contemplation, and so secure myself, by making my recourse to my God, who is our only security.

8

TO WIN A KISS

Robert Herrick (1591-1674)

Robert Herrick was born to a London goldsmith, Nicholas Herrick, and his wife, Julian Stone Herrick. When Robert was fourteen months old, his father died. At the age of sixteen, he went into apprenticeship for some six years, matriculating from Cambridge in 1617. In 1623 he took holy orders and later became vicar of Dean Prior in Devonshire. In 1647 he lost the position because of his royalist sympathies; after the Restoration he was reinstated. He never married, although his love poems are rich and memorable. His poetry was influenced by Roman classics and he developed pastoral themes of English country living.

His poem, 'To His Saviour, a Child: A Present by a Child', is quite charming in its way. It portrays Christ as a child being given gifts by another child. The poem touches the heart as it touches on a 'bib', a 'whistle', on poverty and on love, as to earn a kiss from this child is such a grace it must not be spoiled by repetition. The view of Christ that is portrayed is pleasing, harmless, but answers the purpose for which the poem is made. Indeed, the very insistence on the everyday childhood of the Christ emphasises the fact that the creator God has done something way out of the ordinary by bringing the Son of God into human flesh.

To His Saviour, a Child: A Present by a Child

Go, pretty child, and bear this flower
Unto thy little Saviour;
And tell Him, by that bud now blown,
He is the Rose of Sharon known.

THE OUTLAW CHRIST

When thou hast said so, stick it there
Upon His bib or stomacher;
And tell Him for good handsel, too,
That thou has brought a whistle new,
Made of a clean straight oaten reed,
To charm His cries in time of need.
Tell Him, for coral, thou hast none,
But if thou hadst, He should have one;
But poor thou art, and known to be
Even as moneyless as He;
Lastly, if thou canst win a kiss
From those mellifluous lips of His,
Then never take a second one
To spoil the first impression.

9

GUILTY OF DUST

George Herbert (1593-1633)

Here is a stanza from a poem of George Herbert's, 'Longing':

> Behold, thy dust doth stir,
> It moves, it creeps, it aims at thee:
>   Wilt thou defer
>   To succour me,
> Thy pile of dust, wherein each crumb
> Says, Come?

George Herbert was born in Montgomery, Wales. His father died when he was very young; his mother was patron to the poet John Donne, who dedicated his *Holy Sonnets* to her. When she died in 1627, Donne gave her funeral sermon. In 1618 Herbert was appointed reader in rhetoric at Cambridge and in 1620 was elected public orator. For a time, he was an MP, alongside his friend Nicholas Ferrar, and represented Montgomery in Parliament. In 1629 he married Jane Danvers. He took orders in the Church of England in 1630 and ended his life as rector of Bemerton, near Salisbury. George Herbert's writings were not published in his lifetime but he left them to the care of Nicholas Ferrar of Little Gidding; he asked him to publish them only if he thought they might do good 'to any dejected poor soul'. We are blessed that Ferrar recognised the value of the manuscripts and had them published.

In Herbert's poems Christ is a real, human person, close to the sufferings of humanity and close to the poet's heart and mind; it is in table fellowship that Herbert sought his Christ, his 'Master'. His use of phrases like 'my dear', at times conveys an easy intimacy that is a delight to find in a poetry of faith. This personal response to the person of Christ is new in faith poetry in English and has not been sufficiently taken up by later writers. Several poems speak of humanity's need to respond to the generosity of God, as in 'The Reprisal' (the word is used in the sense of 'reprising' a theme). Humanity is guilty, in Herbert's eyes, of 'dust and sin', by which he means that humanity is always on the road to death and compounds an innate 'guilt', that we see, partly, as entropy, by deliberately going against God's will. R.S. Thomas wrote of him: 'In fact Herbert, like a good Anglican, equates sickness with sin, and good health with holiness, believing implicitly in God's power to heal, if it be also his will.'

Herbert's cautious and exquisite structuring of each individual poem into its own form echoes an ordering imagination and self-confidence in both theme and craft. Herbert uses the word 'dust' frequently; he holds that humanity falls to dust, 'decaying more and more'. If humanity grows in harmony with Christ, then it will rise from that dust into resurrection with Christ: 'Then shall the fall further the flight in me.' This harmony with God to the acceptance of the freely given grace of God allows the soul to grow more and more into Christ, a theme taken up and developed in our own age among writers and philosophers like Teilhard de Chardin, Simone Weil and Ilia Delio. And it is to that point of reference – evolution into Christ – that the poetry of faith is tending in our own time.

Grace is a free gift of God to the soul; humanity, being dust, finds it difficult to accept this gift. George Herbert's poem 'Love' dramatises this offering beautifully, its initial rejection, its gradual inveigling and ultimate acceptance. The last stanza of that fine poem suggests that the final name Herbert finds for Christ is 'Love', because it was Christ who 'bore the blame' for humankind's sin and 'shaming' of life. It is sad to consider how the gentle and beautifully wrought poems of George Herbert seem to have had little effect on later generations and the work was not taken up as a challenge to a Christianity that refused to see the Christ as seeking 'mercy and not sacrifice'. This emphasis on love in spite of guilt already placed Herbert's Christ in the then invidious position of being outside and beyond the legal pretensions of the Church.

Herbert aims his prayer at God, calling the creature 'dust', but a creature that belongs to God, 'thy dust'; this dust aims its existence at God, each crumb of that dust pleading, 'Come'. He calls on God to succour this 'pile of dust'. This recurs in many of his poems; so often the word 'dust' ends a line and is therefore made to rhyme with 'just', sometimes with 'trust', sometimes with 'lust'. And in his greatest poem of all he calls himself, and therefore humanity as a whole, 'guilty of dust and sin'. How is one, then, 'guilty of dust'? Apart from the decorum and decency of his fine verses, Herbert's ongoing appeal lies in his argument, not with God or with himself, but with an inherent 'guilt' in humankind that leads him inevitably to destruction. This, I believe, is the entropy that Teilhard de Chardin later took to its fullest understanding; it is that phrase, 'guilty of dust', that Herbert uses to tell how we are fragile, at all times disintegrating, physically, a falling that may be accompanied by spiritual disintegration, through 'sin'. John Donne had already intuited, in his poetry and life, that this disintegration is a form of evolution in faith and humanity's development. In Herbert's poetry, the deity addressed is most often simply 'Lord', and refers more often than not to God the Creator. It also refers to Christ, whom Herbert addresses often as 'Master', and it is the person of Christ to whom Herbert looks for redemption, not only from sin, but from 'dust'. Two lines from the poem 'Easter' encapsulate this:

> That, as his death calcined thee to dust
> His life may make thee gold, and much more just.

W.H. Auden said of George Herbert 'one does not get the impression from his work that the temptations of the flesh were a serious spiritual menace to him, as they were to Donne'. This, of course, we do not know, but it seems clear from the poems and from his prose passages outlining the ideals he had for the parson, 'The Country Pastor', that he did attempt to keep his life in perfect order. Nor did he seem to suffer from religious doubts – in the seventeenth century very few people did. Herbert's struggles were interior ones, debating in his own heart with God and with his own human appetites. Above all the awareness was one of human frailty and hopelessness without the intervention of a loving God. And here's a passage from 'The Country Parson', neither too cheerful nor too promising: 'The Country Parson is generally sad, because he knows nothing but the Cross of Christ, his mind being defixed on it with those nails wherewith his Master was: or if he have any leisure to look off from thence, he meets continually with two most sad spectacles, Sin, and Misery; God dishonoured every day, and man afflicted.'

One of Herbert's most self-revealing poems is 'The Pilgrimage', a poem written when the Reformation and the Puritan excesses had done away with external forms of worship – icons, incense, even pilgrimages – and, stressing the need for interior pilgrimage, spawning many poems and works like that of Bunyan's *Pilgrim's Progress*:

The Pilgrimage

I travell'd on, seeing the hill, where lay
    My expectation.
  A long it was and weary way.
  The gloomy cave of Desperation
I left on th' one, and on the other side
    The rock of Pride.

And so I came to fancy's meadow strow'd
    With many a flower:
  Fain would I here have made abode,
  But I was quicken'd by my hour.

GUILTY OF DUST

So to care's copse I came, and there got through
                With much ado.

That led me to the wild of Passion, which
                Some call the wold;
        A wasted place, but sometimes rich.
        Here I was robb'd of all my gold,
Save one good Angell, which a friend had ti'd
                Close to my side.

At length I got unto the gladsome hill,
                Where lay my hope,
        Where lay my heart; and climbing still,
        When I had gain'd the brow and top,
A lake of brackish waters on the ground
                Was all I found.

With that abash'd and struck with many a sting
                Of swarming fears,
        I fell, and cry'd, Alas my King!
        Can both the way and end be tears?
Yet taking heart I rose, and then perceiv'd
                I was deceiv'd:

My hill was further: so I flung away,
                Yet heard a crie
        Just as I went, *None goes that way*
        And lives: If that be all, said I,
After so foul a journey death is fair,
                And but a chair.

This is a poem dark with disappointment. The writer's hope in pilgrimage is clear: to get to a better place. There is desperation, care, he is robbed, and even when he reaches the 'gladsome hill', all that was there was a pool of 'brackish waters'. His cry to Christ the King is, 'Can both the way and end be tears?' A sonnet by Gerard Manley Hopkins written during his period of great darkness in Dublin contains the lines: 'Here! creep, / Wretch, under a comfort serves in a whirlwind: all / Life death does end and each day dies with sleep.' Herbert's poem carries the same despair: 'After so foul a journey death is fair, / And but a chair'. Rest, then, is the only hope left, and the path of life leads past and beyond death itself.

The basic groundwork of that strange and modern thinker and philosopher, Simone Weil, insofar as I understand the writing, is that humanity is sinful and is in desperate need of redemption. This redemption is achieved, firstly by Christ's grace, offered without our meriting it, but redemption is also won by reduction and annihilation of the ego, by what she calls 'decreation'. God's act in creating is an act of renunciation and abdication. In this fullness of God's vision, Christ the Son would need to suffer and die, so as to enter most completely into the living, suffering and dying of human beings, thereby sharing everything and thereby, too, redeeming everything to that creating God. This is the necessity for Christ to be seen as an 'outlaw', bringing him to death on the cross, sharing the best and worst that humankind can know. Therefore, Simone Weil says, 'The crucifixion of God is an eternal thing'. This echoes Blaise Pascal many years before, and is rediscovered in the poetry of the late David Gascoyne. It is not God's power, then, but his love that fuels the universe, the diminution of self – in the act of creation – being nothing less than a perfect act of love. As renunciation, then, God is Love; as might and power, in the creation of the material universe, in its ongoing thrust and development, its necessary entropy and construction/destruction, he remains undiminished. There exists a space therefore between God and God, between love and transcendence; it is this space that must be filled by a loving humanity. Christ stands like a beggar imploring humanity for this love. I find that this is, too, the thinking and inspiration of Herbert's poetry, though the language is, of course, different. It is clear, then, that Christ stands in Herbert's work as a link of love between God and creation, and Herbert's poetry chimes (as does John Donne's) most richly with our contemporary Christian thinking.

Calvinism and Puritanism were growing strong in Herbert's age, but Herbert's poetry is a direct and gentle insistence on love, not fear. His focus was always on Scripture. His pilgrimage was an interior one, but it was a struggle, a fight with God as Creator and as absent Lord; but Herbert moved hand in hand with his 'Master', Christ, the proven presence of love as the source and sustenance of God's care for humanity. John Drury writes: 'The primacy of love over theology and everything else is a major reason for the hold Herbert's Christian poetry has on modern readers – secular and even atheist as they may be' (*Music at Midnight*, p.15). This Christ, then, who is he for Herbert?

God is creative power, the source and sustenance of nature, of its calamities and its wonders. But Christ, the 'Master', is God as love, countering and underpinning the creative power. George Herbert, in the earlier poetry, begins at a regulatory distance from his Christ. Gradually he comes to the knowledge that if the struggle in life may be with the Almighty God of the Old Testament and the prophets, the true living is with awareness of, and love of, Christ. And here, being 'guilty of dust', he feels that humankind cannot measure up to the great love that Christ shows. He wishes to be free from sin so that he might return that love, a reprise, a making up and a continuing of that process. It is the suffering Christ underwent for humanity that makes Herbert grow deeper in his own affection for Christ.

The Reprisal

> I have consider'd it, and find
> There is no dealing with thy mighty passion:
> For though I die for thee, I am behind;
> My sins deserve the condemnation.

> Oh make me innocent, that I
> May give a disentangled state and free:
> And yet thy wounds still my attempts defy,
>   For by thy death I die for thee.
>
> Ah! was it not enough that thou
> By thy eternal glory didst outgo me?
> Couldst thou not grief's sad conquests me allow,
>   But in all vict'ries overthrow me?
>
> Yet by confession will I come
> Into the conquest. Though I can do nought
> Against thee, in thee I will overcome
>   The man, who once against thee fought.

Herbert wrote from within tradition, but his grasp of it was imaginative, with each poem carefully wrought, well proportioned and finely structured. This very structure carefully crafts forms that fit each individual poem; it echoes in itself an ordering imagination that works out of sincere and constant meditation, and the delights of constraint. Some poems are didactic, arguments with others, but the best are interior arguments with self and not on doubts generally but on self-doubt. Jesus' death is seen as burning down to ashes the heart of humanity, yet out of these ashes, this dust, gold may be retrieved. The natural progress of human beings, then, is to die, as Jesus did, to become dust, but because of Jesus' resurrection, dust is no longer the final end of life. In 'Easter Wings' humankind is seen as 'Decaying more and more'; if, however, a human being can grow in harmony with the Christ, and rise in praise at his resurrection, then the impetus towards destruction can become its opposite through grace: 'Then shall the fall further the flight in me'.

Christmas (I)

After all pleasures as I rid one day,
My horse and I, both tired, body and mind,
With full cry of affections, quite astray;
I took up the next inn I could find.

There when I came, whom found I but my dear,
My dearest Lord, expecting till the grief
Of pleasures brought me to Him, ready there
To be all passengers' most sweet relief?

Oh Thou, whose glorious, yet contracted light,
Wrapt in night's mantle, stole into a manger;
Since my dark soul and brutish is Thy right,
To man of all beasts be not Thou a stranger:

Furnish and deck my soul, that Thou mayst have
A better lodging, than a rack, or grave.

In this delightful poem, we see how the love of Herbert for Christ becomes almost a friendship, a close and living affection. He speaks to Christ as 'my dearest Lord,' 'my dear'. He wishes his own soul to become a manger, but a purer and more comforting place than a 'rack' – which here means a wooden frame for holding fodder, and, of course, may refer to the cross. The poem portrays the Christ waiting for the soul, who has been seeking only after pleasure, to become aware that pleasure does not last, and that grief follows, when – as if the old way of looking at life has now ended – it is Christ's task to bring 'sweet relief'. We are presented with a 'Christmas' scene, the darkness being broken by the light of Christ's coming, stealing almost unseen into a manger, and the brutes in the stable being the souls of humans won back to God. The prayer is that the brutish soul may be cleansed from the mere search for pleasure and become worthy to house the Lord.

Herbert had studied at Trinity College, Cambridge. When he was elected public orator at the university in 1620 a glittering public career opened up for him. By 1624 Herbert was ordained deacon and appeared to set his mind on the church; he could not, however, be ordained priest and remain public orator and he found himself in a dilemma. He chose to be ordained priest. His choice appears to have depended somewhat on a new awareness of the person of Christ in his life, this incarnation that had altered the course of human history entirely. Suddenly he found that this human dust was enabled to pray, to live a holy life, to aim far higher than mere secular living might offer. That Jehovah, that Yahweh, the Old Testament God who had ruled through punishment, wars, exile, threat and judgement, had become Christ, a human being whose essence was love, an abundance of love. It was now seen that the incarnate God was the one who was taking on the task of redeeming sinners, he was 'cataphatic', approachable, nameable and lovable. A poem called 'Denial' clarifies his thinking on his own poetry and how the world of politics, of 'wars and thunder and alarms', could not satisfy either the poetry, or the untuned heart. This poem, in its broken line-lengths, its sudden switches, its deliberate failure to rhyme the ending of the stanzas and therefore deny expectations, mimics beautifully the movement of the poet, the hesitations, the thinking.

Denial

When my devotions could not pierce
      Thy silent ears,
Then was my heart broken, as was my verse;
   My breast was full of fears
      And disorder.

GUILTY OF DUST

My bent thoughts, like a brittle bow,
        Did fly asunder:
Each took his way; some would to pleasures go,
    Some to the wars and thunder
           Of alarms.

'As good go anywhere,' they say,
        'As to benumb
Both knees and heart, in crying night and day,
    Come, come, my God, O come!
           But no hearing.'

O that thou shouldst give dust a tongue
        To cry to thee,
And then not hear it crying! All day long
    My heart was in my knee,
        But no hearing.

Therefore my soul lay out of sight,
        Untuned, unstrung:
My feeble spirit, unable to look right,
    Like a nipped blossom, hung
           Discontented.

O cheer and tune my heartless breast,
        Defer no time;
That so thy favors granting my request,
    They and my mind may chime,
        And mend my rhyme.

It was a gift of God that his 'bent thoughts' are straightened out, that his soul might be 'tuned' to truth and find contentment; with that, the rhyme will work again. In the long and winding road of history and the development of humanity, the coming of Christ into the world, the clarifying of who and what God is, the incarnation of the Divinity became for Herbert the great crossroads of history and of life, and this crossroads had now a clear signpost. The pilgrim route was clear. Christ, the centre and the focus. It is also clear from these poems that Herbert carried over from the medieval writings some of the traditional imagery, the use of parable and allegory, and a fine sense of the dramatic. What he develops wonderfully is the colloquial tone, while maintaining the power of metaphorical and literal meaning. In 1629 Herbert was ordained priest in Salisbury and given the living of Fugglestone and Bemerton, just a few miles from the centre of Salisbury. He lived and died in the rectory of Bemerton. At this stage, he has come close to Christ, and is aware how the priesthood brings him even closer. The poem 'Aaron', urged on the newly ordained priest brought to the closer service of Christ, is based on the moment where Moses, in Exodus 28, is called on to ordain and dress Aaron to establish a priesthood before Jahweh: 'Have Aaron your brother brought to you from among the Israelites, along with his sons Nadab and Abihu, Eleazar and Ithamar, so they may serve me as priests. Make sacred garments for your brother Aaron to give him dignity and honour. Tell all the skilled workers to whom I have given wisdom in such matters that they are to make garments for Aaron, for his consecration, so he may serve me as priest. These are the garments they are to make: a breastpiece, an ephod, a robe, a woven tunic, a turban and a sash.' This is Herbert's 'putting on the Lord Jesus':

Aaron

> Holiness on the head,
> Light and perfection on the breast,
> Harmonious bells below, raising the dead
> To lead them unto life and rest.
> Thus are true Aarons dressed.

GUILTY OF DUST

  Profaneness in my head,
 Defects and darkness in my breast,
A noise of passions ringing me for dead
 Unto a place where is no rest.
  Poor priest thus am I dressed.

  Only another head
 I have, another heart and breast,
Another music, making live not dead,
 Without whom I could have no rest:
  In him I am well dressed.

  Christ is my only head,
 My alone only heart and breast,
My only music, striking me even dead;
 That to the old man I may rest,
  And be in him new dressed.

  So holy in my head,
 Perfect and light in my dear breast,
My doctrine tuned by Christ, (who is not dead,
 But lives in me while I do rest)
  Come people; Aaron's dressed.

The poem outlines the negative and secular way of being, and the priestly ideal; for Herbert, now 'Christ is my only head … '. Now the 'old man' is dead and the new man is dressed in Christ, 'my doctrine tuned by Christ.' This closeness to Christ is all consuming; Herbert's poems now urge humanity to come closer in affection and love to Christ, the great Lover. So many poems begin as familiar conversations or have lines within them that speak directly to Christ as a close, a very close, friend: 'My love, my sweetness, hear!', 'My God, I read this day … ', 'Ah my dear angry Lord … ', 'My God, if writings may … '. This easy confidence in the presence of his God underlines Herbert's sense of God as love, as Love, as close and concerned. 'Oh my Redeemer dear, / After all this canst thou be strange?' In the great poem to which I have been leading, all of these movements and ideas come together in overwhelming yet simple majesty, a simplicity and directness inspired by the immediate sense of Christ's presence, as a forgiving God and a God that is offering an overwhelming love. Humanity is guilty, of dust and of sin, yet it is God's very urging that insists that the response of the human, even under such drawbacks, must be love, an un-guilty love.

Love (III)

Love bade me welcome: yet my soul drew back,
    Guilty of dust and sin.
But quick-ey'd Love, observing me grow slack,
    From my first entrance in,
Drew nearer to me, sweetly questioning,
    If I lack'd anything.

    Love said, You shall be he.
I the unkind, ungrateful? Ah my dear,
    I cannot look on thee.
Love took my hand, and smiling did reply,
    Who made the eyes but I?

Truth Lord, but I have marr'd them: let my shame
    Go where it doth deserve.
And know you not, says Love, who bore the blame?
    My dear, then I will serve.
You must sit down, says Love, and taste me meat:
    So I did sit and eat.

GUILTY OF DUST

Jesus 'sat down and dined' with sinners, with the outcasts of Jewish society, with beggars, the poor, the crippled, the blind, the lame, with the despised and ostracised, with the tax collectors. He entertained sinners in his home, and was entertained by them. This is, of course, the outlaw Jesus as he was seen by the upper layers of society in his own time. There is the rich parable of the wedding feast to which the wealthy refused to come; it may well have been a distinct memory from Jesus' own life, knowing they would not come because the outcast might also be there. There is the story of Jesus inviting himself to the home of Zacchaeus, the tax collector, the most maligned occupation of them all. This dining with sinners set Jesus apart at once and showed how God himself forgave sinners, indeed went further and sought them out. The invitation to supper with Christ, then, is a very special one, relevant as background to this dramatic poem of Herbert's, relevant, too, to all those invitations to the table of the Lord that Christians of all denominations are party to. Down all the ages, this inviting of the poor and sinners to one's table has been and remains a very uncommon thing; no doubt it was so in Herbert's time too. The more unusual the invitation, the more powerful looms this poem.

I have a cherished fancy to do with the poem I quoted earlier, 'The Pilgrimage', and this poem, 'Love'. The sad and wearily bleak pilgrimage outlined in the first poem ends with the not very reassuring lines:

> After so foul a journey death is fair,
>   And but a chair.

The poem 'Love' ends with the sinner, still conscious of his unworthiness, accepting the invitation to the table of love; and that poem ends: 'So I did sit, and eat'. If we combine the last lines of the two poems, we can dream that that vague 'chair' at the end of 'The Pilgrimage' is indeed the chair at the banquet to which Christ, the outlaw Christ, is inviting us all.

10

DRESSED, AND ON MY WAY

Henry Vaughan (1621-1695)

(Note by James Egan: see the Appendix)

The seventeenth-century poet Henry Vaughan is unquestionably a religious, or faith poet who is the author of sacred poems. He is firmly in that tradition of religious poetry exemplified by John Donne or George Herbert, from whom he clearly draws inspiration. The word 'mystic' is sometimes attributed to him, and while this is often a misused term, the content of his poetry is definitively spiritual. Vaughan connects the supernatural to images and metaphors marked by a simple immediacy, drawing out contrasts between light and darkness, peace and chaos, purity and filth. He has a devotional mind and his religious poetry is often prayerful, offering up the world to God and imploring Christ's redeeming mercy.

Mysticism is so often misattributed to poets, and the term itself becomes so excessively applied as to become more or less meaningless; the term has become so broad and flexible that nearly all poetry could be characterised as such. It comes to mean merely 'deep' or 'meditative' or 'reflective', possessing any sort of otherworldly metaphors and abstract language. This is not an unexpected situation for such a term to find itself in. A term like 'mysticism', however broadly applied, still connotes something strange and extraordinary – words readily associated with the poetic imagination and poetry in general.

The presence of great depth, insight and feeling is not necessarily evidence of mysticism, nor is the presence of mere devotion and religious feeling. Still, mysticism as a spiritual quality, the characteristic or habit of a person in contact with otherworldly, spiritual forces, or at the very least dedicated to meditating on them, is a term that is in need of being recovered. What might it mean for a poet to be mystical, to cross over a spiritual boundary, leaving behind lower tiers of manipulation of language and speech craft, and engaging with some other, grace-filled layer of meaning? Such an event is perhaps too extraordinary, and certainly it does not seem to describe Vaughan, but more so some prophet or visionary. Nevertheless, there is an immediacy to Vaughan's descriptions of the Divine which is well worth analysing.

As in all of Vaughan, the metaphors deployed can be almost immediately grasped. There is a deep connection between thought and feeling which is made present, manifested through poetic metaphors. This is clearly seen in a poem like 'Peace', which simply expresses what is mystical, supernatural and immaterial through the means of simple metaphors and imagery. The thought is felt through the metaphor, as in

> There, above noise and danger
> Sweet Peace sits, crown'd with smiles

The feeling of peace as opposed to noise or danger connects to the thought of Christ as the Lord of Peace. The meaningfulness of the imagery does not take much effort to grasp. Vaughan is speaking of Christ enthroned in heaven with imagery clearly borrowed from the Bible, particularly the Book of Revelation. The immediacy of this imagery may strike the modern reader as contrived, perhaps sometimes a bit saccharine. Yet it is undeniably here that the religious value of Vaughan's writing is most obviously apparent. He constructs devotional imagery, sometimes structured prayers, around an array of images used to speak of the supernatural. In this way, he is able to ground his religious poetry.

Of these images, Vaughan most often applies positive descriptions when he speaks of the divine or heavenly things and negative descriptions when he speaks of death or sin or evil. As noted by Arthur L. Clements (*Poetry of Contemplation*, pp.136–7), Vaughan does not often use the imagery of darkness as a device to speak of *via negativa*, a way of coming to knowledge of God through absence, darkness. Darkness, night, have 'disvalues (or, at best, less positive values than 'light' and 'day'), and symbolise sin, error, ignorance … '. Instead, he speaks of heaven as a 'world of light', where all things are bright and visible and made clear. This is in contrast to the descriptions of darkness and obscurity applied to sin and death, and even to himself: 'I am all filth, and obscene'. It is sin and death which blacken and obscure creation, it is Christ and grace which make it clean again. Eternity, where Christ is enthroned, is

> Like a great ring of pure and endless light,
> All calm, as it was bright

These images connote a sharp contrast, which Vaughan plays with throughout his poetry of faith.

The way Vaughan draws these contrasts may be an important key to interpreting his overall spiritual vision. He sees the world as a dim place, corrupted and covered over by filth. Yet, where Christ and grace enter in, there is light and illumination and salvation. This is markedly different from the picture of the world described by Hopkins in 'God's Grandeur', which acknowledges a darkness in the world, but that 'nature is never spent'; underneath, there is freshness deep down, and the Holy Ghost is bent over all the world, taking care of it. Vaughan clearly has a different vision, as evidenced in 'Christ's Nativity', in which he calls upon the world to praise the newborn Christ. He applies a long list of negative values to himself, who by his sin is an obstacle to Christ. If only Christ might

> Cure him, ease him,
> O release him!

Vaughan's view of Christ is as a saviour who can rescue him from the filth and darkness of the world.

However, there is at least one striking occasion where Vaughan reverses his usual pattern of description and speaks of the Divine in terms of darkness, in his poem 'The Night':

> There is in God, some say,
> A deep but dazzling darkness, as men here
> Say it is late and dusky, because they
> See not all clear.
> O for that night! where I in Him
> Might live invisible and dim!

Here Vaughan says darkness is dazzling, a certainly curious paradox; no longer is this the world of light, where 'I shall need no glass'. In fact the world of light, the world lit by the sun, is 'ill-guiding', quite the opposite of Vaughan's words in 'The World':

> O fools (said I) thus to prefer dark night
> Before true light,
> To live in grots and caves, and hate the day.

Using this imagery of darkness to refer to God is not original to Vaughan, and is seen throughout the entire mystical tradition of Christianity. Perhaps no mystic more exemplifies this than the Spanish saint and poet, John of the Cross, who lived only a hundred years before Vaughan. St John of the Cross's famous poem and spiritual guidebook, 'The Dark Night of the Soul', describes a process of interior conversion in which the soul is brought to closer unity with God precisely through the means of absence and darkness. John too speaks of this darkness in endearing terms, calling it beloved. This strange reversal by Vaughan, which echoes the writings of Christian mystics, perhaps makes for one of his most striking poems.

Once Vaughan's images are analysed, a simple spiritual vision emerges. Vaughan's is a mind marked by devotion and piety, keenly aware of the contrast between himself and the Divine, but still desirous of touching it, even as a beggar. His poems form prayers to his Christ as cries for redemption and mercy, ever eager to be liberated and elevated into a world of light. He may not be a mystic, but the simple, religious power of his poetry is well worth reflecting upon, and even praying with.

John F. Deane continues: As a corollary to his distaste for the earth, the focus of Vaughan's poetry is on the innocence of children and childhood, combined with the notion that the child comes from the hand of God the Creator, and moves further and further away from that God as life develops. Can we move backwards and be born again as innocent children? The same can be said of humankind as a whole; as men and women were expelled from the Garden of Paradise and forced into the misery of human history, gradually humanity moved further from that same God.

Henry Vaughan was born in 1622 to Thomas Vaughan and Denise Morgan in Newton-upon-Usk in Breconshire, Wales. He studied at Oxford with Thomas, his beloved twin brother. Later, he studied law in London, but the Civil War broke out and, as did so many other young Welsh men, he enlisted on the side of the king and served in South Wales for a time. Vaughan returned to Breconshire in 1642 as secretary to Judge Lloyd, and later began to practise medicine. In 1650 he published the first part of a collection of poems, *Silex Scintillans*. The title, 'The Flaming Flint', suggests the hardness of the human heart that needs God or tragedy to strike fire from it. We can draw a distant link with Hopkins here, with his notion that fire comes from flint only when it is struck, and from Hopkins's poem, 'The Windhover', 'and blue-bleak embers, ah my dear, / Fall, gall themselves and gash gold-vermillion'. Vaughan's book was enlarged and reprinted in 1655. His first wife died and he married again about this time. After 1655, however, he published nothing of real interest and died in 1695.

The influence of George Herbert does occasionally intrude too much but it is important for Vaughan that this be continually set aside as both poets part company in so many other ways. Now and again he uses a phrase of some endearment when touching on God, such as 'Haste, haste my dear', but it does not have the same sense of genuine closeness that Herbert achieves. Herbert lives far more contentedly in, and committed to, the actual world; Vaughan despises the world and lives only for the next. No doubt the death of his brother, at the age of about twenty-seven, had a very strong and darkening effect on his own life and feeling. Now the world seems an even darker and emptier place:

> Come, come, what do I here?
> > Since he is gone
> Each day is grown a dozen year,
> > And each hour, one;
> > Come come!
> > Cut off the sum,
> By these soiled tears!

For Vaughan, humanity is formed of vile clay, yet in that clay God has planted a seed that is his own spirit of light; this seed stirs in darkness, which must cast off so that it may grow high into the light. There is a longing for that last day, that final call, the great judgement when Christ's Kingdom will dawn, when the night will be forever expelled and humanity shall at last reach fulfilment, out of vile clay into eternal light. For this Vaughan is waiting; dressed, and ready to go; and meanwhile, of course, this vile earth on which we live and move and have our being, is but a trip and a trap and a distraction:

DRESSED, AND ON MY WAY

>   Yet let my course, my aim, my love,
>   And chief acquaintance be above;
>   So when that day, and hour shall come
>   In which thy self will be the Sun,
>   Thou'lt find me dressed and on my way,
>   Watching the break of thy great day.
>   ('The Dawning')

Many of the great themes of Christian hope and love, of longing and desire, of the awareness of human foibles and the perpetual charging of armies here and there to secure some form of peace, some form of commonwealth, meet in Vaughan's poem, 'Peace'.

Peace

>   My soul, there is a country
>   Far beyond the stars,
>   Where stands a wingèd sentry
>   All skillful in the wars:
>   There, above noise and danger,
>   Sweet Peace sits crown'd with smiles,
>   And One born in a manger
>   Commands the beauteous files.
>   He is thy gracious Friend,
>   And – O my soul awake! –
>   Did in pure love descend,
>   To die here for thy sake.
>   If thou canst get but thither,
>   There grows the flower of Peace,
>   The Rose that cannot wither,
>   Thy fortress, and thy ease.
>   Leave then thy foolish ranges;
>   For none can thee secure,

But One, who never changes,
  Thy God, thy life, thy cure.

Christ's Nativity

Awake, glad heart! get up and sing!
It is the birth-day of thy King.
Awake! awake!
The Sun doth shake
Light from his locks, and all the way
Breathing perfumes, doth spice the day.

Awake, awake! hark how th' wood rings;
Winds whisper, and the busy springs
A concert make;
Awake! awake!
Man is their high-priest, and should rise
To offer up the sacrifice.

I would I were some bird, or star,
Flutt'ring in woods, or lifted far
Above this inn
And road of sin!
Then either star or bird should be
Shining or singing still to thee
I would I had in my best part
Fit rooms for thee! or that my heart
Were so clean as
Thy manger was!
But I am all filth, and obscene;
Yet, if thou wilt, thou canst make clean.

DRESSED, AND ON MY WAY

Sweet Jesu! will then. Let no more
This leper haunt and soil thy door!
Cure him, ease him,
O release him!
And let once more, by mystic birth,
The Lord of life be born in earth.

11

SUCH GREAT FELICITY

Thomas Traherne (1637-1674)

Thomas Traherne was born in Herefordshire. His father was a shoemaker who died when Thomas was still quite young. The boy was brought up by an uncle amidst poverty, which always remained vivid in his mind. He earned an MA in arts and divinity in Brasenose College, Oxford, and in 1657 was given the rectory of Credenhill, near Hereford, where he served as parish priest for ten years. In 1667 he was appointed private chaplain to the Lord Keeper of the Seals under King Charles II, but still appears to have spent most of his life in humble parish duties. He was described as 'a good and Godly man, well learned, a good preacher, a very devout liver'. He died in his patron's house at Teddington, Hampton, and was buried in the church there.

Traherne is seen as one of the last of the so-called metaphysical poets, though very little of his work was published in his lifetime. It took until 1896 for someone to discover a manuscript of his poems at a bookstall in London, after which the publication of his poems began in 1903. Even then some of the poems were thought to be the work of Henry Vaughan. If Vaughan's emphasis is on looking back to a time of innocence, Traherne prefers to look to the present and to take delight in the works of the Creator. This would be a better homage to him, Traherne holds, than the continual nostalgia for better times. Yet he shares, with Vaughan, the wish that humankind should remain childlike, holding on to as much of the innocence in which one is born as possible. Traherne did not marry; he devoted himself to prayer and good works and left after him some houses devoted to the help of the poor in Hereford. A good man, then, and a good poet, if not one of the greatest, and a dedicated and serious Christian.

Traherne lived through an era of terrifying religious controversies. The Puritan movement was gathering force; the Civil War brought terror and death, and the restoration of King Charles II brought back a great deal of corruption into high places. At a moment when he was struggling with agnosticism the following occurred (Traherne has written it in *Centuries of Meditation*):

> Another time, in a lowering and sad evening, being alone in the field, when all things were dead and quiet, a certain want and horror fell upon me, beyond imagination. The unprofitableness and silence of the place dissatisfied me, its wideness terrified me, from the utmost ends of the earth fears surrounded me. How did I know but dangers might suddenly arise from the east, and invade me from the unknown regions beyond the seas? I was a weak and little child, and had forgotten there was a man alive in the earth. Yet something also of hope and expectation comforted me from every border. This taught me that I was concerned in all the world, and that in the remotest borders the causes of peace delight me; and the beauties of the earth when seen were made to entertain me; that I was made to hold a communion with the secrets of divine providence in all the world ... The comfort of houses and friends, and the clear assurance of treasures everywhere, God's care and love, His goodness, wisdom and power, His presence and watchfulness in all the ends of the earth were my strength and assurance forever.

It is a moment of extraordinary epiphany, yet we need read nothing unique into the experience, such epiphanies being common to young men of intellect and integrity everywhere. What may be remarkable is that it affected Traherne's life and work so deeply from that day on. His giving of himself, in his life and in his poetry, to the interior conviction he discovered at that time was quite exemplary, matched perhaps only by the unswerving devotion of a George Herbert.

SUCH GREAT FELICITY

'Concerned in all the world', 'the beauties of the earth made to entertain me'; such phrases matter in the work of Traherne. Here is, perhaps, an early awareness that humanity is part of something much greater than self or the individual soul; an awareness a little like John Donne's that an individual is involved in all humankind, but not only that, involved, too, in all of creation. He is deeply aware of mortality, yet life on earth is the immediate source of his inspiration. Many claims have been made on Traherne's behalf, efforts to draw him into all sorts of esoteric sects and movements, using a phrase like 'Teach me, O Lord, these mysterious ascensions. By descending into Hell for the sake of others, let me ascend into the glory of the Highest Heavens', again from 'Centuries'. This is little more than a prayer that, through suffering, he might rise to the love of God. The fact that he was familiar with Platonic thought and the work of thinkers like Plotinus, does not move him beyond a mild Christian mysticism into secret societies of any kind. Traherne was a searcher for truth, and he was a poet, expressing his deepest emotional life through the medium of rhyme, rhythm and metaphor. None of this makes him a crank. However, it is important to understand aright the notion of joy and light in his concept of happiness on earth and in relation to God; otherwise he can be seen as a rather naïve innocent in this harsh world.

Traherne willed to have no nonsense in his work, wishing to show 'the naked truth', to use 'A simple light, transparent words …' . The object of the exercise was to allow the soul to see its 'great felicity' and know the bliss to which it is heir. This, too, chimes well with the contemporary twenty-first-century Christian awareness, that of our human destiny and that of all of Creation alongside us. Traherne will, then, avoid all 'curling metaphors' and 'painted eloquence'. His will be 'An easy style drawn from a native vein' in an effort to make us wise. His simple metaphor is that of a man richly dressed in 'woven silks and well-made suits', with gems and polished flesh; how men notice such sights but are not aware of God's work, nor the soul where God abides:

THE OUTLAW CHRIST

> Even thus do idle fancies, toys and words,
> (Like gilded scabbards hiding rusty swords)
> Take vulgar souls, who gaze on rich attire
> But God's diviner works do ne'er admire.

The link in the poetry with Henry Vaughan is obvious and has often been remarked upon, but I find Traherne's work moves a great distance away from Vaughan's. It is important to remember how much Traherne was aware of, and appreciated, the physical world around him. An early poem expresses the wonder of being born, a notion common to us all, that we are alive in this place at this time, but here well expressed in the sense of amazement at the gift of living.

> Long time before
> I in my mother's womb was born,
> A God preparing did this glorious store,
> The world, for me adorn.
> Into this Eden so divine and fair,
> So wide and bright, I come His son and heir.
>   ('The Salutation')

Traherne, then, rather than being a simpleton drunk on unfounded joy, sees this world as a prelude to another where everything is filled with light and happiness; because we are already heirs to this wonderful existence, what is needed is to maintain awareness of that world and exult in our awareness of it. An awareness of the wonder of the world to come depends, for Traherne, on an awareness of the beauty of the present world. This awareness is best expressed, according to him, through the eyes of a child that is still unconscious of wickedness. There are multitudes that might not see this world as an 'Eden so divine and fair' but that is not the point here; the emphasis is on the free gift of God's creating. And this is one of the first statements of such a notion, the world up to this time being mostly regarded as a source of sin, to be avoided in favour of purely spiritual notions. If Vaughan sees our arrival on earth as a loss and our growth as a gradually diminishing memory of great times into a miserably sinful living, Traherne prefers to concentrate on the actual moment:

Wonder

How like an Angel came I down!
   How bright are all things here!
When first among His works I did appear
   O how their glory me did crown!
The world resembled His Eternity,
   In which my soul did walk;
And every thing that I did see
   Did with me talk.

The skies in their magnificence,
   The lively, lovely air,
Oh how divine, how soft, how sweet, how fair!
   The stars did entertain my sense,
And all the works of God, so bright and pure,
   So rich and great did seem,
As if they ever must endure
   In my esteem.

A native health and innocence
   Within my bones did grow,
And while my God did all his Glories show,
   I felt a vigour in my sense
That was all Spirit. I within did flow
   With seas of life, like wine;
I nothing in the world did know
   But 'twas divine.

THE OUTLAW CHRIST

Harsh ragged objects were concealed,
   Oppressions, tears and cries,
Sins, griefs, complaints, dissensions, weeping eyes
   Were hid, and only things revealed
Which heavenly Spirits and the Angels prize.
   The state of Innocence
And bliss, not trades and poverties,
   Did fill my sense.

The streets were paved with golden stones,
   The boys and girls were mine,
Oh how did all their lovely faces shine!
   The sons of men were holy ones,
In joy and beauty they appeared to me,
   And every thing which here I found,
While like an Angel I did see,
   Adorned the ground.

Rich diamond and pearl and gold
   In every place was seen;
Rare splendours, yellow, blue, red, white and green,
   Mine eyes did everywhere behold.
Great wonders clothed with glory did appear,
   Amazement was my bliss,
That and my wealth was everywhere;
   No joy to this!

Cursed and devised proprieties,
   With envy, avarice
And fraud, those fiends that spoil even Paradise,
   Flew from the splendour of mine eyes,

And so did hedges, ditches, limits, bounds,
   I dreamed not aught of those,
But wandered over all men's grounds,
   And found repose.

Proprieties themselves were mine,
   And hedges ornaments;
Walls, boxes, coffers, and their rich contents
   Did not divide my joys, but all combine.
Clothes, ribbons, jewels, laces, I esteemed
   My joys by others worn:
For me they all to wear them seemed
   When I was born.

Traherne wished to know no limits, no borders, no boxes that might contain and divide the glory of the world in which we live. We come from the realm of angels and, as Vaughan insists, we remember that realm, although it gradually fades from memory. Traherne is aware of a 'native health and innocence' and, as the poem progresses through its delicately modulated rhymes, its steady rhythmic flow, one keeps expecting a 'but' … There is none, at least, not in this poem. And therefore it is a uniquely refreshing work, one of the very first in the great canon of poetry in English, to betray such pleasure in things of earth. Of course the poem was not read until many years later, hence it had no influence on those who came after him, but it is still good to know that Traherne was writing such poetry at such a time.

There is the word 'mystic', employed without much distinction as to a mere sense of the wonders of nature or an actual and direct contact with 'the Divine'. The latter is, of course, the Christian definition and the word needs to be used carefully. Whether or not Traherne was a mystic in this Christian sense is debatable, and we will never know. A writer like D.H. Lawrence exemplifies the first type of 'nature-mystic', and it is clear that this is not Traherne's bent. It would seem best simply to say that Traherne's sense of wonder in the things of the world drew him to a more sustained attempt to know and love the Creator of the world that moved him deeply.

Traherne's individual poems are linked to one another so that his work can read as one long sequence of poems. He is, then, better read as a whole rather than in individual pieces.

> … Whether it be that nature is so pure
> And custom only vicious, or that sure
> God did by miracle the guilt remove
> And make my soul to feel his love
>
> So early; or that 'twas one day
> Where in this happiness I found,
> Whose strength and brightness so do ray
> That still it seemeth to surround:
>
> What e'er it is, it is a light
>   So endless unto me
> That I a world of true delight
> Did then and to this day do see.

The imagery of light permeates the poetry along with that of being an Adam in Eden before any sense of sin entered the souls of mortals. Before awareness – 'I was an inward sphere of light'. In a poem called 'The Preparative', he is close to echoing Vaughan:

> Unbodied and devoid of care,
> Just as in heaven the holy angels are.
>   For simple sense
> Is lord of all created excellence.

SUCH GREAT FELICITY

Man is born 'as free / As if there were nor sin, nor misery'. And all happiness on earth is bound up with vision, with light, with an awareness of that great life to which we are heir: 'Felicity / Appears to none but them that purely see'. Traherne spent his life seeking that felicity, that vision of the Divine permeating all of creation, that awareness of 'the Jesus body, the Jesus bones' that St Paul outlined as the mystical body of the universe, where God wills the happiness of all creation. The light of a man's living is to be trained towards this vision, this awareness; and the poetry reflects and highlights the progress towards felicity.

Traherne was not so naïve and foolish that he would not admit the darkness of the world, and the forces that continually work to destroy that felicity. But, he states, that awareness will not shake the deepest roots of his vision:

> The first impressions are immortal all;
> And let mine enemies hoop, cry, roar, call,
> Yet these will whisper if I will but hear,
> And penetrate the heart if not the ear.

It is the heart, then, that matters to the work of Traherne, and in his life he exemplified the true Christian sense of charity and service. At times the poetry tends to labour this theme of innocence and complicity with the world, and the rhymes and rhythms tend to remain rather repetitive and dull. But the ongoing work examines the self, for understanding of the human place in the grand scheme of things. 'Nature teacheth nothing but the truth', and by an awareness of nature man comes to knowledge of God: 'The world's fair beauty set my soul on fire'.

> A secret self I had enclosed within
> That was not bounded with my clothes or skin
> Or terminated with my sight, the sphere
> Of which was bounded with the heavens here:

> But that did rather, like the subtle light,
> Secured from rough and raging storms by night,
> Break through the lantern's sides, and freely ray
> Dispersing and dilating every way;
> Whose steady beams, too subtle for the wind,
> Are such that we their bounds can scarcely find.
> It did encompass and possess rare things,
> But yet felt more, and on its angel wings
> Pierced through the skies immediately and sought
> For all that could beyond all worlds be thought.
>
> *(from 'Nature')*

This inward exploration, starting from a love of outward things, brings Traherne to a sense of joy and belonging, to a sense, too, that there is more than all this outward show: 'All which were made that I might ever be / With some great workman, some great Deity'. And all that he saw, by the light of the universe, appeared good: 'Which fountain of delights must needs be love / As all the goodness of the things did prove'. None of this, it is clear, is new or strange to a modern mind, but it must be remembered that Traherne wrote during a period when the things of this world were to be despised in favour of the things of the next, when the beauty of the world was seen as a distraction from the right path, when what was required was a life lived in the darkness of blind faith, rather than in the brightness of God's created day. He lived, too, at a time when there was desperate civil war in England, leading to the beheading of King Charles I, followed by a cruel reign presided over by Oliver Cromwell and the Puritan excesses, where anything to do with the physical world was to be wholly despised; then came the Restoration and a long period of frivolity and foolishness under King Charles II. The Christian churches, too, were at one another's throats. Yet in the midst of all of this, Traherne found a way of harnessing his soul to the other world of allowing the desire for peace and love and fulfilment to take control of his living. He touched on the purity of childhood and to that he returned, for strength.

The Return

To infancy, O Lord, again I come,
   That I my manhood may improve;
  My early tutor is the womb,
     I still my cradle love.
'Tis strange that I should wisest be
When least I could an error see.

Till I gain strength against temptation I
   Perceive it safest to abide
  An infant still, and therefore fly
     (A lowly state may hide
A man from danger) to the womb,
That I may yet new-born become.

My God, thy bounty then did ravish me!
   Before I learnèd to be poor,
  I always did thy riches see
     And thankfully adore:
Thy glory and thy goodness were
My sweet companions all the year.

This rediscovery of innocence in childhood is perhaps the closest Traherne comes to the poetry of Vaughan, yet it is clear from the rest of the work that Traherne is following his own course and that this view of childhood, of man's initial innocence, is his own and part of his overall concerns. Men, he writes, are 'More fools at twenty years than ten'. Out of all of this his vision of a perfect world to which we may aspire forms the heart of Traherne's work. A poem called 'Christendom' outlines his vision of a perfectly attuned city, in harmony with itself and with each inhabitant:

> Beneath the lofty trees
> I saw, of all degrees,
> Folk calmly sitting in their doors, while some
> Did standing with them kindly talk,
> Some smile, some sing, or what was done
> Observe, while others by did walk;
> They viewed the boys
> And girls, their joys,
> The streets adorning with their angel-faces,
> Themselves diverting in those pleasant places.

This is a more down-to-earth vision of the Heavenly City than is offered in the Book of Revelation; it is the town next door uplifted to an ideal place. The people who dwell in this town are perfected, they are innocent like children, they are 'incarnate cherubin':

> In fresh and cooler rooms
> Retired they dine; perfumes
> They wanted not, having the pleasant shade
> And peace to bless their house within,
> By sprinkled waters cooler made
> For those incarnate cherubin.
> This happy place
> With all the grace,
> The joy and beauty which it did beseem,
> Did ravish me and heighten my esteem.

Traherne's quiet vision of Utopia differs in several ways from that of other writers, of his own time and of previous generations. Setting aside the awkward syntax, the repetition of his images and the often simplistic view he elaborated of innocence, Traherne sets his theme firmly on the real world and outlines it in direct language that offers conviction and emphasis on an unswerving faith. He offers no great intellectual debate, unlike the poets who flourished before him, such as Donne, Crashaw, Marvell. Still, it does appear that Traherne's poetry was not unaffected by the enthusiasm of such thinking, and by the scientific examination of the universe that was then beginning to unfold. People like Galileo were opening up the universe and thrusting new questions on the peoples of Europe. In a seemingly expanding universe, human potential appeared to be opening up to vast, unthought-of growth. Oxford, while Traherne was there, became a centre for the study of science. Francis Bacon (1561–1626) had popularised in England his own scientific method, and though this had been born in an era of hermetic studies and alchemical research, Bacon demanded an approach to knowledge that was planned and carefully deductive. Research and science, in other words, begin in actual experience and proceed from there. In his 'Centuries of Meditations' Traherne writes:

> Our Saviour's meaning when He said, 'He must be born again and become a little child that will enter into the kingdom of heaven' is deeper far than is generally believed. It is not only in a careless reliance upon divine providence that we are to become little children, or in the feebleness and shortness of our anger and simplicity of our passions; but in the peace and purity of all our soul. Which purity also is a deeper thing than is commonly apprehended, for we must disrobe ourselves of all false colours, and unclothe our souls of evil habits; all our thoughts must be infant-like and clear, the powers of our soul free from the leaven of this world, and disentangled from men's conceits and customs. Grit in the eye or the yellow jaundice will not let a man see those objects truly that are before it.

Innocence and childlike viewing of our world, then, is not the mere absence of sin and egotism that poets like Vaughan desired; innocence is the conscious stripping away of that egotism that blinds the mind to objective truth. Sin and wrong desires result, Traherne says, from falling away from that clear approach to the world that finds its deep justification in the actions and words of Christ.

One of the strangest poems in Traherne's output, one that joins itself most obviously to the age in which he was writing, that famous 'metaphysical' age, is:

On Leaping Over the Moon

I saw new worlds beneath the water lie,
    New people; yea, another sky
    And sun, which seen by day
    Might things more clear display.
    Just such another
    Of late my brother
Did in his travel see, and saw by night,
    A much more strange and wondrous sight:
Nor could the world exhibit such another,
    So great a sight, but in a brother.

Adventure strange! No such in story we,
    New or old, true or feigned, see.
    On earth he seemed to move
    Yet heaven went above;
    Up in the skies
    His body flies
In open, visible, yet magic, sort:
    As he along the way did sport,
Like Icarus over the flood he soars
    Without the help of wings or oars.

SUCH GREAT FELICITY

As he went tripping o'er the king's high-way,
    A little pearly river lay
    O'er which, without a wing
    Or oar, he dared to swim,
    Swim through the air
    On body fair;
He would not use or trust Icarian wings
    Lest they should prove deceitful things;
For had he fallen, it had been wondrous high,
    Not from, but from above, the sky:

He might have dropt through that thin element
    Into a fathomless descent;
    Unto the nether sky
    That did beneath him lie,
    And there might tell
    What wonders dwell
On earth above. Yet doth he briskly run,
    And bold the danger overcome;
Who, as he leapt, with joy related soon
    How happy he o'er-leapt the moon.

What wondrous things upon the earth are done
    Beneath, and yet above the sun?
    Deeds all appear again
    In higher spheres; remain
    In clouds as yet:
    But there they get
Another light, and in another way
    Themselves to us above display.
The skies themselves this earthly globe surround;
    We are even here within them found.

THE OUTLAW CHRIST

On heavenly ground within the skies we walk,
    And in this middle centre talk:
    Did we but wisely move,
    On earth in heaven above,
    Then soon should we
    Exalted be
Above the sky: from whence whoever falls,
    Through the long dismal precipice,
Sinks to the deep abyss where Satan crawls
    Where horrid death and despair lies.

As much as others thought themselves to lie
    Beneath the moon, so much more high
    Himself and thought to fly
    Above the starry sky,
    As that he spied
    Below the tide.
Thus did he yield me in the shady night
    A wondrous and instructive light,
Which taught me that under our feet there is
    As o'er our heads, a place of bliss.

* * *

To the same purpose; he, not long before
    Brought home from nurse, going to the door
    To do some little thing
    He must not do within,
    With wonder cries,
    As in the skies
He saw the moon, 'O yonder is the moon
    Newly come after me to town,
That shined at Lugwardin but yesternight,
    Where I enjoyed the self-same light.'

SUCH GREAT FELICITY

    As if it had even twenty thousand faces,
       It shined at once in many places;
       To all the earth so wide
       God doth the stars divide
       With so much art
       The moon impart,
They serve us all; serve wholly every one
       As if they served him alone.
While every single person hath such store,
       'Tis want of sense that makes us poor.

The poem is quite carefully constructed, beginning with the poet's vision of day, followed by his brother's vision of the moon, back to the poet's wisdom and ending once more with the brother and the moon. We start with an experience of sunlight in which the poet sees beyond what mere sunlight on the earth will display; his brother, then, in leaping over the moon reflected in a stream of water, gets another view of creation. The image of Icarus is cleverly used and developed for it is the sunlight that destroyed the wings in the original myth and the fall of Icarus was a disaster. If the poet's brother had fallen into the water he would have fallen through, as far as the moon itself; a beautiful 'conceit', the fall being down and up at the same time, painful and revealing, a vision and a hurt. And always it is the existence of another view of the world that is in question. If he had fallen through into the reflected sky, he could have described to the inhabitants what it was like on the earth above them, thus once again turning our physical world on its head. There are echoes of phrases from the Bible: 'What wondrous things upon the earth are done ... on earth as it is in heaven ... '. There are worlds held within worlds. While we are on earth we are in heaven and while in heaven we are on earth and how rightly does the first conclusion come: 'Did we but wisely move, / On earth in heaven above, / We then should be / Exalted high / Above the sky'. The lovely word 'tripping', along the king's high-way, suggests the danger and the joy of moving in the actual world, all of which eventually comes down to the use of neither oar nor wing, but 'swimming', and in this case swimming in the air; the cleverness of this is admirable. All of this 'unreasonable' and highly imaginative work, is yet fully earthed, particularly in the final two stanzas where the brother, after a stint in hospital, 'brought home from nurse', has to go outside to use the toilet: 'To do some little thing / He must not do within'; even the name of the village where Thomas and Philip lived is used. Like the moon and the stars, that shine always somewhere in the world, God too is available to everyone and it is our poor minds alone that are unwilling to open up to the wonder and mercy of God's presence.

    The special grace of Traherne's poetry, and its concern for this study, is its positive response to the story of Christ's revelation of God, of the glories of his creation and of the human destiny. Reading this poet almost inevitably arouses an answering hope, almost a conviction, in the reader. The surface innocence of the verse, with its often-repeated memories of childhood integrity, is still carefully focused on his theme, and the individual poems are constructed with intelligence and purpose.

12

THE SCRIBE EVANGELIST

Christopher Smart (1722-1771)

Christopher Smart was born in Shipbourne, Kent. His father, a steward on the estate of Lord Vane, died when Smart was eleven. He studied at Pembroke College, Cambridge, and became known for his Latin verses and his translation of the works of Horace. He earned a living in London doing occasional writing work and spent time drinking and carousing. He was arrested for debt in 1747. He married in 1752. He developed a form of religious mania and was confined in a hospital in Bethnal Green. Here he wrote some magnificent verse, mainly 'A Song to David' and 'Jubilate Agno'. Towards the end of his life he was again arrested for debt. Smart saw himself as 'the Lord's News-Writer and scribe evangelist', working to spread the good news of God. His poems carried in rich and unusual language his awe before the person of Christ, whom he called 'this stupendous stranger'. Smart also foreshadowed John Clare, who found praise and honour offered to Christ, not only by humanity but by the whole of creation.

The Nativity of Our Lord and Saviour Jesus Christ

Where is this stupendous stranger,
    Swains of Solyma, advise?   *[Judaea]*
Lead me to my Master's manger,
    Show me where my Saviour lies.

THE OUTLAW CHRIST

O Most Mighty! O MOST HOLY!
   Far beyond the seraph's thought,
Art thou then so mean and lowly   *[weak]*
   As unheeded prophets taught?

O the magnitude of meekness!
   Worth from worth immortal sprung;
O the strength of infant weakness,
   If eternal is so young!

If so young and thus eternal,
   Michael tune the shepherd's reed,
Where the scenes are ever vernal,
   And the loves be Love indeed!

See the God blasphem'd and doubted
   In the schools of Greece and Rome;
See the pow'rs of darkness routed,
   Taken at their utmost gloom.

Nature's decorations glisten
   Far above their usual trim;
Birds on box and laurels listen,
   As so near the cherubs hymn.

Boreas now no longer winters
   On the desolated coast;
Oaks no more are riv'n in splinters
   By the whirlwind and his host.

THE SCRIBE EVANGELIST

Spinks and ouzels sing sublimely, *[chaffinch and blackbird]*
   'We too have a Saviour born';
Whiter blossoms burst untimely
   On the blest Mosaic thorn.

God all-bounteous, all-creative,
   Whom no ills from good dissuade,
Is incarnate, and a native
   Of the very world He made.

13

THE VERY VOICE OF GOD

John Clare (1793-1864)

To begin with, early work by John Clare presents an Edenic morning, perfectly and delicately delineated, with a sense that this is the morning of creation, Adam and Eve at peace, until the first sense of human interference enters. Here is no 'peasant poet', ignorantly painting the rural scene; here is experience of cosmic magnificence already threatened:

> Come early morning with thy mealy grey
> Moist grass and fitful gales that winnow soft
> And frequent – I'll be up with early day
> And roam the social way where passing oft
> The milking maid who greets the pleasant morn
> And shepherd with his hook in folded arm
> Rocking along across the bending corn
> And hear the many sounds from distant farm
> Of cackling hens and turkeys gobbling loud
> And teams just plodding on their way to plough
> Down russet tracks that strip the closen green
> And hear the mellow low of distant cow
> And see the mist up-creeping like a cloud
> From hollow places in the early scene ...
>
> There's more than music in this early wind
> Awaking like a bird refreshed from sleep
> And joy what Adam might in Eden find

> When he with angels did communion keep
> It breathes all balm and insence from the sky
> Blessing the husbandman with freshening powers
> Joy's manna from its wings doth fall and lie
> Harvests for early wakers with the flowers
> The very grass in joy's devotion moves
> Cowslaps in adoration and delight
> This way and that bow to the breath they love
> Of the young winds that with the dew pearls play
> Till smoking chimneys sicken the young light
> And feelings' fairey visions fade away

Here is a cosmic consciousness of the wonders of creation and only the human's actions 'sicken' the scene. Adam features, and communion with the angels, the whole earth and sky are also in communion. There is cosmic unity and fellowship and the joy and gladness only fade away before human interference. This awareness comes in a countryman early in the nineteenth century just before the world was shattered by the industrial revolution.

John Clare was born in the village of Helpstone, Northamptonshire, in 1793. He was born into the home of an agricultural labourer and had little or no formal education. He read and loved James Thompson's 'The Seasons' and started to write his own verses, publishing his first book and paying for it himself. It did not do well, but John Taylor, the publisher of Keats, read and liked it, and in 1820 published Clare's *Poems Descriptive of Rural Life*. This brought Clare into a society that was utterly alien to his private, agricultural background, a youth where joy in nature, in creation, was in his blood. In London's elite literary society he felt himself an outsider, a country bumpkin but with talent, a romantic innocent abroad. This, of course, was also the experience of Patrick Kavanagh, and both of these odds and sods men failed to cope adequately with city and literary life. At home John Clare was very poor, finding a small income by doing odd jobs, as lime-burner, gardener, haymaker, jack-of-all-trades. As he moved and worked in the fields he composed his poems and became, for the literary society of London, a fine curiosity.

One of the great delights of Clare's work is the occasional use of Northamptonshire dialect, as in 'the sailing puddock's shrill peelew'. This kind of thing, together with his accurate and loving description of the countryside about him, adds to the sense of curiosity and weirdness so beloved of the literary hangers-on. And of course, John Clare was in love. He had married and was trying to support a wife and seven children. His strange fame called him away from home too often; he visited London, where he met writers like Hazlitt, De Quincey and Coleridge, who liked him but could not make him a permanent part of their company. His great hope was to meet and talk with John Keats, but they missed one another in the comings and goings. Patrick Kavanagh, too, became a curiosity in Dublin and someone who was seen as a 'character', not to be taken too seriously.

Clare suffered from occasional 'swoonings', a kind of panic attack. By 1823 a heavy depression began to settle on him from which he never fully recovered. He was eventually admitted to an insane asylum where he immediately became more delusional. He spent some four years there before he discharged himself and walked home; he had to walk over eighty miles, which took him well over three days, and he lived for that period on grass and herbs he found by the roadside. Later in that same year, 1841, he was certified as insane and committed to the Northampton Asylum, where he stayed until his death in 1864. Twenty-three years! Whatever the nature of his sorry disorder, it is clear that Clare really suffered greatly. His mental confusions were serious and hurtful, as he lost a sense of who he was and what life was about. And yet, when he carries his self-awareness and his simplicity of thought and language into an honest appraisal of life, his poetry touches deeply.

It has become the norm to associate John Clare and Patrick Kavanagh as 'peasant poets', but nothing could be further from the actual truth. Their influences in upbringing were somewhat similar, but then so many poets brought up in rural areas tend to work their poetry and its influences from their birthplace. Underneath Clare's unsophisticated forms, though rarely expressed, is a strong and unshaken sense of God's existence as the ultimate arbiter of truth, of the certainty that his frustrated love and his frustrated dreams will at last find fulfilment. He placed himself wholly in God's care. This God he saw mostly as the Creator of wonders, the universe about him he knew as a source of joy and pleasure, though perpetually threatened by human greed. Humanity's response to being in the world was inimical to how Clare saw it; he wrote

> And he who studies nature's volume through
> And reads it with a pure unselfish mind
> Will find God's power all round in every view
> As one bright vision of the almighty mind
> His eyes are open though the world is blind
> No ill from him creation's works deform
> The high and lofty one is great and kind
> Evil may cause the blight and crushing storm
> His is the sunny glory and the calm

This is a rare and almost contemporary view of creation that finds God's power everywhere; here is a man who knows creation as 'one bright vision of the almighty mind'. The dealing with such a creation ought to be by a humanity that has 'a pure unselfish mind'. Clare, in another early poem, 'Summer Happiness', speaks of creation itself as having God's blessing in it everywhere:

> I marvel, well I may,
> To see such worlds of insects in the way
> And more to see each thing however small
> Sharing joy's bounty that belongs to all

THE VERY VOICE OF GOD

> And here I gather by the world forgot
> Harvests of comfort from their happy mood
> Feeling God's blessing dwells in every spot
> And nothing lives but owes him gratitude

This is a poem, and a poet, which continually reminds the reader of those psalms where the psalmist calls on all of creation to praise the goodness of the Lord. And soon you come across these lines, in 'Summer Images': 'And droning dragonflye on rude bassoon / Striveth to give God thanks / In no discordant tune.' For Clare, then, the wonder of creation is thanks to God's blessing, and creation itself attempts to give God thanks. This ultimately builds to a poem that he calls 'The Peasant Poet', but down the years since then, that title has garnered little respect; instead we should read the poem as the work of a great lover of creation, a person cognizant of the abundance of a creating God, and the goodness that lies behind all that we see. For John Clare, self-knowledge and humility held together his awareness of the possibilities of the world in spite of his own poverty and building illness. And it is a self-knowledge in touch with and sustained by God, not the God of theologians, of pastors or mystics, but the God of the countryside, the Cosmic Creating God who has made a world that Clare loved and would be part of.

The Peasant Poet

> He loved the brook's soft sound
> The swallow swimming by
> He loved the daisy-covered ground
> The cloud-bedappled sky
> To him the dismal storm appeared
> The very voice of God
> And where the Evening rock was reared
> Stood Moses with his rod

> And every thing his eyes surveyed
> The insects i' the brake
> Were creatures God almighty made
> He loved them for his sake
> A silent man in life's affairs
> A thinker from a Boy
> A Peasant in his daily cares –
> The Poet in his joy

The work should also call on those who do damage to this world to think again:

> He that can meet the morning wind
> And o'er such places roam
> Nor leave a lingering wish behind
> To make their peace his home –
>
> His heart is dead to quiet hours
> No love his mind employs
> Poesy with him ne'er shares its flowers
> Nor solitude its joys:

And this, from the same poem: 'Emmonsales Heath'

> I thought how kind that mighty power
> Must in his splendour be
> Who spread around my boyish hour
> Such gleams of harmony
> Who did with joyous rapture fill
> The low as well as high
> And make the pismires round the hill
> Seem full as blest as I

THE VERY VOICE OF GOD

And in 'Summer Evening' he says: 'Thus nature's human link and endless thrall: / Proud man still seems the enemy of all'.

Clare's self-knowledge grew apace, and he suffered disappointment in love while his mind seemed to lose hold on reality. The last part of his life was deeply unhappy and fraught with madness. It is sad now, too, in our time, to think that a cure would be probably quite easily available, instead of the cruel and hopeless regimes of the Bedlam, of Northampton County Lunatic Asylum.

I Am

I am – yet what I am, none cares or knows;
    My friends forsake me like a memory lost:
I am the self-consumer of my woes –
    They rise and vanish in oblivion's host
Like shadows in love-frenzied stifled throes
    And yet I am, and live – like vapours tossed

Into the nothingness of scorn and noise,
    Into the living sea of waking dreams,
Where there is neither sense of life or joys,
    But the vast shipwreck of my life's esteems;
Even the dearest that I love the best
    Are strange – nay, rather, stranger than the rest.

I long for scenes where man hath never trod
    A place where woman never smiled or wept
There to abide with my Creator, God,
    And sleep as I in childhood sweetly slept,
Untroubling and untroubled where I lie
    The grass below – above, the vaulted sky.

The directness, simplicity and humility of that word 'Untroubling' are deeply touching; Clare was aware that his life caused difficulties to others, to his wife, his children, even his carers in the asylum. He knew in his deepest core that he was not made for human companionship and longed for, and found peace only in solitude and amid the loveliness of Nature (creation). Here is a poet, troubled beyond what most of us will ever know, who peers out of his darkness now and again and grasps with the naturalness of his birth and station the energies of life and creation that he knows are real. His faith continues unquestioning, even in the depths of his wrecking and being wrecked.

> God looks on nature with a glorious eye
> And blesses all creation with the sun
> Its drapery of green and brown, earth, ocean, he
> In morning as Creation just begun
> That saffron East foretells the rising sun
> And who can look upon that majesty
> Of light brightness and splendour nor feel won
> With love of him whose bright all-seeing eye
> Feeds the day's light with Immortality?

This gentle, distraught and grieving soul, did not keep his sorrowing out of the poetry. There is a poem where this suffering is given its place, and because of the immediacy of his writing, and his awareness, the suffering is brought close to the reader, who feels it in phrases like 'My bones like hearth-stones burn away', and 'But thou hast held me up awhile and thou hast cast me down'. This poem reads powerfully as it takes into itself all Clare's poetic achievement, all his self-knowledge, all his acute observation, not only of creation and himself, but also of the attitude of other people towards him. And the poem ends with the unquestioning acceptance of his fate under the watchful eye of the Creator who has laid all things out:

THE VERY VOICE OF GOD

Lord hear my prayer when trouble glooms
Let sorrow find a way
And when the day of trouble comes
Turn not thy face away
My bones like hearth-stones burn away
My life like vapoury smoke decays

My heart is smitten like the grass
That withered lies and dead
And I so lost to what I was
Forget to eat my bread
My voice is groaning all the day
My bones prick through this skin of clay

***

But thou Lord shalt endure forever
All generations through
Thou shalt to Zion be the giver
Of joy and mercy too
Her very stones are in their trust
Thy servants reverence her dust
Heathens shall hear and fear thy name
All kings of earth thy glory know
When thou shalt build up Zion's fame
And live in glory there below
He'll not despise their prayers though mute
But still regard the destitute

As with Hopkins later on, it is the sense of the loss of innocence in life that brings certain sadness to the soul. In Clare's poetry youth is relished and is almost a paradise that is lost as life goes on and that will not be found again save in eternity. Kavanagh moved along this road, too. And, like Hopkins, Clare rejoiced in 'the weeds and the wilderness':

THE OUTLAW CHRIST

Pleasant Spots

There is a wild and beautiful neglect
About the fields that so delights and cheers
Where nature her own feelings to effect
Is left at her own silent work for years
The simplest thing thrown in our way delights
From the wild careless feature that it wears
The very road that wanders out of sight
Crooked and free is pleasant to behold
And such the very weeds left free to flower
Corn poppys red and carlock gleaming gold
That makes the cornfields shine in summer's hour
Like painted skys – and fancy's distant eye
May well imagine armys marching bye
In all the grand array of pomp and power

Between about 1809 and 1820, Helpston and the surrounding area were 'enclosed', with open fields being fenced off and land divided to provide greater production; rights of way were closed, fences and hedges were built; trees were cut down, streams stopped so that ditches could be made straight and No Trespassing signs went up. These actions were known as 'the Enclosures' and Clare saw it all as giving unrestricted power to big landowners. Gypsies, loved by Clare, were among those greatly affected. Commonages and waste grounds were also restricted and all of this infringed on Clare's right to wander. In his later depressions and madness he sometimes thought himself damned and sought reassurance; he had once tried a primitive Methodist movement: he needed enthusiasm, simplicity and freshness, though his inborn sense of restraint drew him back. Clare was not fond of going to church, preferring to read his bible or a religious treatise. He had little trust in priests; indeed, he gradually lost his trust in people in general. Like Hopkins he kept notes on his observations in the fields, and did drawings, too, detailed and delicately observed. Indeed, his later mental difficulties sometimes make one think of Hopkins's depressions, symptoms of physical distress. And his sense of a loss of the innocence he knew in childhood always haunted him, as it did, later on, with Patrick Kavanagh. Now the Enclosures restricted his life even further.

> Inclosures came and trampled on the grave
> Of labour's rights and left the poor a slave …
> Fence now meets fence in owners' little bounds
> Of field and meadow large as garden grounds
> In little parcels little minds to please
> With men and flocks imprisoned ill at ease …
> Each little tyrant with his little sign
> Shows where man claims earth glows no more divine.
>
> (*from* The Mores)

His belief in the worth and wonder of creation never failed him, even under such sadness and virtual imprisonment that he suffered. In a poem called 'The Eternity of Nature' he speaks of how the child will forever be a kind of Adam or Eve in the garden, filled with wonder and loving the small and beautiful things of creation; this is 'the child hid in the womb of time' who will, in the future, still love and appreciate the daisy for, though it be 'trampled underfoot / The daisy lives and strikes its little root / Into the lap of time'.

> 'Tis nature's wonder and her maker's will
> Who bade earth be and order owns him still
> As that superior power who keeps the key
> Of wisdom, power, and might through all eternity.

THE OUTLAW CHRIST

Trying to find labour he tried his hand at all kinds of odd jobs, even joining the militia for a time, in expectation (all England was on tenterhooks) of an invasion by Napoleon's armies. He was given some training but was quickly dismissed, being small and seemingly weak, an 'odds and sods man', with a uniform too big for him and a helmet too small. What made his life worth living, then, he came to find in poetry, and in his mind he later associated poetry with love unfulfilled, Mary Joyce and her absence tormenting him. Gradually, the love of poetry took him over, though he enjoyed drinking (often far too much) with his friends, though he tended to despise those very same co-revellers' lack of awareness of the glories of creation. The poem 'The Robin's Nest' shows how he wishes to be

> Far from the ruder world's inglorious din
> Who see no glory but in sordid pelf   *[money]*
> And nought of greatness but its little self
> Scorning the splendid gift that nature gives
> Where nature's glory ever breathes and lives

This is where he finds comfort and relief, even in memory and imagination later on:

> there is no curb
> Of interest, industry, or slavish gain
> To war with nature, so the weeds remain
> And wear an ancient passion that arrays
> One's feelings with the shadows of old days
> The rest of peace the sacredness of mind
> In such deep solitude we seek and find.

Out in the countryside he is found gathering joy from the bounty of summer:

THE VERY VOICE OF GOD

> And here I gather by the world forgot
> Harvests of comfort from their happy mood
> Feeling God's blessing dwells in every spot
> And nothing lives but owes him gratitude

So many of the poems and parts of poems contain the phrase 'I love …', and he goes on to describe in delightful and moving detail what has stirred him. He is deeply and sorrowfully aware that the lovely things of creation are vulnerable and mortal, and so he expresses his love over and over again. This sense of being with creation in all things, even in the ugly stinging nettles, in his sheer immersion in creation and his exquisite use of language to capture both the detail of what he experiences and his sense of the innocence and fragility of beauty around him, make him unique in English poetic work.

Here is a stanza from 'The Moorhen's Nest':

> And man the only object that disdains
> Earth's garden into deserts for his gains
> Leave him his schemes of gain – 'tis wealth to me
> Wild heaths to trace –

There is quite a late poem written during his final years in the asylum; he has retained, all through his life, his love of creation, and has, of course, lost all faith in humanity. His fidelity to nature, to the details and sense of belonging, is quite extraordinary, given his physical and mental problems; the wisdom he has acquired over his frustrated longings and his long sufferings come across in this poem, as well in its statements as in its perfectly flowing language, rhymes and rhythms; it is the work of a wise man, perfectly wrought, not what one would expect from a man in his condition.

THE OUTLAW CHRIST

> Would'st thou but know where Nature clings
>   That cannot pass away
> Stand not to look on human things
>   For they shall all decay:
> False hearts shall change and rot to dust
>   While truth exerts her powers
> Love lives with Nature, not with lust.
>   Go find her in the flowers.
>
> Dost dream o'er faces once so fair,
>   Unwilling to forget?
> Seek Nature in the fields and there
>   The first-loved face is met
> The native gales are lovers' voices
>   As nature's self can prove
> The wild field-flowers are lovers' choices
>   And Nature's self is Love.

'To a Lark Singing in Winter' has this delightful piece:

> The god of nature guides her well
> To choose best dwellings for hersel'
> And in the spring her nest we'll tell
>   Her choice at least
> For God loves little larks as well
>   As man or beast

There is a passage in Shakespeare's 'A Midsummer-Night's Dream' in which Theseus says:

> The lunatic, the lover and the poet
> Are of imagination all compact:

THE VERY VOICE OF GOD

> One sees more devils than vast hell can hold,
> That is, the madman: the lover, all as frantic,
> Sees Helen's beauty in a brow of Egypt;
> The poet's eye in a fine frenzy rolling,
> Doth glance from heaven to earth, from earth to heaven;
> And as imagination bodies forth
> The form of things unknown, the poet's pen
> Turns them to shapes, and gives to airy nothing
> A local habitation and a name.

I am quite certain that John Clare never heard of ecology, nor of Christology, nor of bi-polar affective disorder … yet to read his poetry is to be deeply moved by his sense of faith and his instinct for the God of the cosmos. His vision moved from the beauty of the daisy at his feet to the spirit of creation itself. For a poet so much in love with creation and the things of earth, the greatest suffering was his incarceration.

Written in Prison

> I envy e'en the fly its gleams of joy
> In the green woods from being but a boy
> Among the vulgar and the lowly bred
> I envied e'en the hare her grassy bed
> Innured to strife and hardship from a child
> I traced with lonely step the desert wild
> Sighed o'er bird-pleasures but no nest destroyed
> With pleasure felt the singing they enjoyed
> Saw nature smile on all and shed no tears
> A slave through ages though a child in years
> The mockery and scorn of those more old
> An Esop in the world's extended fold
> The fly I envy settling in the sun
> On the green leaf and wish my goal was won

THE OUTLAW CHRIST

I sometimes think of John Clare on his deathbed and wonder if he could have sighed softly and repeated to himself, over and over, as Hopkins did, 'I am so happy, I am so happy ...', this I would wish for him. The reports merely say: early in 1864 he was 'very helpless and quite childish', and on 20 May 'he simply ceased to breathe'. Clare had at last stepped out of the constrictions of his life into the wide meadows of light; he had gone home, to the Cosmic God and the original Eden of his dreams. Alongside his Christ, John Clare could be termed an outlaw.

14

THE QUEEN OF CALVARY

Emily Dickinson (1830-1886)

Emily Dickinson was born in Amherst, Massachusetts, in 1830 to a family well known for educational and political activity. Her father, an orthodox Calvinist, was a lawyer and treasurer of Amherst College, and also served in Congress. She was educated at Amherst Academy (1834–47) and Mount Holyoke Female Seminary (1847–8). Of her father, Dickinson said: 'you know he never played'. She started writing poems around 1850 and assembled them in packets bound with needle and thread. She guarded her independence jealously and became a recluse, spending most of her time in her room. She read a great deal: Keats, Ruskin, Byron and many more. There has been speculation about a possible disappointment in a love affair. Apart from that there is little to report of Dickinson's life. If she held herself apart from the world going on outside her home, she yet developed an interior life infinitely more deep and powerful than that of so many of her predecessors. She is a strange and very rich phenomenon, emerging from such a dark and delaying world, yet penetrating that world with her own strong and individual grace.

Her emphasis on self-reliance in religion sprang from what she perceived as choice between a temporal goal and the elusive promise of Christ's heaven. She preferred to take a risk and bet on faith. She never seems to have doubted the existence of God, yet often in her work she places herself before him as a child, hoping to hide the desperation of her living and her search. No doubt partly due to a reaction against her father's Calvinism, something grew in her of Byron's sense of rebellion in rejecting a visible Church, yet the Jesus she chose to put her faith in was

Jesus, the man of grief, the one who stood outside the confines of that visible Church. The Outlaw. She was unhappy with the prevailing Puritan conservative theology. Perhaps one of the great delights in following the development of her faith poetry is that there is no systematic argument behind it; she simply accepts gratefully the moments of joy that come to push the soul along, and many of her poems address her suffering and her non-responding God.

In the quiet of her own room, poetry became the centre of her existence. The God she was given, and this was a relic of the Puritan outlook, was incomprehensible as a Person and remained faceless and menacing for her. The Deity she sought was a kindlier one, yet she found her relationship with any Deity intensely problematical. How much this was due to the fact that she closed herself away from any real contact with other human beings will remain a moot question.

An early poem contains still some curiosity about the world of nature beyond her room:

79

> Going to Heaven!
> I don't know when –
> Pray do not ask me how!
> Indeed I'm too astonished
> To think of answering you!
> Going to Heaven!
> How dim it sounds!
> And yet it will be done
> As sure as flocks go home at night
> Unto the Shepherd's arm!
>
> Perhaps you're going too!
> Who knows?

THE QUEEN OF CALVARY

If you should get there first
Save just a little space for me
Close to the two I lost –
The smallest 'Robe' will fit me
And just a bit of 'Crown' –
For you know we do not mind our dress
When we are going home –

I'm glad I don't believe it
For it would stop my breath –
And I'd like to look a little more
At such a curious Earth!
I'm glad they did believe it
Whom I have never found
Since the mighty Autumn afternoon
I left them in the ground.

This somewhat whimsical piece is a fine mixture of sorrow and playfulness, of simplicity and humility, all spiced with a gentle sarcasm. She says her parents believed what she finds hard to take and envies them. Her ambivalence about faith – 'I'm glad I don't believe it' – continues right to the end. It is Christ she comes closest to, and in the next poem she expresses a hope that Christ himself will manage to explain all the anguish she knows when she gets to the 'schoolroom' of heaven:

193

I shall know why – when Time is over –
And I have ceased to wonder why –
Christ will explain each separate anguish
In the fair schoolroom of the sky –

> He will tell me what 'Peter' promised –
> And I – for wonder at his woe –
> I shall forget the drop of Anguish
> That scalds me now – that scalds me now!

The word 'scalds', repeated, remains in the memory. Her great and ongoing dilemma was that the heaven she dreamed of, or had heard so much about from Calvinist and Puritan sources, was not one she thought she would be restful in. Her difficult and demanding father, together with the difficult and demanding Puritan outlook on life, kept her sense of religion one of gloom and sadness. This she wished to reject, but the ambivalence and doubt remained with her and peppered the poems in this still early stage of her poetry and life.

413

> I never felt at Home – Below –
> And in the Handsome Skies
> I shall not feel at Home – I know –
> I don't like Paradise –
>
> Because it's Sunday – all the time –
> And Recess – never comes –
> And Eden'll be so lonesome
> Bright Wednesday Afternoons –
>
> If God could make a visit –
> Or ever took a Nap –
> So not to see us – but they say
> Himself – a Telescope –

THE QUEEN OF CALVARY

> Perennial beholds us –
> Myself would run away
> From Him – and Holy Ghost – and All –
> But there's the 'Judgment day'!

An astute awareness and memory of the difficulties of the schoolroom, and of the demands of a Puritan Sunday, the drag of it, the insistence. But there is an unmissable echo of George Herbert's poem 'Love' in another of Emily's poems; a rather whimsical echo, where the hesitation and the doubt are more palpable than the final sense of acceptance of God's unquestioning generosity that is found in Herbert. The dialogue form she uses here is delightful and echoes the Herbert poem, too.

964

> 'Unto Me?' I do not know you –
> Where may be your House?
>
> 'I am Jesus – Late of Judea –
> New – of Paradise' –
>
> Wagons – have you – to convey me?
> This is far from Thence –
>
> 'Arms of Mine – sufficient Phaeton –
> Trust Omnipotence' –
>
> I am spotted – 'I am Pardon' –
> I am small – 'The Least
> Is esteemed in Heaven the Chiefest –
> Occupy my House' –

'You must sit down and eat' is the conclusion of Herbert's poem; Jesus tells Dickinson, at the end of this poem, 'Occupy my House'. Her suffering appears to have been great, as she feels herself abandoned, alone and loveless in this life, and she finds her God, her Christ, was unresponsive.

341

After great pain, a formal feeling comes –
The nerves sit ceremonious, like Tombs –
The stiff heart questions was it He, that bore,
And Yesterday, or Centuries before?

The Feet, mechanical, go round –
Of Ground, or Air, or Ought –
A Wooden way
Regardless grown,
A Quartz contentment, like a stone –

This is the Hour of Lead –
Remembered, if outlived,
As Freezing persons recollect the Snow –
First – Chill – then Stupor – then the letting go –

'After great pain' was written in 1862 when she was about thirty years of age. The pain she knew was, perhaps, the kind of pain Hopkins knew in his hours of deep distress: the sense of abandonment, the whole body and spirit numbed by suffering, isolation, loss. What she calls a 'formal feeling' is a kind of accepting quiet where life will continue in a wooden, mechanical way, without overt purpose, or like a stone, dulled. And such pain will be remembered – and here comes the hard thought – she says 'if' that pain can be 'outlived'. She felt it terribly deeply then. She outlines the progress of that outliving, first the chill, then a stupor and at last the 'letting go'. But lines three and four come to the nub of the question: she asks, after such suffering and when she is recollected in stiffness, was all this suffering just yesterday, or centuries ago? There is the echo in this question of the idea of Christ's crucifixion being an eternal one, and we shall meet it again in a great poem by David Gascoyne. The fragility of the person settling 'ceremonious, like Tombs' is wonderfully caught in the two reasonably formal stanzas surrounding a broken one that has a line that does not rhyme with any other line. The fine analysis of the progress of settling down, recovering, then letting go, is quite startlingly accurate.

Another poem, written also in 1862 and shortly after the above, is 'I dreaded that first Robin, so … '.

348

> I dreaded that first Robin, so,
> But He is mastered, now,
> I'm accustomed to Him grown,
> He hurts a little, though –
>
> I thought if I could only live
> Till that first Shout got by –
> Not all Pianos in the Woods
> Had power to mangle me –
>
> I dared not meet the Daffodils –
> For fear their Yellow Gown
> Would pierce me with a fashion
> So foreign to my own –
>
> I wished the Grass would hurry –
> So – when 'twas time to see –
> He'd be too tall, the tallest one
> Could stretch – to look at me –

THE OUTLAW CHRIST

> I could not bear the Bees should come,
> I wished they'd stay away
> In those dim countries where they go,
> What world had they, for me?
>
> They're here, though; not a creature failed –
> No Blossom stayed away
> In gentle deference to me –
> The Queen of Calvary –
>
> Each one salutes me, as he goes,
> And I, my childish Plumes,
> Lift, in bereaved acknowledgment
> Of their unthinking Drums –

Inevitably, this poem brings to mind the famous lines of T.S. Eliot:

> April is the cruellest month, breeding
> Lilacs out of the dead land, mixing
> Memory and desire, stirring
> Dull roots with spring rain.

The lines are from 'The Burial of the Dead' section of *The Waste Land*. Spring, the coming to life of everything in creation, brings its demands to the soul that is cowering in dread of life. The consciousness of the life that is not being lived, the memory of all that has been missed, or lost, hurts 'the dull roots'. Hopkins wrote: 'Mine, O Thou Lord of life, send my roots rain'. But Dickinson is not wishing for new life for herself. There is a quiet humour and self-mockery in this poem, 'me, the Queen of Calvary', look at me, see how I suffer when I notice how everything that is coming alive comes to 'salute me' as it passes on. She sees herself as 'bereaved', and all that the wonders of spring give to her is the annoying sound as of drums beating. All of creation, then, in its stirring, is indifferent to Dickinson's suffering as she cowers behind the window, scared to look or to listen.

That drum appeared in an earlier poem and perhaps clarifies why she uses the image here. The poem, 'I felt a Funeral, in my Brain', was written in 1861, a poem in which she imagines her own funeral taking place.

280

I felt a Funeral, in my Brain,
And Mourners to and fro
Kept treading – treading – till it seemed
That Sense was breaking through –

And when they all were seated,
A Service, like a Drum –
Kept beating – beating – till I thought
My Mind was going numb –

And then I heard them lift a Box
And creak across my Soul
With those same Boots of Lead, again,
Then Space – began to toll,

As all the Heavens were a Bell,
And Being, but an Ear,
And I, and Silence, some strange Race
Wrecked, solitary, here –

And then a Plank in Reason, broke,
And I dropped down, and down –
And hit a World, at every plunge,
And Finished knowing – then –

Here is the young woman, alone, cooped up in her room in Amherst where she spends most of her life, thinking, reading, watching out the window – and writing. She feels a great lack of loving in her life, she feels alone, living almost a pointless life apart from her writing. She rarely reaches towards the world outside. This poem comes out of that brooding and self-watching, imagining her funeral, all the noise and movement around her, and the great rhythmic movement of the poem echoes these sounds, 'to and fro', 'treading, treading', a drum 'beating, beating'. The poem moves from these sense awareness sounds of moving to a numbness of the mind; then there is the soul and the dreadful sounds, 'boots of lead', a tolling bell. The form of nightmare comes in where there is nothing but space and the sky itself and all of being is an ear and she alone is silence. She is wrecked, solitary, and then even her reason fails and she passes into a strange situation; she has finished all knowing … or she has finished by knowing? Perhaps she touches the shore of madness, Reason wrecked, and that final word 'then …' leaving us all hanging.

Christian Wiman speaks of Dickinson in terms of an awareness of our earthly longing, that there is something missing in life, but what is that something, and where is its source?

959

A loss of something ever felt I –
The first that I could recollect
Bereft I was – of what I knew not
Too young that any should suspect

A Mourner walked among the children
I notwithstanding went about
As one bemoaning a Dominion
Itself the only Prince cast out

THE QUEEN OF CALVARY

> Elder, Today, a session wiser
> And fainter, too, as Wiseness is —
> I find myself still softly searching
> For my Delinguent Palaces —
>
> And a Suspicion, like a Finger
> Touches my Forehead now and then
> That I am looking oppositely
> For the site of the Kingdom of Heaven

The poem tells how she felt, in childhood, something precious had been lost, something of real worth whose source is unknown, though there are several causes that could be brought to bear; she lived in a time of Calvinist bleakness and Puritan negativity; she lost her parents, her father was distinctly harsh and committed to a dark and judgemental God; she was so young that nobody around her could guess her feeling. She was aware, even as a child, of the existence of death, something that was not spoken of amongst the young. But when she grew older, wiser and 'fainter', because the garnering of wisdom is a long and difficult process, she still tries to understand what palaces (the word 'delinguent seems deliberate, perhaps associating the fact that conversation about death was avoided, with the fulfilment of her dream kingdom being still absent) she has always missed in her life, and at times now believes she had always been seeking the kingdom of heaven. The poem beautifully nets that sense of longing we all share, the awareness that the human spirit is ever unfulfilled. Even the acquisition of wisdom does not destroy that sense. Where is the answer? She knows, so late, that she has been seeking 'the kingdom of Heaven'.

The depth and integrity of Dickinson's self-probing has resulted in a poetry that we may all inhabit, a special room, immaculately kept, where her soul struggled with innumerable doubts and hopes and fears, and with an early sense of sin and guilt imposed on her from without. Those of us who have spent our lives in the wild and rushing world, who still find guilt and a need for forgiveness holding our minds in thrall, need but follow and understand that long and wonderfully productive journey Emily Dickinson made within her poetry. Yet she clearly did suffer, and suffer deeply, nor is there resolution to her suffering, save her sense of being a 'bride' to her absent Christ. She called herself, after all, the 'Queen of Calvary'.

She was still prepared to think of religion as schooling and God as a perpetually watchful head teacher; the only escape from the dimness of Sunday rigidity is to run away, to mitch from it all. But there is sin, there is judgement, there is hell! Or is there? Quickly, the sadness and emptiness of her life, apart from her own room and her poetry, placed a weight of sorrow on her spirit, a sense of the hard journey that is life. One of her most powerful poems takes up again that theme of horse and carriage to take the soul away. It adds the notion of school and holiday, the loveliness of the world, however small the garden and acreage she knew and allowed herself to know, with that heavy awareness that mortality is not a childhood game, but a reality.

712

Because I could not stop for Death –
He kindly stopped for me –
The Carriage held but just Ourselves –
And Immortality.

We slowly drove – He knew no haste
And I had put away
My labour and my leisure too,
For His Civility –

THE QUEEN OF CALVARY

We passed the School, where Children strove
At Recess – in the Ring –
We passed the Fields of Gazing Grain –
We passed the Setting Sun –

Or rather – He passed Us –
The Dews drew quivering and chill –
For only Gossamer, my Gown –
My Tippet – only Tulle –

We paused before a House that seemed
A Swelling of the Ground –
The Roof was scarcely visible –
The Cornice – in the Ground –

Since then – 'tis Centuries – and yet
Feels shorter than the Day
I first surmised the Horses' Heads
Were toward Eternity –

Dickinson works, as did George Herbert, by reasoning with herself, and by willing that the answer may be love, and generosity beyond what our human nature may expect. In the poem Christ has the last word and basically assures her that death's carriage was his arms and would bring her to eternity. And so her life and poetry pass, and the temptation is to see Emily Dickinson all the time sad and alone and removed from the world, looking into the mirror of her own spirit and stitching away at her poetry. And so, no doubt, a great deal of her life was spent. But there are moments of sparkle and light, as there are in all our lives, in spite of the 'I am spotted' and 'I am small' of the poem quoted earlier. And in the development of her sense of God, there are moments of light, too, but they are rare and are always darkened by her uncertainty. God had been presented to her in such a way that she wished to shun it, but that left in her a longing which has appeared in so many of the poems. If Christ is introduced to the soul with a love that one is sensually aware of, if it is presented with a positive and joyful earnestness rather than a dour and demanding portentousness, then the possibilities of answering positively are more sure; in things of the spirit 'I am small': 'and the Christ told us that it is the children, those of unquestioning and selfless acceptance, that will inherit the kingdom'.

1258

Who were 'the Father and the Son'
We pondered when a child,
And what had they to do with us
And when portentous told

With inference appalling
By Childhood fortified
We thought, at least they are no worse
Than they have been described.
Who are 'the Father and the Son'
Did we demand Today
'The Father and the Son' himself
Would doubtless specify –

But had they the felicity
When we desired to know,
We better Friends had been, perhaps,
Than time ensue to be –

THE QUEEN OF CALVARY

>We start – to learn that we believe
>But once – entirely –
>Belief, it does not fit so well
>When altered frequently –
>
>We blush, that Heaven if we achieve –
>Event ineffable –
>We shall have shunned until ashamed
>To own the Miracle –

This poem has a slowness and sad awareness to it that has thrown out all the little bits of humour and irony the earlier work had allowed into her poems of faith and seeking. The doubt is still there, but the sense that life would have been much more fruitful if the faith had been well presented to her at the beginning is a deeply tragic sense of loss and wastefulness. Her growing awareness of the weakness of her own faith and her wish to have a much stronger belief, deepen the later poems and slow them to a kind of dirge, where the lines plod more heavily; even though they remain short, the rhymes are much less full, thus creating a sense of unease in the reading.

1433

>How brittle are the Piers
>On which our Faith doth tread –
>No Bridge below doth totter so –
>Yet none hath such a Crowd.
>
>It is as old as God –
>Indeed – 'twas built by him –
>He sent his Son to test the Plank,
>And he pronounced it firm.

That word 'firm' is rich with irony, I believe; and the Plank that God sent his Son to 'test' surely reminds the reader of the wood of the cross. Faith then depends on such suffering; it must take that same 'test' and, if the firmness is there, then perhaps we shall not 'totter' so much on the bridge we have to cross.

As her quiet life progressed, this sense of condemnation and evil associated with her early belief in God remained strong in Emily's mind as if she continued in an effort of belief, but found the negativities she was introduced to as a child ever daunting. It will always be impossible to know if she might have developed her faith had she gone out 'into the world' and lived a more traditional lifestyle, had a job, had a family, mixed with people whose faith was stronger. The opposite, indeed, held sway, as a late poem testifies.

1551

Those – dying then,
Knew where they went –
They went to God's Right Hand –
That Hand is amputated now
And God cannot be found –

The abdication of Belief
Makes the Behaviour small –
Better an ignis fatuus
Than no illume at all –

What a sad conclusion she has come to! Better, perhaps, to hold to a will-o'-the-wisp than to the religion she was introduced to. And there is another piece, also late in her life and writing, where she sees life as a prison, even though it may be a magical one; life itself has not allowed her the happiness she knows would have been possible; and if, in her side-lined living, there have been faults, she pleads for forgiveness, but in a vague, uncertain way. Finally, what happiness she may have known has been undershot all through her living by the early negativities she found thrust upon her. It is our good fortune that Emily Dickinson spent her life in the small room of her poetry, a room that has expanded through the honesty of the self-examination she conducted through her poems into a universe we all might better understand.

1601

Of God we may ask one favour,
That we may be forgiven –
For what, he is presumed to know –
The Crime, from us, is hidden –
Immured the whole of Life
Within a magic Prison
We reprimand the Happiness
That too competes with Heaven.

A note on Emily Dickinson

by Teresa Vasquez
[see the Appendix]

There is little known about Emily Dickinson's life, a recluse to the extreme. As a lawyer, congressman and treasurer of Amherst College, her father worked to keep her family well connected during his lifetime. Educated, she attended Amherst Academy from 1834 to 1847. Wanting to continue her education, she joined the Mount Holyoke Female Seminary for one year before leaving. She was known to have an extensive reading interest, from Keats to Byron. About two years after leaving the seminary, she began to write poetry. Though never confirmed, rumours swirled that she had suffered a romantic disappointment. Not much more can be said definitively about her life, but her poetry enlightens us on intimate parts of her life, inside the walls of her bedroom. Born to an orthodox Calvinist family, Emily Dickinson's inherited religiosity during her lifetime contributed to much of her poetry, though it is far from remaining in line with Calvinist doctrine. She expresses a true Christian faith through the suffering depicted in her writing.

She decided to place her faith in Jesus, a man of grief and pain. In her resistance to organised religion, she writes of her dissatisfaction: 'I never felt at Home – Below.' Here, she conveys her unmet needs as a follower of Christ. Within this poem, Dickinson teases her yearning for freedom and her inability to achieve it through the institutionalised version of God. She writes, 'I don't like Paradise – / Because it's Sunday – all the time' (lines 4–5). Unable to escape the confines of her family's conservative Calvinism, all that is left for her is to hate the heaven she knows. She does not want her heaven to be Sunday with strict rules every single day for the rest of eternity. She expresses her disinterest, yet she does not denounce religion, or God, altogether. Continuing her desire to step away from such practices, she adds at the end of the poem, 'Myself would run away / From Him – and Holy Ghost – and All – But there's the 'Judgement Day'! (lines 14–16). These lines send the clear message that she is not connected to her religion but believes in God. She wants to distance herself from the religion that had been forced upon her, but she still keeps God close. This contradiction marks the beginning of her identification with a suffering Jesus.

Enduring her road of grief, she focuses on God's abandonment of her years later. She led her life alone in her room, and in 'After great pain, a formal feeling comes – ,' she attacks this abandonment head on. The first stanza uses words like 'formal' and 'stiff' to describe aspects of life that are usually filled with great personal and volatile emotions. She begins by distancing the movement allowed between 'feeling' and 'heart,' but this distance only occurs after the pain, specifically after her isolation. The second stanza echoes the first in its depiction of an automatic way of everyday living. It mirrors her own life. Her dissatisfaction with the god of her family's church gradually solidifies after her lifetime of loneliness. After the agony she has endured because of this unrelenting God, she feels no connection to him. Despite the mechanical living of her life and her rejection of any emotional investment in God, Dickinson still yearned to connect to a God. She ends the poem with the hope of moving past the pain and, eventually, the aloofness. She concludes with a hope of letting go and being able to connect once again.

Following this need to reconnect, she writes, 'I dreaded the first Robin, so … '; later the same year that 'After great pain, a formal feeling comes – ' was written. For the length of the poem, she berates nature as springtime arrives, bringing with it new life, and is unfeeling towards her internal suffering. Beginning with the song of a robin, she mentions the ache she experiences with the first bird of the season in spite of her knowledge of what is to come: 'I'm accustomed to Him grown, / He hurts a little, though' (lines 3–4). Life cultivates around her whilst ignoring the pain she carries. 'Each one salutes me, as he goes,' indifferent to her need for quiet (line 25). She merely asks to suffer in peace. It is within this detailed description of her hurt that she expresses a link between Jesus and herself by proclaiming to be 'The Queen of Calvary' (line 24). Here, she links herself to the ultimate form of suffering, yet she does it in a religious context. Despite her uneasiness with religion, she alludes to it constantly. Her faith has become grounded in her pain. Through this pain, she sees herself as the bride of Christ.

Her life is filled with the thought of death, with loneliness, and unresolved agony. By comparing her ache to the death of Jesus, she suggests that she understands Jesus' pain in his last moments. This trap of hurt allows her last few years to know a need for forgiveness. Here, she finds comfort and forgiveness of all of her life's anguish. She knows that her way of life may have been heavily influenced by the negative events of her youth, which deprived her of any potential future happiness. In 'Of

God we may ask one favour,' she portrays life as a jailhouse full of magic, for she could not find joy. Unsure of her god, but noticing her flaws, she prays rather ambiguously for forgiveness from God. All she knows is that she needs forgiveness to find ' … the Happiness / That too competes with Heaven' (lines 7–8).

Being a recluse, Emily Dickinson limited her world to the four walls of her bedroom and her richly telling poetry. Her small world expanded beyond her room with the help of words and thoughts as she reflects on her life. She experiences the world around her through poetry. The truthfulness found in her poems allows us to see inside a life that may otherwise have been lost to history. Very little may be known factually of her life, but the intimate details of her thoughts are outlined in the poetry.

15

BECOMING JESUS

Gerard Manley Hopkins (1844-1889)

The world itself, the physical universe, in Hopkins's sense of things, is shot through with sanctity; it is the bones of God, the body of Christ, it is the atmosphere we breathe in and breathe out. From 'The Wreck of the Deutschland':

> I kiss my hand
> To the stars, lovely-asunder
> Starlight, wafting him out of it; and
> Glow, glory in thunder;
> Kiss my hand to the dappled-with-damson west:
> Since, tho' he is under the world's splendour and wonder,
> His mystery must be instressed, stressed;
> For I greet him the days I meet him, and bless when I understand.

In a letter to his old school friend, E.H.Coleridge, on 1 June 1864, Hopkins said that the main object of Christian belief was the doctrine of the Real Presence: that is, belief in the actual presence of Christ's body and blood in the Eucharist. It was this that brought him to Catholicism. Conscious all his life, then, of both the wonder and grandeur of the created universe about him, and of the person of Jesus Christ, it is interesting to focus on his actual and changing view of the relationship with Christ. An early poem of 1864, 'New Readings', has this first stanza:

THE OUTLAW CHRIST

> Although the letter said
> On thistles that men look not grapes to gather,
> I read the story rather
> How soldiers platting thorns around Christ's head
> Grapes grew and drops of wine were shed.

Not too promising, perhaps, but here is a young poet practising his craft and thoughtful about the Christ. About a year later, Hopkins's fluency with the sonnet form comes together with a slightly more promising relationship to the Christ:

> Myself unholy, from myself unholy
> To the sweet living of my friends I look –
> Eye-greeting doves bright-counter to the rook,
> Fresh brooks to salt sand-teasing waters shoaly:–
> And they are purer, but alas! not solely
> The unquestion'd readings of a blotless book.
> And so my trust, confused, struck, and shook
> Yields to the sultry siege of melancholy.
> He has a sin of mine, he its near brother;
> Knowing them well I can but see the fall.
> This fault in one I found, that in another:
> And so, though each have one while I have all,
> No *better* serves me now, save *best*; no other
> Save Christ: to Christ I look, on Christ I call.

Echoes of the serious playfulness with the language of George Herbert may be heard, but not the argument with Christ that Herbert had. The consciousness of faults in himself and in others leads him to a seeking of what is purest and best, and this may be foreseeing, but the awareness of faults suggests a response of 'melancholy', something that will take over

BECOMING JESUS

Hopkins's life in later years. Then again he will call upon Christ, but the relationship will have greatly matured.

After his conversion to Catholicism, Hopkins joined the Jesuits and spent his novitiate in St Beuno's in North Wales, having earlier urged himself to give up the writing of poetry as being an occupation unfit to the serious business of being a priest. It is well known how the wreck of the ship, the *Deutschland*, and the loss of so many souls aboard, followed by the hint given to him by his superior that somebody ought to write about the event, moved Hopkins back to poetry. In the intervening years, he had prayed and studied, following the laid-down methods of the Spiritual Exercises of St Ignatius. There he would have drawn closer to Christ in meditation and in prayer ,and the need for expression that he always had would have grown towards a dam-burst of language. It came out in the magnificent 'The Wreck of the Deutschland' in late 1875. What struck Hopkins most about this was the fact that five nuns of the Franciscan order had been expelled from Germany and were on the ship. One of them, 'the chief sister', as Hopkins described her, was 'a gaunt woman 6ft. high, calling out loudly and often "O Christ, come quickly!" till the end came.' This pushed Hopkins to think more closely of his own relationship to Christ. He recalls a period of spiritual distress he had suffered:

> I did say yes
> O at lightning and lashed rod;
> Thou heardst me truer than tongue confess
> Thy terror, O Christ, O God.

He feels that, in a state of spiritual doubt or difficulty, Christ frowns at him, and hell beckons; how is he to get out of it, and answers

> I whirled out wings that spell
> And fled with a fling of the heart to the heart of the Host.

THE OUTLAW CHRIST

This is what the frailty of human faith requires, a complete yielding to the presence and the commandments of Christ, knowing there is within the self, 'a vein / Of the gospel proffer, a pressure, a principle, Christ's gift.' The gospel has promised grace; we are to open the heart to receive that gift of grace. The poem outlines that this grace comes from Christ's incarnation, 'dates from day / Of his going in Galilee', through the Passion, and it is only when the human heart is suffering, is 'at bay', that the person will call out in anguish for help.

> Hither, then, last or first,
> To hero of Calvary, Christ's feet –
> Never ask if meaning it, wanting it, warned of it – men go.

In her utter distress, the nun called upon Christ. And Hopkins, who knew he was 'Away in the loveable west, / On a pastoral forehead of Wales, / I was under a roof here, I was at rest, / And they the prey of the gales', is brought to tears at her strength. They were Franciscan nuns, and St Francis bore the stigmata, 'the finding and sake and cipher of suffering Christ'. Out of the bewildering and destroying storm that struck the *Deutschland*, the nun calls on 'A master, her master and mine!' He asks himself what she may have meant: was it to suffer death as Christ had done?

> Or is it that she cried for the crown then,
> The keener to come at the comfort for feeling the combating keen?

His conclusion is that it is Christ who tests the soul, and it is Christ who brings relief.

> There then! the Master,
> *Ipse*, the only one, Christ, King, Head:
> He was to cure the extremity where he had cast her.

Thus Christ wins glory, in Hopkins's view, and Hopkins, in stanza 34 of this powerful poem, offers a hymn of praise to that Christ:

> Now burn, new born to the world,
> Double-naturèd name,
> The heaven-flung, heart-fleshed, maiden-furled
> Miracle-in-Mary-of-flame,
> Mid-numberèd he in three of the thunder-throne!
> Not a dooms-day dazzle in his coming nor dark as he came;
> Kind, but royally reclaiming his own;
> A released shower, let flash to the shire, not a lightning of fire hard-hurled.

A tour-de-force of description, awed and awe-smitten language, but modulating into a more personable softness in the last few lines, this paean of praise remains far from being a personal response to a friend, but an adequate response to a taskmaster and a demanding God. We are still far from the Herbertian love of 'my dear', though Hopkins's earlier poems, such as 'The Half-Way House', are distinctly influenced by Herbert.

While in St Beuno's, Hopkins wrote his most distinctive and happy poems, in the glory of the natural environment of that part of North Wales, and in the certainty of his studies and his awareness of his coming ordination to the priesthood. In 1877 he wrote:

The Lantern out of Doors

> Sometimes a lantern moves along the night,
>   That interests our eyes. And who goes there?
>   I think; where from and bound, I wonder, where,
> With, all down darkness wide, his wading light?
>
> Men go by me whom either beauty bright
>   In mould or mind or what not else makes rare:
>   They rain against our much-thick and marsh air

Rich beams, till death or distance buys them quite.

Death or distance soon consumes them: wind
 What most I may eye after, be in at the end
 I cannot, and out of sight is out of mind.

Christ minds: Christ's interest, what to avow or amend
 There, eyes them, heart wants, care haunts, foot follows kind,
 Their ransom, their rescue, and first, fast, last friend.

Hopkins remains the watcher, from a distance, and his final three lines read somewhat gratuitous, though, of course, it is part of his ongoing and developing awareness of who Christ is, and what Christ means. The long and accurate description of the strangers passing in the darkness is, indeed, richly meaningful from the point of view of the watcher: how people are a light in the darkness of one another, and how, then, they pass out of one another's ken. The Christ in this poem is a caring Christ; there is no sense of awe or dread, no insistence on a testing or demanding God, merely one whose heart is with the traveller, caring, following, and their 'first, fast, last friend'. There is fine fellow feeling in the poem, and it moves Hopkins closer to Herbert's stance on Christ.

Then, in 1878, another wreck moved him to write 'The Loss of the Eurydice'. In late 1877 Hopkins had left St Beuno's and moved to Stonyhurst, the Jesuit school where he taught classics and was suddenly very busy. He found it difficult to write now, but the *Eurydice* got him stirring again. The *Eurydice* was a training ship and was on its way home after a stint in Bermuda. There were some 327 sailors on board and many of them were young men. The ship ran into a freak gale off the Isle of Wight and all but two on board were lost. Hopkins wrote a very different poem from the *Deutschland* one, this being far more of a narrative and a tribute to the youths; Hopkins kept a strong affection for the young soldiers of the Empire! But the very beginning harks back to the *Deutschland* and

BECOMING JESUS

Christ's relationship to the tragedy:

> The Eurydice – it concerned thee, O Lord: ...
> Lads and men her lade and treasure ...
> Death teeming in by her portholes
> Raced down decks, round messes of mortals.

What worries Hopkins greatly is that these souls, caught so suddenly, may well be 'in Unchrist', perhaps unshriven, and he wonders why his 'master bore it'. He does not pursue the question, simply urges prayers.

> But to Christ lord of thunder
> Crouch; lay knee by earth low under:
>   'Holiest, loveliest, bravest,
> Save my hero, O Hero savest ... '

So there is little comfort; the prayer Hopkins asks for is a prayer 'in retrospect': that those who may have been in Unchrist may have been given grace. If eternity is unconcerned with time, then a prayer at a specific point in time will touch the eternal Christ and may have effected something before the actual event occurred in time. But the sense that Hopkins is so moved by Christ in moments of great tragedy and grief does not yet convince that he has actually come to understand and accept Christ as friend. Christ is the Hero yet, as in 'The Dream of the Rood', and it is, perhaps, difficult to feel close to a 'hero' with a capital H!

This would suggest that the sonnet 'As Kingfishers Catch Fire', which is undated in the manuscripts, may have been written around 1881, when Hopkins's sense of Christ has developed. Here is a very thoughtful Hopkins, examining how human beings can grow in perfection and worth.

> As kingfishers catch fire, dragonflies draw flame;

THE OUTLAW CHRIST

> As tumbled over rim in roundy wells
> Stones ring; like each tucked string tells, each hung bell's
> Bow swung finds tongue to fling out broad its name;
> Each mortal thing does one thing and the same:
> Deals out that being indoors each one dwells;
> Selves – goes itself; myself it speaks and spells,
> Crying *What I do is me: for that I came*
>
> I say more: the just man justices;
> Keeps grace: that keeps all his goings graces;
> Acts in God's eye what in God's eye he is –
> Christ. For Christ plays in ten thousand places,
> Lovely in limbs, and lovely in eyes not his
> To the Father through the features of men's faces.

Hopkins wrote of this piece: ' … Christ in his member on the one side, his member in Christ on the other. It is as if a man said: That is Christ playing at me and me playing at Christ, only it is no play but truth. That is Christ being me and me being Christ'. The thought is based on the Scotist idea that individuals of any sort, when they act or behave according to the metaphysical fullness of their being, achieve perfection in that act. A human is perfected by the self-being that is his will, and that person is made perfect when the self becomes Christ-like in his act, indeed 'becomes' Christ. This comes about only in full correspondence with the gift of grace. Hopkins elsewhere insists that this is by no means the destruction but the fulfilment of one's individual person. The human is perfected in becoming Christ. In his poem 'The Soldier', written much later when he was in Ireland, he makes the analogy that a soldier, if he does his work well for his king and country, is Christ-like; 'He knows war, served this soldiering through'. To see Christ's life as a war and Christ a soldier serving the kingdom of heaven, may be thought somewhat forced and a little distasteful for this age, though St Ignatius saw his followers as 'soldiers of Christ', and St Paul writes, in 2 Timothy: 'Thou therefore endure hardships, as a good soldier of Jesus Christ'. That poem, 'The Soldier', ends:

> ... seeing somewhere some man do all that man can do,
> For love he leans forth, needs his neck must fall on, kiss,
> And cry 'O Christ-done deed! So God-made-flesh does too:
> Were I come o'er again' cries Christ 'it should be this'.

Hopkins came to work in Ireland in 1884 and was unwell, suffering from spiritual and physical trials, and while there wrote the sonnets that are referred to as the 'terrible sonnets'. These present a study in themselves but what concerns me here is the relationship he develops during this time of fierce suffering, loneliness, depression, illness … with Christ. He was brought to such a pitch of pain that he writes:

> Here, creep,
> Wretch, under a comfort serves in a whirlwind: all
> Life death does end and each day dies with sleep.

There is no complaint save that the Christ is unresponding. 'And my lament / Is cries countless, cries like dead letters sent / To dearest him who lives alas! away.' Herbert appears to whisper to him in the darkness, using that Herbertian phrase: 'dearest him'. Though life has become almost a curse to him, there is no loss of faith in Christ, indeed it appears the opposite, that he draws much closer to Christ. The reason for this is clear and important and comes in a poem written when some peace has been achieved and he can face the world again. That poem is from July 1888, a poem that begins with a resumption of the delight in creation that brought Hopkins to poetry in the first place. 'That Nature is a Heraclitean Fire and of the Comfort of the Resurrection' begins with a powerfully vivid and language-rich description of the world in the aftermath of a storm: 'Delightfully the bright wind boisterous ropes, wrestles, beats earth bare / Of yestertempest's creases.' How creation, then, deals with the things of earth, sky, tree: 'in pool and rutpeel parches / Squandering ooze to squeezed dough, crust, dust ... '. And when faced with this, how 'Million-fuelèd, nature's bonfire burns on', human beings are quickly irrelevant to creation and lost to it. Human fragility and suffering are pointed out:

> Manshape, that shone
> Sheer off, disseveral, a star death blots black out; nor mark
> Is any of him at all so stark
> But vastness blurs and time beats level.

With death, there is nothing left, 'his mark on mind, is gone!' Hopkins now accepts all of this and bursts out with 'Enough! The Resurrection.' With suffering and death, with the fading of flesh and life, all that is left is ash. And now comes the resolution Hopkins had struggled for, from the nun in the wreck of the *Deutschland* and the sailors in the sinking of the *Eurydice*, he knows that all must come 'to hero of Calvary, Christ's feet'. Christ became incarnate and suffered as all men do, as Hopkins has done; but Christ took on all the sufferings and the death of humanity and therefore humanity itself can become Christ: this wildly optimistic, triumphantly exuberant language, the heart-music of the lines, rhythms and rhymes; all come together in the poem at its majestic and awe-smitten end:

> In a flash, at a trumpet crash,
> I am all at once what Christ is, since he was what I am, and
> This Jack, joke, poor potsherd, patch, matchwood, immortal diamond,
> Is immortal diamond.

Christ in his death and resurrection has overcome the flux that Heraclitus consigned all of creation to. And, as Teilhard de Chardin later developed, this is a human being's destiny, to become divinised, as Christ.

This identification with Christ that Hopkins found his way to became a faith for him in his deepest darkness and suffering, and this theme has become common and central to Christian thinking in more recent times. Cardinal Walter Kasper, in his book *Jesus the Christ*, says, 'Faith means ceasing to rely on one's own capabilities, admitting human powerlessness' (p. 69). The Kingdom of God is no longer hidden, it is visible and knowable in the incarnation, in the passion and the resurrection of Christ. During Jesus' lifetime his disciples still believed in a political liberation, but after his death and resurrection they came to believe in a suffering and redeeming Son of God. 'For Luther,' as Kasper writes, 'the hidden God is the God hidden in the suffering and the Cross' (p. 168), and this, too, Hopkins came to believe. The fourteenth-century German Dominican mystic, John Tauler, in a piece titled 'Christmas Season', wrote that the Christ enters the soul 'when we are no longer putting ourselves in his way'; in Hopkins's case, as in so many others, it was deep and prolonged suffering that opened him to the birth of God in himself. Tauler wrote: 'If one would prepare an empty place in the depths of the soul, there can be no doubt that God must fill it at once'. For Hopkins, then, the suffering Christ became the reason and answer to human suffering and was born, at last, into the Hopkins self. This identity with the suffering and resurrected Christ is a central focus for Christian hope.

And again: Gerard Manley Hopkins (1844–1889)

Hopkins made detailed sketches of plants, trees, clouds, even animals, and called the work 'My treasury of explored beauty'. In language, too, he described what he saw in great and loving detail; for instance, speaking of a fall of snow: 'It tufted and toed the firs and yews and went on to load them till they were taxed beyond their spring. The limes, elms, and Turkey-oaks it crisped beautifully as with young leaf'. Many years before the word 'ecology' came into anybody's mind this poet was urging the absolute beauty of creation and how such a creation must lead inevitably to the love of Christ. He was born and brought up an Anglican; it was love for the 'true presence' of Christ in the Eucharist that eventually brought him to Catholicism and to ordination as a Jesuit priest. The love of the world about him and the love of Jesus gave his poetry a special thrust towards awareness of how Christ will rescue humanity, through his death and resurrection, into life. The world itself, the cosmos, is shot through with holiness; it is the bones of God, the body of Christ, it is the air we breathe and it is our duty to care for it. We get a strong feeling of a cosmic awareness in Hopkins, alongside the conviction that it was a trusting in Christ, even through the overwhelming sense that the Christ appears not to be responding that brought Hopkins through his deeply troubled time in Dublin in the last years of his life. 'God's Grandeur' is a central poem in any awareness of Christian ecology and evolution.

God's Grandeur

The world is charged with the grandeur of God.
   It will flame out, like shining from shook foil;
   It gathers to a greatness, like the ooze of oil
Crushed. Why do men then now not reck his rod?
Generations have trod, have trod, have trod;
   And all is seared with trade; bleared, smeared with toil;
   And wears man's smudge and shares man's smell: the soil
Is bare now, nor can foot feel, being shod.

And for all this, nature is never spent;
   There lives the dearest freshness deep down things;
And though the last lights off the black West went
   Oh, morning, at the brown brink eastward, springs –
Because the Holy Ghost over the bent

BECOMING JESUS

World broods with warm breast and with ah! bright winds.

Humankind has not been sensitive to 'nature', to creation, particularly from the beginning of the Industrial Revolution, through the twentieth century and into our own. Hopkins knew that between God and humanity, between God and his creation, there is an ongoing contract, an agreement, a testament, and it is the way of creation to show forth God's grandeur. The word 'charged' in this poem is loaded with meaning. From Genesis onwards, humankind has a duty to care for the earth and be aware of how the wonder of the world shows forth God's glory as a kind of electric current. A further poem by Hopkins emphasises this and points out how creation embodies and shows forth God, in his Christ.

The Starlight Night

Look at the stars! Look, look up at the skies!
   O look at all the fire-folk sitting in the air!
   The bright boroughs, the circle-citadels there!
Down in dim woods the diamond delves! The elves'-eyes
The grey lawns cold where gold, where quickgold lies!
   Wind-beat white beam! Airy abeles set on a flare!
   Flake-doves sent floating forth at a farmyard scare! –
Ah well! It is all a purchase, all is a prize.
Buy then! Bid then! – What? – Prayer, patience, alms, vows.
Look, look: a May-mess, like on orchard boughs!
   Look! March-bloom, like on mealed-with-yellow sallows!
These are indeed the barn; withindoors house
The shocks. This piece-bright paling shuts the spouse
   Christ home, Christ and his mother and all his hallows.

Hopkins associated the detailed wonders of creation with the presence of Christ. He has discovered the work of Duns Scotus, the thirteenth-century Franciscan philosopher and theologian. Here he found a framework for his faith which is not strictly Thomist, nor a Jesuit view, holding that Christ's incarnation was not an act of reparation for the original 'Fall', but a free act of love that would have taken place with or without humanity's failure. Here, too, Hopkins anticipates the great work of Teilhard de Chardin where the notion of a static cosmos needs not one great moment of redemption to counter that 'Fall', but a cosmogenesis, an ongoing evolution towards the fullness of Christ in the final coming of God's kingdom.

Scotus had also prompted Hopkins to an awareness of 'inscape', the individual difference that makes each created thing distinct in itself, with its own unique being. Hopkins took 'inscape' to be that individual excellence, distinctive and patterned as the kernel of each being, and that perfection to be aimed at and expressed in every individual created thing. While in the seminary in Stonyhurst Hopkins wrote: 'The ashtree growing in the corner of the garden was felled … a great pang and I wished to die and not to see the inscapes of the world destroyed any more.'

If the world is 'charged' to take care of the beauty of creation, if the covenant offered between humanity, creation and God is to be upheld, humanity must be aware and careful. He saw this beauty and worth of creation made flesh, incarnated in Christ.

Hurrahing in Harvest

Summer ends now; now, barbarous in beauty, the stooks rise
Around; up above, what wind-walks! what lovely behaviour
Of silk-sack clouds! has wilder, wilful-wavier
Meal-drift moulded ever and melted across skies?

> I walk, I lift up, I lift up heart, eyes,
> Down all that glory in the heavens to glean our Saviour;
> And, eyes, heart, what looks, what lips yet gave you a
> Rapturous love's greeting of realer, or rounder replies?
>
> And the azurous hung hills are his world-wielding shoulder
> Majestic – as a stallion stalwart, very-violet-sweet –
> These things, these things were here and but the beholder
>
> Wanting; which two when they once meet,
> The heart rears wings bold and bolder
> And hurls for him, O half hurls earth for him off under his feet.

Hopkins also saw his Christ as Hero, as in 'The Dream of the Rood' centuries before, and through the Incarnation this hero is humanity's friend. In one of his sermons he wrote: 'Our Lord Jesus Christ is our hero, a hero all the world wants … Often mothers make a hero of a son; girls of a sweetheart and good wives of a husband … but Christ, he is the hero.' This is hero with a lower-case h! An approachable hero, admirable, too, as friend, and more than that; as with the Scotus notion of 'inscape', he saw the human heart as inscaped by Christ – Christ in his Incarnation being the source, sustenance and end of all human endeavour.

In February 1884 Hopkins was sent to St Stephen's Green, Dublin, 'reluctant and apprehensive', as Professor of Greek and Examiner in Classics for the Royal University. He suffered greatly under the regime of classes and examinations, and in being far from all he loved and knew. He developed eye problems and gradually fell into deep depression. What appears to have helped him hold his sanity was a series of carefully ordered and organised sonnets that explored and opened up his hurts. He held to Christ, though for a time he felt wholly abandoned even by God … 'My life is determined by the Incarnation down to most of the details of the day'. At times his pleas and prayers to Christ appear futile:

I Wake and Feel …

I wake and feel the fell of dark, not day.
What hours, O what black hours we have spent
This night! what sights you, heart, saw; ways you went!
And more must, in yet longer light's delay.
   With witness I speak this. But where I say
Hours I mean years, mean life. And my lament
Is cries countless, cries like dead letters sent
To dearest him that lives alas! away.
   I am gall, I am heartburn. God's most deep decree
Bitter would have me taste: my taste was me;
Bones built in me, flesh filled, blood brimmed the curse.
   Selfyeast of spirit a dull dough sours. I see
The lost are like this, and their scourge to be
As I am mine, their sweating selves; but worse.

Christ remains the focus; he now feels that it is through suffering that Christ draws humanity closer to himself. But for most of this terrible time, it is the hidden, the absent Christ. Indeed, he comes near to despair by touching in the next sonnet as deep into pain and misery as a human being may go without wishing to take his own life. He can still choose: even choose 'not to be':

Carrion Comfort

Not, I'll not, carrion comfort, Despair, not feast on thee;
Not untwist – slack they may be – these last strands of man
In me ór, most weary, cry *I can no more*. I can;
Can something, hope, wish day come, not choose not to be.
But ah, but O thou terrible, why wouldst thou rude on me
Thy wring-world right foot rock? lay a lionlimb against me? scan
With darksome devouring eyes my bruisèd bones? and fan,

> O in turns of tempest, me heaped there; me frantic to avoid thee and flee?
>
> Why? That my chaff might fly; my grain lie, sheer and clear.
> Nay in all that toil, that coil, since (seems) I kissed the rod,
> Hand rather, my heart lo! lapped strength, stole joy, would laugh, chéer.
> Cheer whom though? the hero whose heaven-handling flung me, fóot tród
> Me? or me that fought him? O which one? is it each one? That night, that year
> Of now done darkness I wretch lay wrestling with (my God!) my God.

After this long period of almost unbearable suffering, held somewhat in check by the mastery of will and the accomplishment of superbly wrought sonnets, that same will to faith finally brought him respite. In July 1888 he wrote a strange, rich 'sonnet' in which he takes again the wonders of the created world, expressing them in a word-grappling, sound-amazing series of descriptions, which echo the twists and tortures of his mind:

> Cloud-puffball, torn tufts, tossed pillows 'flaunt forth, then chevy on an air-
> built thoroughfare: heaven-roysteres, in gay-gangs 'they throng; they glitter in marches …

The poem is in the name of a sonnet, but the lines are long and there are 'codas'. But still the basic structure of movement of a sonnet is there, the 'turn' coming in the second line of the first coda. If, Hopkins believes, the wonderful things of creation pass quickly, human beings do also, is there anything left behind?

> But quench her bonniest, dearest 'to her, her clearest-selvèd spark
> Man, how fast his firedint, 'his mark on mind, is gone!
> Both are in an unfathomable, all is in an enormous dark
> Drowned. O pity and indignation! Manshape, that shone
> Sheer off, disseveral, a star, 'death blots black out; nor mark
>   Is any of him at all so stark
> But vastness blurs and time 'beats level.'

This rather bleak view suddenly switches with the phrase: 'Enough! The Resurrection' and so, even if flesh fades and 'mortal trash fall to the residuary worm', yet a human, being habited by Christ, does not disappear but becomes something of lasting worth:

> I am all at once what Christ is,
> since he was what I am, and
> This Jack, joke, poor potsherd,
> 'patch, matchwood, immortal diamond
>   Is immortal diamond.

St Paul wrote, in Romans 8, 'For I reckon that the sufferings of the present time are not worthy to be compared with the glory which shall be revealed in us. For the earnest expectation of the creature waits for the manifestation of the sons of God. For the creature was made subject to vanity, not willingly, but by reason of him who has subjected the same in hope, because the creature itself also shall be delivered from the bondage of corruption into the glorious liberty of the children of God. For we know that the whole creation groans and labours in pain together until now. And not only they, but ourselves also, who have the first fruits of the Spirit, even we ourselves groan within ourselves, waiting for the adoption, namely, the redemption of the body.'

In May 1889 Hopkins fell ill with a fever that was soon diagnosed as a type of typhoid. Mariani writes: 'And while the official diagnosis is typhoid, it is quite possible that the illness has been made worse by another complaint, which will not even be named until 1932: Crohn's, a disease marked by constant fatigue' (p. 424), with other symptoms that Hopkins had manifested over the years: stomach cramps, indigestion, diarrhoea, exhaustion. Around noon on Saturday, 8 June, just short of his forty-fifth birthday, Hopkins died. He had been heard to whisper, over and over, 'I am so happy, I am so happy … '.

16

THE COST OF DISCIPLESHIP

Dietrich Bonhoeffer (1906-1945)

Before moving into the twentieth century and the poets who wrote on their relationship with the Christ, it is well to remember that the Industrial Revolution, two world wars, and the challenging awareness of evolution taking over from the notion of the seven-day creation of the Book of Genesis, threw the commitment to faith and to Jesus Christ into some chaos. Before and during the Second World War, it was Dietrich Bonhoeffer's work and writings that urged an even greater commitment to Christ as the way humanity might still survive. It is worth remembering his life and work.

Dietrich Bonhoeffer was born in Breslau, Germany in 1906. He began life with a great enthusiasm for music but surprised everyone by announcing he would become a priest. He studied at the University of Berlin, graduating in 1927 with a doctorate in theology. He worked in Spain and in America where he quickly grew conscious of the poor and the oppressed and vowed to devote himself to their care. He was ordained a Lutheran priest in Berlin in 1931, and just two years later Adolf Hitler was elected chancellor. Bonhoeffer was angry that many members of the church appeared to be supportive of Hitler and the Nazi programme, and he vociferously opposed the Nazification of Germany and of his church. He spoke out, on radio and elsewhere, against Hitler and the persecution of the Jews, urging that the church had responsibilities in this area. In 1933 he broke away from those in the church who supported the Nazi regime. He formed a 'Confessing Church' to stand against Nazism. In 1936 he had his authorisation to preach and teach revoked and he was denounced as an enemy of the state.

Nazism was continually gaining ground and resenting all opposition. In 1937, the Confessing Church was closed down. Bonhoeffer began to travel around Germany preaching and urging seminarians and the established Lutheran Church to resist the Nazi influence. He was also working on a book, *The Cost of Discipleship*, which was published in 1937. One of the regime's techniques of finding dissidents was to force people to take an oath of allegiance to Hitler. Anxious not to be forced into this, Bonhoeffer left for America but, after a short time there, his conscience brought him back to share in the sufferings of his people. 'I have made a mistake in coming to America. I must live through this difficult period of our national history with the Christian people of Germany'. He was denied the right to preach or speak in public and was not allowed to publish. He succeeded in joining the Abwehr, the military intelligence agency, working to oppose Hitler, where he became aware of plots to assassinate the dictator. Now he had to question the value of pacifism, seeing that Nazism would only be overcome by violence. He was once asked what he was praying for at this time and he replied, 'I am praying for the defeat of my nation.'

There were always attempts being made to get German Jews out of Germany into Switzerland, and Bonhoeffer helped in this. For this he was arrested in April 1943 and imprisoned in Tegel Military prison on the shores of Lake Tegel, Berlin. He continued to write and his letters and essays were smuggled out to his family by sympathetic guards. He was later moved to Buchenwald and on to the concentration camp at Flossenburg, in Bavaria. Here, on 8 April 1945, he was court-martialled and sentenced to death by hanging. He was executed the following day. Two weeks later the camp was liberated by American soldiers. A doctor who witnessed the execution wrote:

> I saw Pastor Bonhoeffer kneeling on the floor praying fervently to God. I was most deeply moved by the way this lovable man

prayed, so devout and so certain that God heard his prayer. At the place of execution, he again said a short prayer and then climbed the few steps to the gallows, brave and composed. His death ensued after a few seconds. In the almost fifty years that I worked as a doctor, I have hardly ever seen a man die so entirely submissive to the will of God.

In Flossenburg, and in the other camps where he was imprisoned, Bonhoeffer knew that he had gained almost heroic status in the eyes of his jailers and fellow prisoners, but in some of the poems that he wrote he revealed his own sense of self-worth: 'weary and empty at praying, at thinking, at doing, faint, and ready to say farewell to it all'. And yet he knew this: 'In Jesus, God has said Yes and Amen to it all, and that Yes and Amen is the firm ground on which we stand'. He had come early on, in his time in Barcelona, Spain, and in America, to share solidarity with the innocent victims of racial hatred and with those suffering in war. He was influenced in theology by Karl Barth but he saw God's freedom as *for* us, not *from* us, as Barth saw it; Barth being more Calvinist towards God's glory, Dietrich more Lutheran, God being '*pro me*', for me. He saw Christ as community: God more tangible because Christ lives in community in word, sacrament and the mutual love of members. His work and writings focused on Christ's credible presence in the world. As pastor, his aim was to share as closely as possible the lives of the poor. He was deeply angry at the accommodation of teachers and church leaders to Nazism's denial of civil rights.

Christianity was, for Dietrich Bonhoeffer, not so much a religion, but a person – Christ – who made difficult demands on those who followed him. He worried that Christ had become a church matter, not a matter of life, and he saw that church and real life seemed to be splitting from each other, a division that has almost reached completion in our own time. He would hope that the churches would bring God, in the person of Jesus Christ, back to form a force in the context of human social existence. Here the Holy Spirit would impel Christians towards Christ, the real presence of Christ; the church, he saw, is the presence of Christ, in the way that Christ is the presence of God. So he saw the teaching of theology as urging the search for personal meaning in Christ. He called for an international brotherhood and sisterhood in Christ. Hence the church, like Jesus, must be a presence in the midst of the world. The debris of centuries, which had hidden in mythical, other-world fog, had to be cleared away. Creation needed to be won again for Christ and by Christ.

For Bonhoeffer, Christ was the centre of existence and, in the context of Hitler's time, Christ was an outlaw. Hitler's Germany saw atheist Bolshevists and non-Aryan Jews as threats to the state, and the 'Enabling Law' of March 1933 granted absolute dictatorial powers to Hitler to deal with these 'threats'. In that same month concentration camps had been set up and, a month later, Goering instituted the Gestapo. Bonhoeffer delivered his last university lectures where his life and theology converged. Christ in all the robustness of the prophetic Sermon on the Mount now stood at the centre of his vocation as minister. 'Christ goes through the ages, questioned anew, misunderstood anew, and again and again put to death'. Christ as outlaw. His church, the Evangelical Church in Germany, comprising both Lutheran and Reformed confessions, was considered a state church. State officials were expected to enforce Nazi policies in public life, civil and ecclesial. In July 1933 a rigged church election brought in a Hitler sympathiser, Ludwig Müller, as Reich bishop, an ecclesiastical counterpart to the political leadership of Adolf Hitler. Bonhoeffer kept calling for church action in defence of Jews, regardless of their baptismal status.

The Cost of Discipleship, published in 1937, finds its roots and strength in his own life. He had dedicated his life to the church and to social justice, seeking always 'what Jesus Christ himself wants of us'. He saw the situation as like that of the early church, where the great questions boiled down to a choice: whether or not to follow Christ. The real trouble he identified as the pure word of Jesus being overlaid with so much human ballast: rules and regulations, false hopes and consolations, forcing on them man-made

THE COST OF DISCIPLESHIP

dogmas. 'Grace is costly because it compels a person to submit to the yoke of Christ and follow him.' 'Luther had said that grace alone can save; his followers took up his doctrine and repeated it word for word. But they left out its invariable corollary, the obligation of discipleship'.

One of his repeated arguments centred on the notion of 'cheap grace': 'Cheap grace is the grace we bestow on ourselves. Cheap grace is the preaching of forgiveness without requiring repentance, baptism without church discipline, Communion without confession … Cheap grace is grace without discipleship, grace without the cross, grace without Jesus Christ, living and incarnate.' The follower of the person of Christ is called on to give full commitment to the message of the Sermon on the Mount. 'When Christ calls a man, he bids him come and die.' Bonhoeffer was a gift of grace to the Germany of his time, and is still to all who wish to know, love and follow Christ.

'Jesus Christ lived in the midst of his enemies. At the end all his disciples deserted him. On the Cross he was utterly alone, surrounded by evildoers and mockers. For this cause he had come, to bring peace to the enemies of God. So the Christian, too, belongs not in the seclusion of a cloistered life but in the thick of foes. There is his commission, his work. "The kingdom is to be in the midst of your enemies. And he who will not suffer this does not want to be of the Kingdom of Christ; he wants to be among friends, to sit among roses and lilies, not with the bad people but the devout people. O you blasphemers and betrayers of Christ! If Christ had done what you are doing who would ever have been spared" (Luther).'

17

ART'S NEUROSIS

R.S. Thomas (1913-2000)

R.S. Thomas was born in Cardiff, Wales, in 1913, and his family moved to Holyhead in 1918. He was ordained a priest by the Church of Wales, serving as curate for many years. He married and had a son, Gwydion, in 1945. He worked among the poor Welsh hill peasants, remained poor and lacked the amenities of modern life. He wrote prose in Welsh, but his poetry, in his many collections, was written in English. He became one of the most popular poets writing in the UK and was nominated for the Nobel Prize. He retired in 1978, and devoted more time to advocating Welsh nationalism. He was fiercely opposed to England and its 'occupation' of his country.

Thomas takes the reader by the lapel and forces him to exclaim: 'By thy long grey beard and glittering eye now wherefore stoppest thou me?' Apart from the long grey beard, this is a wholly legitimate question. If it is asked of the poems, the poems answer, and then a sadder and a wiser man, the reader, will wake the following morn. In his introduction to the *Faber Selected Poems of George Herbert*, Thomas writes: 'The poet invents the metaphor and the Christian lives it.' He goes on to quote Simone Weil: 'Every true artist has had real, direct and immediate contact with the beauty of the world, contact that is of the nature of a sacrament'. In an early poem, 'The Moor', he himself can relish the sacramental nature of the landscape: 'It was like a church to me. / I entered it on soft foot, / Breath held like a cap in the hand ... There were no prayers said. But stillness / Of the heart's passions – that was praise / Enough; and the mind's cession / Of its kingdom'.

THE OUTLAW CHRIST

R.S. Thomas began by slowly coming to know the difficulties and darkness of the hill farmer's soul, made strong not by faith in God but 'By the earth's incense, the wind's song.' He grows aware of the farmers' struggles and sufferings and gradually comes to believe in them. There follows, through the poems, a map of his own struggle with himself and with his faith. There is little sense of the presence of his God, rather he pushes his will towards belief. Yet, at times, the person of Christ appears to touch him, as in this poem:

In a Country Church

To one kneeling down no word came,
Only the wind's song, saddening the lips
Of the grave saints, rigid in glass;
Or the dry whisper of unseen wings,
Bats, not angels, in the high roof.

Was he balked by silence? He kneeled long,
And saw love in a dark crown
Of thorns blazing, and a winter tree
Golden with fruit of a man's body.

This is Christ, dwelling in absence and silence, named 'love', perhaps after George Herbert's influence; because the poet kneels long, Christ is glimpsed as a figure of suffering. This is a touch of presence, but at a distance. This standing apart from his God, his Christ, is normal for Thomas; he writes out of his hesitations and doubts, he steers his ambiguities and his shadowing through his verses, and he quizzes the person of Christ. For him there is never any doubt about the historical presence of Christ, but Thomas focuses on the suffering, comparing him in one poem to the artist at work, and to Christ's self-awareness as a neurosis, his very being a work of art. In the same poem it is God who listens most closely, the God that remains unclear in Thomas's mind and work, that Christ who stands for human pain.

The Musician

A memory of Kreisler once:
At some recital in this same city,
The seats all taken, I found myself pushed
On to the stage with a few others,
So near that I could see the toil
Of his face muscles, a pulse like a moth
Fluttering under the fine skin
And the indelible veins of his smooth brow.

I could see, too, the twitching of the fingers,
Caught temporarily in art's neurosis,
As we sat there or warmly applauded
This player who so beautifully suffered
For each of us upon his instrument.

So it must have been on Calvary
In the fiercer light of the thorns' halo:
The men standing by and that one figure,
The hands, bleeding, the mind bruised but calm,
Making such music as lives still.
And no one daring to interrupt
Because it was himself that he played
And closer than all of them the God listened.

Kreisler, the artist, suffers on our behalf, toiling, twitching in the work of producing music, and his suffering is beautiful. The comparison with Christ is both close and distant: the light is 'fiercer', there are thorns, the hands are bleeding but the mind remains calm. The artistic labour of the Christ makes a music that is with us still because he played himself, his own life's music, the music of suffering that draws God's attention to humankind. There is no hint of love in this poem, nor indeed of faith or doubt. It is art outlining an experience of growing aware of another artist.

Song

I choose white, but with
Red on it, like the snow
In winter with its few
Holly berries and the one

Robin, that is a fire
To warm by and like Christ
Comes to us in his weakness,
But with a sharp song.

This poem, too, touches the same strings, the same notes, though in a different register. Here, too, Christ is seen in 'weakness' and his song is sharp as thorns. The gaze in these poems may be turned towards God but there is no personal response adumbrated here – save that of pointing out the suffering of humankind. Is there redemption? Is there faith? Is there acceptance? Or is this poet touching on the Christ that is emblem only of the suffering of twentieth-century humankind in its urgency towards war and self-destruction? We live on an earth that is 'a scorched land of fierce colour', according to another poem. God's Son was shown this land 'as through water', so that a river looked like the serpent. When the Son saw the people of this land, they were holding out 'their thin arms' on a hill, waiting for the bloom of April.

The Coming

And God held in his hand
A small globe. Look, he said.
The son looked. Far off,
As through water, he saw
A scorched land of fierce
Colour. The light burned
There: crusted buildings
Cast their shadows: a bright
Serpent, a river
Uncoiled itself, radiant
With slime.
         On a bare
Hill a bare tree saddened
The sky. Many people
Held out their thin arms
To it, as though waiting
For a vanished April
To return to its crossed
Boughs. The son watched
Them. Let me go there, he said.

Thomas tells a story well but again, there seems to be no *personal* response. The poem does not suggest that Christ came to these poor people out of love or care. The emphasis once more is on barrenness and minimal expectation. Is it mere curiosity on the part of the son? Thomas's passivity in this sense can be disconcerting. One does not come to poetry seeking answers to the great questions, but there is always expectation of a deeper understanding; these poems often remain in that area of expectation the reader wanders through. Another poem retells the story:

THE OUTLAW CHRIST

Amen

It was all arranged:
the virgin with child, the birth
in Bethlehem, the arid journey uphill
to Jerusalem. The prophets foretold
it, the scriptures conditioned him
to accept it. Judas went to his work
with his sour kiss; what else
could he do?
            A wise old age,
the honours awarded for lasting,
are not for a saviour. He had
to be killed; salvation acquired
by an increased guilt. The tree,
with its roots in the mind's dark,
was divinely planted, the original fork
in existence. There is no meaning in life,
unless men can be found to reject
love. God needs his martyrdom.
The mild eyes stare from the Cross
in perverse triumph. What does he care
that the people's offerings are so small?

The word 'Amen' signifies acceptance. In this poem there is a strong sense of predestination, or pre-arranged history. Even Judas had no choice – Christ had to be killed. There is the tree again, its roots in the darkness of the human mind. If all is pre-arranged by the Creator who is offering love, then if that love is rejected the arrangement is void and this gives life a meaning beyond predestination. Love was rejected; Christ is on the Cross 'in perverse triumph'. And so he cares nothing about the people's offerings; the meaning of life is a negative one.

ART'S NEUROSIS

A late poem speaks with a more tender awareness. A poem called 'The Coming' in which he sees the Christ coming still: 'I think he still comes / stealthily as of old … / an impression of eyes, quicker than / to be caught looking, but taken / on trust like flowers in the dark country towards which we go.' Here the people are indifferent rather than antagonistic to God. The question of faith is no longer a question. But here we have the 'I' word: 'I think he still comes / stealthily as of old'. The Christ comes, then, but the coming is so still, so slight it is scarcely noted. This is, perhaps, the closest R.S. Thomas gets to a statement of faith.

The Word

Enough that we are on our way;
never ask of us where.

Some of us run, some loiter;
some of us turn aside

to erect the Calvary
that is our signpost, arms

pointing in opposite directions
to bring us in the end

to the same place, so impossible
is it to escape love. Imperishable

Scarecrow, recipient of our cast-off,
shame us until what is a swear-

word only becomes at last
the word that was in the beginning.

THE OUTLAW CHRIST

Is it indeed 'enough that we are on our way'? Even though we do not know where we are going, save into 'some dark country'. The Calvary remains our signpost though Christ's crucified hands point in both directions, forward to our end, backward to our beginnings. However, the word we use as a swearword: Jesus Christ! has become the Word of the Gospel of John, the one recipient of our cast-off shame, because he has taken it upon himself and made himself an 'imperishable scarecrow'. This appears to be the limit of Thomas' faith and hope: this strange scarecrow Christ, this Christ not now, not here the 'Christ of Revolution and of Poetry', but in a dark and war-torn age, perhaps this Christ will have to do.

18

LATE END OF THE MIDDLE AGES

Simone Weil (1909-1943)

Alongside the thinking and life of Dietrich Bonhoeffer were two other writers and thinkers greatly affected by the wars of the twentieth century and probing the importance of the response of the individual to the person of Jesus Christ. Bonhoeffer's commitment to Christ was total and brought him to his martyrdom. The other two writers, Simone Weil and Teilhard de Chardin, also put Jesus Christ at the centre of their thinking: de Chardin making him the Alpha and Omega of all of creation, Weil making him the exemplar of the need for suffering and the destruction of the ego, her approach taking the teaching of the Scholastic theologians to a logical and difficult conclusion. Weil stands and falls at the end of the medieval world, Bonhoeffer suffered a period of desperate transition, de Chardin takes us forward from the medieval world into a challenging and very hopeful future.

Susan Sontag, in a review of Weil's *Selected Essays*, says, 'We read writers of such scathing originality for their personal authority, for the example of their seriousness, for their manifest willingness to sacrifice themselves for their truths, and – only piecemeal – for their 'views' … I am thinking of the fanatical asceticism of Simone Weil's life, her contempt for pleasure and for happiness, her noble and ridiculous political gestures, her elaborate self-denials, her tireless courting of affliction; and I do not exclude her homeliness, her physical clumsiness, her migraines, her tuberculosis … Yet so far as we love seriousness, as well as life, we are moved by it, nourished by it. In the respect we pay to such lives, we acknowledge the presence of mystery in the world – and mystery is just what the secure possession of the truth, an objective truth, denies … '.

This is a fine summing up of the life and urgent work of Simone Weil, a writer whom I came across by the sheer mystery of a book I saw in a bookshop, entitled *Gravity and Grace*. It was at a time when I was at a loss in my life and faith as to where and how I should find depth and serious meaning – even to a deepening of the lyrical impulse of my poems. Weil was difficult to understand until I realised she was almost an Old Testament prophet in the style of Jeremiah or Job, calling out the bleakness of living and the woe of the flesh and its desires. The simplicity of seeing 'original sin' as gravity (in the widest sense of that word), and the beauty of the earth and of God's love as grace, gave me a breathless excitement to understand her thinking.

Simone Weil was born in Paris in 1909. Her parents were Alsatian Jews who had moved to Paris after the annexation of Alsace-Lorraine by Germany. She was a precocious student, proficient in ancient Greek by the age of twelve. For me, this was a frightening intellect! Her first attempt at the entrance examination for the École Normale Supérieure in June 1927 ended in failure due to her low marks in history, but in 1928 she was successful in gaining admission. She finished first in the exam for the certificate of general philosophy and logic; Simone de Beauvoir finished second. At the École Normale Supérieure, Weil studied philosophy and earned her DES (diplôme d'études supérieures, roughly equivalent to an MA) in 1931 with a thesis under the title 'Science et perfection dans Descartes' ('Science and Perfection in Descartes'). She received her Agrégation that same year. Teaching was her primary employment during her short life. She wished to pursue her vocation to improve social conditions for the disadvantaged.

She immersed herself in political action in order to understand and share the lives of the working class. She wrote political tracts, marched in demonstrations and advocated workers' rights. She was a Marxist, pacifist and trade unionist. She supported the unemployed and striking workers. The rise of Hitler from 1933 moved Weil to help German communists going abroad. In 1934 she took a twelve-month leave of absence from her teaching position to work as a labourer in factories, one of them owned by Renault, believing that this experience would allow her to connect with the working class. In 1936, despite her pacifism, she fought in the Spanish Civil War on the Republican side. On returning to Paris, she continued to write essays on labour, on management, on war and peace.

She became attracted to the Christian faith around 1935. While in Assisi in the spring of 1937, she experienced a religious ecstasy in the Basilica of Santa Maria degli Angeli. She had another, more powerful revelation a year later while reciting George Herbert's poem 'Love';, from 1938 on, her writings became more mystical and spiritual, while retaining their focus on social and political issues. She was attracted to Roman Catholicism, but would not be baptised, preferring to remain outside due to 'the love of those things that are outside Christianity'. If indeed Simone Weil had been deeply stirred by George Herbert's poem, it also seems quite clear she did not take its meaning and urgency fully to heart. The poem is an invitation by 'love', or Christ, to come closer and partake of the bounty of God's love; it begins:

> Love bade me welcome but my soul drew back
> Guilty of dust and sin.

This consciousness of dust and sin, of original guilt, is overcome in the poem by the gentle insistence of love that the soul should come to the table. Weil continued her resistance, and her sense that 'guilt' kept her standing at the door and would not allow her to enter. She did not, as the poem ends, 'sit and eat'.

In 1942, she traveled to America to help safeguard her family. She also hoped to be able to get to Britain from there, and then on to France to help in the Resistance. She made it to London, where she finally joined the French Resistance. By May 1943, it became clear that she was in very poor health. Her exhausting work-regime took its toll and in 1943 she was diagnosed with tuberculosis and instructed to rest and eat well. Again, it is inveigling to see this as a living out of the George Herbert poem and the invitation to 'sit down and taste my meat', to live a life more dedicated to the love of Christ than to the attempt to drive away the darkness that surrounds us. But she refused special treatment because of her political idealism and her detachment from material things. Instead, she limited her food intake to what she believed residents of German-occupied France ate. Her condition quickly deteriorated, and she was moved to a sanatorium in Ashford, Kent, England. Weil died from cardiac failure in August 1943, aged thirty-four. The coroner's report said that 'the deceased did kill and slay herself by refusing to eat whilst the balance of her mind was disturbed'.

Simone Weil saw herself as being 'captured by Christ'. It was partly through Herbert's poem that she understood the great grace and generosity of the love of God towards an unworthy humanity. The response to God's love was, to use Weil's term, 'decreation', the unmaking of the ego, the dismantling of desire and purposes in life and the lying at God's feet as a particle of creation. My efforts at understanding the outlook of Weil brought me to a memory of childhood innocence, under the influence of the 'old faith'; I confessed, in the under-the-stairs out-of-this-world sin-cupboard: to spitting, the telling of lies, the use of bad words; the priest, amongst the dust-motes, railed at my sinfulness; I was small; I deserved annihilation; to be unmade; a childhood experience that was not exorcised until I had read and loved the poetry of Herbert.

In Weil's view of the world, as I understand it, we are basically sinful and need redemption; to reduce the self as a human being by refusing the steps that build the ego helps restore the gap between us and God. It is our egotistic and egoic urges and efforts, our desires and aims and longings, that come between our face and the face of God. God is both necessity and love. Necessity is the simple movement of creation, the response to its inner energies by tree, fish, star or human being; our egoic tendencies attempt to push necessity aside and make it work in our favour. 'Before' creation, God was all in all, and then creation was a renunciation by God of his absolute apartness. Weil echoes the words of Blaise Pascal who said: 'Jésus est à l'agonie jusqu'à la fin des temps,' when she wrote: 'the crucifixion of God is an eternal thing'. The English poet, David Gascoyne, also took up this notion in his own work (see page 00). Weil would see God's love for creation as a willing diminution of God. The Father is might and power; the Son is love. Necessity shows itself in the cosmos in its violence, its blindness, its indifference, its impersonality, its ongoing thrust. Necessity is the limit God places on Chaos; it bears God's name as a principle of order. 'Necessity is one of the eternal dispositions of Providence … God wills necessity'. Then she writes: 'Genesis separates creation and original sin because of the requirements of a narration made in human language'. Genesis, creation, includes the necessary losing of energy that growth brings about. Free will gives the creature autonomy, which it must deny to find its way to God. Brute matter is in perfect continuity with God, but the human will tries to defeat necessity and hence separates the human from God; 'Evil is the distance between the creature and God.'

This is hard stuff and clearly it borders on the very extreme edges of self-destruction and negativity. God exists; basically, human beings do not exist – by fighting our own existence as separate individuals, by 'decreating' ourselves, we lay ourselves open to God. This would be the extreme interpretation of the soul's work at self-denial, at selfless contemplation in order to allow God's love to penetrate the soul. Weil wrote, 'God creates a finite being who says I, who cannot love God. By the effect of grace, little by little the I disappears, and God loves himself through the creature, who becomes empty, who becomes nothing'. The self-affirming ego comes between God and creation. One's desires, beliefs and ambitions make the ego a centre; so imagination 'fabricates the void-filling imagination'. Self is the negation of others and Other. God 'forgives us for existing at the moment when we no longer wish to consent to exist except to the extent it is the will of God'. Her labour in the factories showed her how the workers, in order to survive with mind somehow intact, had to become almost automatons, almost matter.

Suffering and death, too, are methods of decreation, but the suffering must come from within. We are subject to necessity but have the power not to consent to evil. Something in us corresponds to God as love: obedience, consent to the existence of others. Weil saw suffering as a privilege; the highlight of the Incarnation, its culmination, she saw as the cross, and not the resurrection. She knew that suffering could also be 'useless and degrading'; one must consent and embrace it. When it comes to human violence, both victim and perpetrator may be dehumanised; the perpetrator has to be cold and unyielding as inert matter. But if one consents to affliction, it becomes grace. This is a hard reasoning; but it *is* reasoning, logical, and one feels glad, reading this, to know that God does not work by reasoning and logic, but by love. All of Simone's thinking was influenced by her own difficult life, her illness, her depression and – as with Dietrich Bonhoeffer – her awareness of the dreadful negativities of the approaching Nazi threat.

Something in me found genuine response to something in Simone Weil. I was greatly taken by her notion of gravity and grace; gravity has, in a way, taken the place in my mind of 'original sin'. We are not born in guilt, but we are born with our lives dominated by gravity, in every sense of that word, the ultimate sense being our own death. Here, too, George Herbert comes to mind. From the moment of our birth, every growth is weighted with a corresponding falling away until, eventually, we die. And her notion of grace: that all that is good and beautiful is of God's doing and lifts the spirit towards him, the beauty of creation, kindness, mercy, the beatitudes …

The beautiful is the sensible experience of the order of creation; the cosmos is obedient, and this obedience is beautiful and may be identified with the Incarnation that gives creation radiance. Weil writes: 'The desire to love the beauty of the world in a human being is essentially desire for the Incarnation.' Jesus the Christ, as the origin, energy and goal of creation, gives it its radiance. We have a choice: to appropriate the beautiful or contemplate it; we should watch, and wait. That means detachment: 'Perfect joy excludes the very feeling of joy, because in the soul filled by the object there is no corner free to say 'I'.' 'The circle is the model for the beautiful kind of monotony, the oscillation of a pendulum for the atrocious kind'. When she thinks of time she writes: 'The arrogance of the flesh consists in believing it has a hold over the future'. Aims and purposes are necessary to us, but she holds that striving towards the future merely disguises attempts to escape from God.

For Simone Weil the world around us is something beautiful, but it must be treated as an instrument of gravity and decreation. What she has emphasised is the 'indifference' of the cosmic movement around us, matter is brute and must not distract us from our asceticism and self-immolation. The work of Teilhard de Chardin will counter this approach. In Weil there is darkness and emptying, which was the negative and destructive force of much of the troubled ages of Christian living. She held that there must be attention, emptied of ego, to reality; the creative faculty of genius in all areas of human existence is based upon extreme attention: … 'the utmost ecstasy is the fullness of attention'. So, 'remain still, implore in silence'. There is a great need to purify desire. All of this is true; but there is more, much more. The powerful awareness, in our time, of the possibility of ecological disaster because we have treated creation as merely brute matter, is something that must, at last, focus our minds with love and care on that creation.

Weil, in her way, almost closes the brackets on the notion of original sin, the response to the human predicament of evil promoted by Augustine many centuries before, a notion based on the literal interpretation of the myth of Adam and Eve, that we are all born with the stain of guilt already on our souls. Weil's demand was to develop 'desire without an object', a return to the disappearance of the ego, the sinful ego, a decreation to leave us fully open to the infinite. It is an impossible task, achieved perhaps by saints *in extremis*, for the everyday layperson, and therefore a very small part of God's plan for humanity. What it comes down to is an acceptance of God's will, a coming closer to the obedience of non-human creatures to the necessity of creation. Give up, in other words, all human desire and give your whole being to God. She says: 'Is it not ridiculous to abandon that which is for that which perhaps is not? Not at all, if that which is, is not the good and that which perhaps is not, is the good'. Attention must be focused at its highest level on God, and desire must be to love and consent, no more.

Energy, according to Weil, is of two types: vegetative and supplementary; the first corresponds to mere necessity, the latter is autonomy and this must be suppressed: 'The perfection offered to us is the direct union of the divine spirit with inert matter. Inert matter seen as thinking is a perfect image of perfection'; so the abolition of the self is necessary, a redemptive suffering to make up for sin. Desire and motives incite energy and this must be destroyed, bringing about a void in the soul, allowing God full space. This is one definition of the Dark Night, living without a motive, a profound asceticism. Weil may well have been the last to advocate such extremist acceptance of the basics of Scholastic theology. She urged the impossible, an embracing of the void. 'For only they possess nature and earth whose bodies these have entered into through the daily suffering of limbs broken by fatigue. The days, the months, the seasons, the heavenly vault endlessly turning above us all belong to those who must cross the expanse of time separating dawn from sunset each day by going painfully from tiredness to tiredness. They accompany the firmament in its rotation, they live out each day, they are not dreaming'. This is destructive labour. Teilhard de Chardin will, shortly after Simone Weil's outline of her thinking, shift the focus back into love of the whole of God's creating power. Death and labour, for Weil, are the wages of sin. These become our way of being obedient to God, and may not be much different from the ants or the trees; we, however, can consent to labour, and consent to our death.

All of this appears to lead inevitably to a rejection of what most of us would regard as an ordinary, well-regulated and working life; our normal desires and objectives give us enough energy to suffer the demands of labour, the earning of our daily bread. It appears to suggest the rejection of the world itself as merely something to be aloof from, and the possibility of taking part in the glory and beauty of the cosmos is anathema to Simone Weil.

Weil's resentment towards being, her elevation of death and nothingness, bring the old self-abnegation tradition to its climax and logical conclusion. She appeared to be against progress and had no sense of the Christian evolution of the world Teilhard de Chardin was then working towards. She was the last wave, a personal tidal wave, of the grand negativities of Old Testament moralities. We are indebted to her for many images and movements of the spirit, particularly for her awareness of the grace and gravity to which we are subject and subjected; we are grateful, too, for the honesty and penetrating gaze of her intellect towards the Christ, and saddened for her that she could not finally yield her spirit to the imaginative love and abundance of the Christ– focusing perhaps too much on the crucifixion and setting aside the resurrection.

19

DEMENTED WRESTLER

David Gascoyne (1916-2001)

Gascoyne was born in Harrow, England, and published his first collection of poems at the age of sixteen. He lived in Paris and became one of the only true 'surrealist' poets to have written in English. He also translated some of the work of the leading French surrealists: Breton, Eluard, Ernst. Already, in pre-war Paris, Gascoyne was deeply serious about his life's task: to find truth through words. In *A Short Survey of Surrealism* he wrote: 'The most vital feature of surrealism is its exclusive interest in that point at which literature and art give place to real life, at that point at which the imagination seeks to express itself in a more concrete form than words or plastic images.' By allowing the imagination to 'express itself' he hoped to get beyond mere realism and words. In Paris he also joined the Communist Party, but at a meeting Breton accused him of Stalinism and of being a Roman Catholic. 'I was excommunicated,' he wrote. In 1936 he took part in the Spanish Civil War against Franco. By now, he was also beginning to suffer from depression.

With the Second World War his depression deepened; he also began to take amphetamines. He went through some two decades of suffering, 'the most drastic consequences for me of the persistent assault on the central nervous system that amphetamine abuse represented', he wrote in the *Collected Journals*. He had to enter Whitecroft Asylum on the Isle of Wight. While there he met Judy Lewis who later wrote: 'I used to visit Whitecroft Hospital and read poetry to the patients there. One of my favourite poems was called "September Sun". I read it one afternoon and one of the patients came up to me afterwards and said "I wrote that".

I put my hand on his shoulder and said, "Of course you did, my dear." Then of course when I got to know him I realised he had.' David married Judy in 1975 and together they travelled through many countries and he came to see that his poetry was still being read. He came back to it. Judy had given him new life and the poetry he wrote grew greatly in strength and popularity. He died in 2001.

For Gascoyne, the search for truth and meaning in life was absolute and the poetry he wrote echoes that seriousness and intensity. His destiny, and that of all humanity, troubled him and the poetry followed his changing thoughts and shades. The poem that drew him and Judy together, 'September Sun', looks back and forward: back through his own life, through war and humankind's 'self-darkened spirits', to the origins of Chaos itself. If living in the September phase, the sun is yet strong and still offers a pristine light and the hope is that the poet's work may achieve something better.

September Sun

Magnificent strong sun! in these last days
So prodigally generous of pristine light
That's wasted only by men's sight who will not see
And by self-darkened spirits from whose night
Can rise no longer orison or praise:

Let us consume in fire unfed like yours
And may the quickened gold within me come
To mintage in due season, and not be
Transmuted to no better end than dumb
And self-sufficient usury. These days and years

May bring the sudden call to harvesting,
When if the fields Man labours only yield

Glitter and husks, then with an angrier sun may He
Who first with His gold seed the sightless field
Of Chaos planted, all our trash to cinders bring.

When he finds Christianity and the person of Christ, Gascoyne glimpses a way that reconciliation between a broken humanity and a loving and creating God might be possible. He writes how the accidents of an individual's experience may lead towards the numinous, the transcendent, and in this way finds common cause with poets like Vaughan, Herbert, Traherne and Donne. He believes that a rejection of mere empiricism and atheism allows a human to face death with some equanimity.

The Three Stars

A Prophecy
The night was Time:
The phases of the moon,
Dynamic influence, controller of the tides,
Its changing face and cycle of quick shades,
Were History, which seemed unending. Then
Occurred the prophesied and the to be
Recounted hour when the reflection ceased
To flow like unseen life-blood in between
The night's tenebral mirror and the lunar light,
Exchanging meaning. Anguish like a crack
Ran with its ruin from the fulfilled Past
Towards the Future's emptiness; and black,
Invading all the prism, became absolute.

Black was the No-time at the heart
Of Time (the frameless mirror's back),
But still the Anguish shook

THE OUTLAW CHRIST

As though with memory and with anticipation: till
Its terror's trembling broke
By an unhoped-for miracle Negation's spell:
Death died and Birth was born with one great cry
And out of some uncharted spaceless sky
Into the new-born night three white stars fell.

And were suspended there a while for all
To see and understand (though none may tell
The inmost meaning of this Mystery).

The first star has a name which stands
For many names of all things that began
And all first thoughts of undivided minds;
The second star
Is nameless and shines bleakly like the pain
Of an existence conscious only of its end,
And inarticulate, alone
And blind. Immeasurably far
Each from the other first and second spin;
Yet to us at this moment they appear
So close to one another that their rays
In one blurred conflagration intertwine:
So that the third seems born
Of their embracing: till the outer pair
Are separate seen again
Fixed in their true extremes; and in between
These two gleams' hemispheres, unseen
But shining everywhere
The third star balanced shall henceforward burn
Through all dark still to come, serene,
Ubiquitous, immaculately clear;

DEMENTED WRESTLER

> A magnet in the middle of the maze, to draw us on
> Towards the Bethlehem beyond despair
> Where from the womb of Nothing shall be born
> A Son.

There are nods to William Blake in this strange, brave piece, a form of cosmic history and evolutionary development that Teilhard de Chardin himself might have enjoyed. We start with a sort of Genesis, when Time appears and it is night, with History becoming no more than the movements of darkness, tides, moon phases, and all appearing endless. But something or Someone (the Creator God?) had already spoken of the 'prophesied and the to be' when that seeming unending self-regarding of darkness changed. Anguish appeared in a crack in that darkness; all is still chaos and seething and unshaped. There was, though, movement in that Anguish, a cosmic memory and anticipation, bringing about a form of Birth and therefore an ending of Death. There appeared three stars. It is not wholly clear what these three stars are, the first suggesting beginnings of all things including thought, the second anguished by its awareness of what lies ahead, namely its end. These two stars are close and have in between them the third, balanced and facing forward through all the darkness; it will shine, or burn, serene, ubiquitous and immaculately clear. This is the Christ, already born and to be born again. Christ the light, the Good Shepherd, the one who shines at last 'beyond despair'. Here Gascoyne has discovered Bethlehem and is gazing beyond death to a second Bethlehem. There is optimism in spite of the seething darkness of most of the poem, optimism strikingly different from Yeats's beast that 'slouches towards Bethlehem to be born'. Gascoyne's poetry has shifted towards the Divine transcendent, through suffering, and towards light.

The Christ he comes to know is darkened by Gascoyne's experience of despair and misery during the Second World War. He remains ever aware of the extent of destructive lust that can overwhelm humanity. Both belief and unbelief are mingled with fear.

THE OUTLAW CHRIST

Lachrymae

Slow are the years of light:
                              and more immense
Than the imagination. And the years return
Until the Unity is filled. And heavy are
The lengths of Time with the slow weight of tears.
Since Thou didst weep, on a remote hill-side
Beneath the olive-trees, fires of unnumbered stars
Have burnt the years away, until we see them now:
Since Thou didst weep, as many tears
Have flowed like hourglass sand.
The tears were all.
And when our secret face
Is blind because of the mysterious
Surging of tears wrung by our most profound
Presentiment of evil in man's fate, our cruellest wounds
Become Thy stigmata. They are Thy tears that fall.

We know about that 'remote hill-side', those 'cruellest wounds'; we know how, especially after the horror of that war, and of every war before and since (and they grow more furious and more intense all the time), the Christ has taken it all upon himself and will bear the fears and sorrows humanity imposes upon itself until the 'Unity' is fulfilled. How telling that line: 'They are Thy tears that fall'. In the context of the current and developing view of Christian evolution, that sense that there will be a unity at the end of time, is most interesting. Our hope against the dread of oblivion and nothingness will appear to be the cross; Gascoyne still finds this 'incomprehensible'. Christian thinking has always insisted that the way through to eternity is by endurance, by accepting and going beyond, the cross. But endurance is required, and here Gascoyne touches on a theme that Samuel Beckett was to take to its extreme. Beckett's piece from the end of *The Unnamable*: 'You must go on. I can't go on. I'll go on', captures it to perfection. The will alone, for Gascoyne, is the spring and source of faith, based on the knowledge of Christ's participation in our pain.

Shortly after this, David Gascoyne wrote his most powerful poem, 'Behold the Man'.

Ecce Homo

Whose is this horrifying face,
This putrid flesh, discoloured, flayed,
Fed on by flies, scorched by the sun?
Whose are these hollow red-filmed eyes
And thorn-spiked head and spear-stuck side?
Behold the Man: He is Man's Son.

Forget the legend, tear the decent veil
That cowardice or interest devised
To make their mortal enemy a friend,
To hide the bitter truth all His wounds tell,
Lest the great scandal be no more disguised:
He is in agony till the world's end,

And we must never sleep during that time!
He is suspended on the cross-tree now
And we are onlookers at the crime,
Callous contemporaries of the slow
Torture of God. Here is the hill
Made ghastly by His spattered blood

Whereon He hangs and suffers still:
See, the centurions wear riding-boots,

THE OUTLAW CHRIST

Black shirts and badges and peaked caps,
Greet one another with raised-arm salutes;
They have cold eyes, unsmiling lips;
Yet these His brothers know not what they do.

And on his either side hang dead
A labourer and a factory hand,
Or one is maybe a lynched Jew
And one a Negro or a Red,
Coolie or Ethiopian, Irishman,
Spaniard or German democrat.

Behind his lolling head the sky
Glares like a fiery cataract
Red with the murders of two thousand years
Committed in His name and by
Crusaders, Christian warriors
Defending faith and property.

Amid the plain beneath His transfixed hands,
Exuding darkness as indelible
As guilty stains, fanned by funereal
And lurid airs, besieged by drifting sands
And clefted landslides our about-to-be
Bombed and abandoned cities stand.

He who wept for Jerusalem
Now sees His prophecy extend
Across the greatest cities of the world,
A guilty panic reason cannot stem
Rising to raze them all as He foretold;
And He must watch this drama to the end.

DEMENTED WRESTLER

Though often named, He is unknown
To the dark kingdoms at His feet
Where everything disparages His words,
And each man bears the common guilt alone
And goes blindfolded to his fate,
And fear and greed are sovereign lords.

The turning point of history
Must come. Yet the complacent and the proud
And who exploit and kill, may be denied –
Christ of Revolution and of Poetry –
The resurrection and the life
Wrought by your spirit's blood.

Involved in their own sophistry
The black priest and the upright man
Faced by subversive truth shall be struck dumb,
Christ of Revolution and of Poetry,
While the rejected and condemned become
Agents of the divine.

Not from a monstrance silver-wrought
But from the tree of human pain
Redeem our sterile misery,
Christ of Revolution and of Poetry,
That man's long journey
May not have been in vain.

'Behold the Man'; 'Ecce Home'; behold humankind. The Latin word 'homo' really means all humankind, while the individual person, man, in Latin is 'vir'. Christ had been scourged, mocked, slapped, spat on … and Gascoyne spares no adjective to catch all this: 'putrid flesh, discoloured,

THE OUTLAW CHRIST

flayed, fed on by flies'. The title will, of course, reach all of humankind in its degradation, in the pits and trenches of the war. Christ is Man's Son and Gascoyne has found him. Did all of this happen two thousand years ago? Yes, and it is forever happening: 'the centurions wear riding-boots, / Black shirts and badges and peaked caps'. Nazis, fascists and, by extension, all the horrific human uniforms put on to attempt to justify and make anonymous the horrors human beings can commit; haven't we all seen it, and continue to see it? It is up to human beings now to watch this drama until the end; we are all, individually, guilty, as 'each man bears the common guilt alone'. On Christ's right and on his left, there were thieves, also crucified; Gascoyne names them, too, in contemporary terms, labourers, Jews, Negroes, Communists, Irishmen, German democrats. Sadly, every age can draw up its own lists, and these may well be growing greater with every new and Satanic invention, killing machines, cluster bombs, drones … Gascoyne addresses Christ directly, this 'Christ of Revolution and of Poetry', a most telling phrase, filled with a vibrant immediacy and a small suggestion of hope in the development of the arts. The self-declared 'demented wrestler', David Gascoyne, has discovered a place of rest, not a place where complacency has a part, because the poet remains alive to the fact that this struggle will go on to the very end of time and will affect each individual. The response is Christ: Man's Son will be waiting, watching and suffering on our behalf until the end of the ages.

20

O EVER-GREATER CHRIST

Teilhard de Chardin (1881-1955)

Ursula King wrote, in the Preface to her masterly biography of Teilhard de Chardin: 'Teilhard was an ardent seeker, in love with all of life, a modern scientist, a dedicated priest, and a fervent mystic, but also a great friend and spiritual adviser to many, and a great writer.'

Teilhard de Chardin was born in 1881, in Sarcenat near Clermont-Ferrand in the Auvergne. His mother was from Picardy and his father was deeply interested in all aspects of geology. Teilhard's family life was happy and sheltered. He later wrote: 'Under the influence of my mother I was devoted to the Child Jesus ... To my father I owe a certain balance, on which all the rest is built, along with a taste for the exact sciences.' He was sent to a Jesuit boarding school where he did well in every subject save religion! In 1899 he joined the Jesuits. He studied at the scholasticate in Jersey and came to love the rock-strewn shore; here, too, he developed his scientific studies. Later he was sent to Cairo and studied many fossils there. At this time he wrote of Christ: 'You the Centre at which all things meet and which stretches out over all things so as to draw them back into itself: I love you for the extensions of your body and soul to the furthest corners of creation through grace, through life, and through matter'. In August 1911 he was ordained priest in Hastings, England; here he read Henri Bergson's 'Creative Evolution', which opened his eyes to the notion of evolution, and found himself thinking how his Catholic faith might bind with this new notion.

In 1912, at the age of thirty-one, he returned to Paris to do research in geology and palaeontology. 'The man who is filled with an impassioned love for Jesus hidden in the forces which bring death to the earth, him the earth will clasp in the immensity of her arms as her strength fails, and with her he will awaken in the bosom of God.' In 1914 he joined the military as a medical orderly, requesting stretcher-bearing duties at the front. Through the war he became deeply engaged with the suffering of the soldiers and people, working through some of the main battles: Ypres, Arras, Dunkirk, Verdun, the Marne. He was awarded the medal of Chevalier de la Légion d'Honneur after the war: the citation says it all: 'An outstanding stretcher-bearer who, during four years of active service, was in every battle and engagement the regiment took part in, applying to remain in the ranks in order that he might be with the men, whose dangers and hardships he constantly shared.'

By now he held that 'one is an atom in the body of the mystical and cosmic Christ'. He knew that religious faith must forward the common task of evolution, feeling that he had touched, during the war, 'the heart of matter', knowing the sufferings of the world and yet aware of God's transforming power. 'Lord, it is you who, through the imperceptible goadings of sense-beauty, penetrated my heart in order to make its life flow out into yourself. You came down into me by means of a tiny scrap of created reality; and then, suddenly, you unfurled your immensity before my eyes, and displayed yourself to me as a Universal Being.' By 1919 he was studying at the Sorbonne and teaching in the Institut Catholique. He saw the need to integrate what he called 'living pantheism' into the Christian faith: 'to revere an omnipresence in the universe', the presence and action of God in all things. He developed the theory of the noosphere: a sphere of mind and spirit surrounding the globe.

In 1923 he was invited to Tianjin, not far from Beijing, to analyse fossils, and sailed from Marseilles to a Jesuit house in that city. In remote areas of Mongolia he felt the power of the heart of Christ as 'a fire with the power to penetrate all things'. In China he wrote a seminal book, *Le milieu divin* (*The Divine Milieu*), though he was not allowed to publish it and it did not appear until 1957, after his death. In 1928, in Paris, he began work on *Le phénomène humain* (*The Human Phemomenon*). He travelled a great deal in India, Pakistan, Egypt, Myanmar, Java and America. 'The world is being converted spontaneously to a sort of natural religion of the universe, which is wrongly turning it away from the God of the Gospel; it is in this that 'unbelief' consists.' In the late 1930s he could say: 'What we are all more or less lacking at this moment is a new definition of holiness.' He was developing his notion of the Omega Point: 'Omega, in which all things converge, is reciprocally that from which all things radiate. Impossible to place it as a point at the peak of the universe without at the same time diffusing its presence within each smallest advance of evolution. The meaning of this is nothing less than this: that *for him who has seen it* everything, however humble, *provided it places itself in the line of progress*, is warmed, illumined and animated, and consequently becomes an object to which he gives his *whole* adhesion.'

Teilhard was in Beijing when the Second World War began and was almost a prisoner in the city. 'By making plain the splendours of the universal Christ, Christianity, without ceasing to be for the earth the water that purifies and the oil that soothes, acquires a new value. By the very fact that it provides the earth's aspirations with a goal that is at once immense, concrete and assured, it rescues the earth from the disorder, the uncertainties and the nausea that are the most terrible of tomorrow's dangers. It provides the fire that inspires man's effort'. He had finished *The Human Phenomenon* by mid-1940, and in 1944 Rome refused permission to publish. He saw the human phenomenon as the centre of perspective and of construction of the whole universe in the name and being of Christ. Even during the war, when he lost friends from Beijing and often came close to despair, while even the Jesuit authorities ruled against him, yet he could write: 'Through and beyond matter, spirit is hard at work, building'. He returned to Paris in 1946 but was forbidden to teach or give public lectures. 'Since it has become human, the world cannot continue to advance towards greater complexity and consciousness except by making an ever more explicit place for the forces of expectation and hope, that is to say for religion.' He suffered a serious heart attack in June 1947. Rome then even forbade him to visit Paris, and he couldn't return to communist China; Rome would not let him accept the chair he was offered at the Collège de France.

Humanity, he held, has a collective responsibility to shape the 'noosphere', the future. This was the development of consciousness, which is the direction in which he believed evolution was moving, and moving unstoppably. He sought a unity of complexity with respect for pluralistic differences: this, of course, is one definition of love. His studies had brought him from Fossil Man to Man of Tomorrow. And his cry continued to be: 'O ever-greater Christ!' In 1951, he signed over his essays to Jeanne Mortier, in the hope of future publication. He spent some short time in South Africa, then back to New York, to the Jesuits at 980 Park Avenue. He now found himself an exile in America. He continued, in New York, reading and writing, with support from the Wenner Gren Foundation. He came back for a few months to France in 1954, though he knew he was not welcome in Paris; he visited his home at Sarcenat. On his way back to New York, he was refused a visa permit for longer than six months. He wrote to Mortier: 'It is most certainly in shadow and exile that I must work'. His position is one of the most scandalous failures of the Church to open itself to new ideas, to accept the scientific obvious and to develop Christian thinking along the new paths that evolution had shown. That December, he became ill when out walking and fell on the sidewalk. Thanks to the blindness of the authorities, this saintly man, prophet and scientist, and deeply Christian thinker, was made to suffer loneliness and a form of inner martyrdom; yet he could say, in those last weeks, that he felt he now lived permanently in the presence of God. He had prayed that his death might occur on Easter Sunday, and on that day in 1955, 10 April, he suffered a massive heart attack and died. He is buried in the Jesuit cemetery at St Andrew-on-Hudson, near Poughkeepsie, New York. Teilhard de Chardin remains the most important thinker and Christian for a new age, and a new view of the whole Christian undertaking. For him, Christ and cosmogenesis together form the heart of the whole of creation.

O EVER-GREATER CHRIST

'Not only among the Gentiles or the rank and file of the faithful, but even in the religious orders themselves, Christianity still to some degree provides a shelter for the 'modern soul,' but it no longer clothes it, nor satisfies it, nor leads it. Something has gone wrong and so something, in the area of faith and religion, must be supplied without delay on this planet. The question is, what is it we are looking for?' (from *The God of Evolution*).

'We must admit that if the neo-humanisms of the twentieth century de-humanise us under their uninspired skies, yet on the other hand the still-living forms of theism – starting with the Christian – tend to under-humanise us in the rarefied atmosphere of too lofty skies. These religions are still systematically closed to the wide horizons and great winds of Cosmogenesis, and can no longer be said to feel with the Earth – an Earth whose internal frictions they can still lubricate like a soothing oil, but whose driving energies they cannot animate as they should' (from *The Heart of Matter*).

The entire cosmos, for Teilhard de Chardin, is 'the divine milieu'; it is seen as the theatre of God's saving action, the means of drawing the whole of creation to himself, and the gift of God to a conscious and caring humanity to help the evolution of all of creation towards the Omega-God. So, Teilhard worked, hands-on, in the earth, as an honoured palaeontologist. In the midst of the physical creation, we plunge into the being of God. It is only in the love of the milieu, in which Christ is being born, crucified and resurrected, that we will be able to find again all that we have lost. Because the cosmos is divinised by God's presence in it, and by Christ's incarnation in our world, all our activities and even our passivities are part of the divine work, and our task is to be a cooperation with Christ to complete God's plan.

In communications technology, it would seem we are going through a type of convergence. We can speak of the law of complexity-consciousness. The earth is weaving around itself something analogous to a brain. Isn't it possible something new and unimaginably complex is being created? We speak of 'vital dust', those carbon compounds that make up as much as forty per cent of interstellar dust. God is not 'up above' but 'up ahead', the way the shepherds in Palestine lead the sheep by walking ahead of them, rather than driving them along. God is the world's future and the world's ultimate support.

The modern world tries to understand itself without reference to Christ. Teilhard wrote: 'The only thing that counts for me is not to propagate God, but to discover Him; from this conversion follows somewhat automatically.' As a soul of sorts unites the elements in a cell so there is a Soul of sorts drawing humans together into a higher form. If the human ideal is merely 'humanity', this could lead to the mechanisation of the individual. The personalising force Teilhard calls Omega, that is Christ, who is indeed the Alpha and the Omega of creation and its evolution, the Soul uniting individuals to each other and uniting them to itself. Thus Teilhard resolved a dualism between love of this world and love of Christ as the evolutionary world leads to Jesus. So, the world itself has a loving Soul (it is Christ Jesus). This Soul shines through the matter of Earth.

Teilhard's theology is emphatically focused on the cosmic Christ. He identifies the World Soul with the Holy Spirit. The cosmic dimension of our existence has been too often ignored. Theologians of the Reformation saw Christ in his role of redeemer from sin, not in relation to creation and the cosmic process. Cosmic concern passed to the scientists who had to struggle with the religious establishment in order to vindicate the autonomy of their method, which became more and more secularised. Linking World Soul with Holy Spirit brings together the highest reality, the Trinity, with the lowest level of matter. Teilhard wrote: 'Through the soul of the world, and through the soul alone the Word, becoming incarnate in the universe, has been able to establish a vital, immediate, relationship with each one of the animate elements that make up the cosmos. Through the soul, accordingly, and for all time, the humano-divine influence of Christ encompasses us, penetrates us, identifies itself with all the forces of our growth as individuals and as a social whole.' Cosmogenesis leads on to Christogenesis. Teilhard cites Gregory of Nyssa who wrote, 'The bread of the Eucharist is stronger than our flesh; that is why it is the bread that assimilates us, and not we the bread, when we receive it.' 'Complexity-consciousness' culminates in the Omega Point, God's fulfilment of the creation in Christ. 'By means of all created things, without exception, the divine assails us, penetrates us and moulds us. We imagined it as distant and inaccessible, whereas in fact we live steeped in its burning layers. *In eo vivimus.*'

21

THE FUNCTIONAL WARD OF A CHEST HOSPITAL

Patrick Kavanagh (1904-1967)

There is an entrance into the work of Patrick Kavanagh through a poem written by W.B. Yeats in 1916. It is a poem evoking an ideal reader of Yeats's work, John Millington Synge. The poem speaks of the popularity versus isolation that nuances Yeats's own sense of aristocracy and artistic integrity. In many ways John Millington Synge, playwright, friend of Yeats, is himself this ideal fisherman, this audience Yeats hoped for. Somebody simple, immediate and direct yet wise; who would understand what Yeats was about in his poetry and public activity; for him Yeats would wish to write, but knows that such a man, apart from Synge, does not exist as audience for the work.

The Fisherman

Although I can see him still,
The freckled man who goes
To a grey place on a hill
In grey Connemara clothes
At dawn to cast his flies,
It's long since I began
To call up to the eyes
This wise and simple man.
All day I'd looked in the face
What I had hoped 'twould be
To write for my own race
And the reality,

THE OUTLAW CHRIST

The living men that I hate
The dead man that I loved,
The craven man in his seat,
The insolent unreproved,
And no knave brought to book
Who has won a drunken cheer,
The witty man and his joke
Aimed at the commonest ear,
The clever man who cries
The catch-cries of the clown,
The beating down of the wise
And great Art beaten down.

Maybe a twelvemonth since
Suddenly I began
In scorn of this audience,
Imagining a man,
And his sun-freckled face
And grey Connemara cloth,
Climbing up to a place
Where stone is dark under froth,
And the down-turn of his wrist
When the flies drop in the stream –
A man who does not exist,
A man who is but a dream;
And cried, 'Before I am old
I shall have written him one
Poem maybe as cold
And passionate as the dawn.'

    Wise and simple, to write for his own race, hope and the reality, a man who does not exist: all of this is realism and idealism combined, anger and hope, determination and doubt. A poem 'cold and passionate as the dawn', a poem that might avoid and obliterate all the negativities of insolence, of those who play to the common crowd; it would be a poem of complete authenticity, a poem that would hold on to the dream with which the poet always sets out. It is the dream of every serious poet: to write a poem cold and passionate as the dawn, with the rise, the roll, the carol, the creation that Gerard Manley Hopkins demanded of a great poem; a poem that would inhabit its audience for ever, just as the audience ought to inhabit the poem, as Synge might inhabit the Yeats poem. Patrick Kavanagh was well aware of Yeats's dreams and his successes in poetry, and was envious of his certainties and natively contemptuous of his aristocratic insistencies. But Kavanagh, too, had a dream for his poetry, and for his life, a very different dream, but it, too, concerned truth, anger, loss and insistence.

Wordsworth's great poem, 'Ode on the Intimations of Immortality …' is essentially a poem about the loss of joy that growing older and more 'philosophical' can bring, as the sense of intimacy, love and happiness in the simple presence of natural beauty in the world begins to give way to the cold intellect of the growing man.

from 'Ode on Intimations of Immortality from Recollections of Early Childhood'

There was a time when meadow, grove, and stream,
The earth, and every common sight
To me did seem
   Apparelled in celestial light,
The glory and the freshness of a dream.
It is not now as it hath been of yore –
   Turn wheresoe'er I may,
   By night or day,
The things which I have seen I now can see no more.
…

> What though the radiance which was once so bright
>   Be now for ever taken from my sight,
> Though nothing can bring back the hour
> Of splendour in the grass, of glory in the flower;
> We will grieve not, rather find
> Strength in what remains behind;
> In the primal sympathy
> Which having been must ever be;
> In the soothing thoughts that spring
> Out of human suffering:
> In the faith that looks through death,
> In years that bring the philosophic mind.

And there are those memorable lines from 'Tintern Abbey'

> For I have learned
> To look on nature, not as in the hour
> Of thoughtless youth; but hearing oftentimes
> The still, sad music of humanity …

In youth, then, creation brings a careless joy, an unquestioning acceptance, a delight in the things of nature, 'every common sight', 'meadow, grove and stream'; as youth passes, so, it appears, does this joy fade away. Wordsworth puts it in an interesting way: 'I have learned / To look on nature … ' Learned? This love of the natural world, then, may appear to be something to be got rid of; are there better ways of looking at the world that must be learned? And what is the recompense for this learning? It's a little vague, here, a little uncertain: 'Soothing thoughts' that come from suffering? 'The faith that looks through death'? And what is that faith? Is it merely 'the philosophic mind'? And must we live while hearing 'oftentimes / The still, sad music of humanity'? One can understand how Wordsworth lost

THE FUNCTIONAL WARD OF A CHEST HOSPITAL

his inspiration, his will to write poetry in later life, while he settled into a quiet, dulling middle and old age.

Patrick Kavanagh spent the months of March and April 1955 as a patient in the Rialto Hospital in Dublin and was operated on for lung cancer on 31 March.

The Hospital

A year ago I fell in love with the functional ward
Of a chest hospital: square cubicles in a row,
Plain concrete, wash basins – an art lover's woe,
Not counting how the fellow in the next bed snored.
But nothing whatever is by love debarred,
The common and banal her heat can know.
The corridor led to a stairway and below
Was the inexhaustible adventure of a gravelled yard.

This is what love does to things: the Rialto Bridge,
The main gate that was bent by a heavy lorry,
The seat at the back of a shed that was a suntrap.
Naming these things is the love-act and its pledge;
For we must record love's mystery without claptrap,
Snatch out of time the passionate transitory.

Kavanagh had left Monaghan many years before to try and find a place in Ireland's cultural and social heart in Dublin. But he had brought his heavy boots with him, his guttural language, his love of the soil, and he fought with Dublin's society and its mores, its poets and its poetry. He was in his fifties when he spent that time in hospital. He had been hoping to rediscover his earlier excitement and innocence in a part of Dublin he had discovered: 'I have been thinking of making my grove on the banks of the Grand Canal near Baggot Street Bridge where in recent days I rediscovered my roots. My hegira was to the Grand Canal bank where again I saw the beauty of water and green grass and the magic of light. It was the same emotion I had known when I stood on a sharp slope in Monaghan … '. By now, Kavanagh relied more on satire and complaint than on lyrical poetry, and, even though 'nothing whatever is by love debarred', a bent gate and a gravelled yard are not what gave him his elan in Monaghan in his childhood years. His wish to 'Snatch out of time the passionate transitory' was now almost as much a dream as was Yeats's dream of the ideal reader, or Wordsworth's talk of 'the radiance which was once so bright'. As Seamus Heaney wrote (Douglas Dunn, ed.: *Two Decades of Irish Writing*: Carcanet, UK 1975): ' … one might say that when he had consumed the roughage of his Monaghan experience, he ate his heart out.'

It is intriguing how this initial innocence before the love of creation and created things appears to peter out rather quickly in most lives. Indeed, the 'Romantic' movement in poetry towards the end of the eighteenth and into the nineteenth century may have first opened humanity's eyes to the glories of 'nature' (creation), but it did not take that movement long to diminish into the Victorian sense of decorum, dignity and mastery over created things. It is my belief that faith, and I mean all religions, by focusing the eyes of the soul on transcendent things and accusing the physical creation of being mere distraction or, at worst, temptation, may have had a great deal to do with all of that. In his early living, at home on the farms and dark hillsides of Monaghan, Patrick Kavanagh was a child, innocent and in love with 'nature'. This love he attempted to ally to his Catholic faith, and although his poetry does not explicitly and consciously explore his relationship to the Christ, a sense of that faith stayed with him all his life.

An early poem explicitly links his love of the earth to his awareness of God; although it has been claimed that this was written to endear AE (George William Russell) to Kavanagh's poetry so that it might be published, I find that claim to be somewhat fanciful and unfounded. In the

THE FUNCTIONAL WARD OF A CHEST HOSPITAL

poem 'Ploughman' he speaks of his pleasure when out ploughing, but somewhat gratuitously goes on to add: 'I find a star-lovely art / In a dark sod. / Joy that is timeless! O heart / That knows God!'

Perhaps that last stanza is pushing it, but there is no doubt of his awe and even love of the world about him. If the sentiment at the end is pulled out of the air, at least there is still an innocence in the whole thing that rings true. In 1939, when he was already thirty-five years of age, he wrote this poem:

Primrose

Upon a bank I sat, a child made seer
Of one small primrose flowering in my mind.
Better than wealth it is, said I, to find
One small page of Truth's manuscript made clear.
I looked at Christ transfigured without fear –
The light was very beautiful and kind,
And where the Holy Ghost in flame had signed
I read it through the lenses of a tear.
And then my sight grew dim, I could not see
The primrose that had lighted me to Heaven,
And there was but the shadow of a tree
Ghostly among the stars. The years that pass
Like tired soldiers nevermore have given
Moments to see wonders in the grass.

The child has now become 'seer' and the poem moves into the young man's mind; the primrose is seen, not as a primrose, but an image of what is Truth. In the primrose he sees Christ and the transfiguration and the Spirit blessing the moment, touching the poet to tears. He is aware, then, that the actual primrose that had begun by turning his thoughts to the afterlife is no longer a primrose, and what was about him now was merely the shadow of a tree. Ever since then, he concludes, he has failed to see 'wonders in the grass'. It appears that already he has lost, as Wordsworth did, 'the hour / Of splendour in the grass, of glory in the flower'. And yet another poem written after this, while he was still in Monaghan in 1939, touches gladly on childhood innocence; it is a poem that links that innocence with both poetry and his Catholic faith.

Christmas, 1939

O Divine Baby in the cradle,
All that is poet in me
Is the dream I dreamed of Your Childhood
And the dream You dreamed of me.

O Divine Baby in the cradle,
All that is truth in me
Is my mind tuned to the cadence
Of a child's philosophy.

O Divine Baby in the cradle,
All that is pride in me
Is my mind bowed in homage
Upon Your Mother's knee.

O Divine Baby in the cradle,
All that is joy in me
Is that I have saved from the ruin
Of my soul Your Infancy.

Childhood, innocence, a child's philosophy, the ruin of his soul, and the joy that is still left to him is associated with Christ's infancy. One of his best known poems of this time is 'A Christmas Childhood', which catches with great skill and beautiful musical language the joyful memories of a child at Christmas. He praises the sounds, the light, the frost: 'Now and then / I can remember something of the gay / Garden that was childhood's.' He talks of the world as Eve and its temptation, and this poem of memory is written when the years have cast him out of Eden. The accuracy of the details is such that they show without doubt Kavanagh's relish in what he had known:

> I nicked six nicks on the door-post
> With my penknife's big blade –
> There was a little one for cutting tobacco.
> And I was six Christmases of age.

However, it is in the poem 'Advent', written in 1942, that Kavanagh makes an attempt to revivify that innocence that he has known as a child, and renew the dream as an adult. He speaks to a 'lover' and admits to having 'tested and tasted too much', and the sense of wonder in life will be lost if the opening out into the world is too large. Advent, preparation-time, the lead-in to the birth of Christ, used to be designated by the Catholic Church as a time for penance. Penance now may bring back that childhood innocence before knowledge of the world was 'stolen' from him. Penance done, the world seen afresh, then Christmas will return them to 'ordinary plenty', to a state beyond reason when there is no need to question that innocence. However, the ending of the poem offers a caveat: all of this will be won at the giving up of pleasure, of knowledge and full consciousness, allowing innocence and imaginative living to take over. This somewhat negative victory will usher Christ in to their lives!

THE OUTLAW CHRIST

Advent

We have tested and tasted too much, lover –
Through a chink too wide there comes in no wonder.
But here in this Advent-darkened room
Where the dry black bread and the sugarless tea
Of penance will charm back the luxury
Of a child's soul, we'll return to Doom
The knowledge we stole but could not use.

And the newness that was in every stale thing
When we looked at it as children: the spirit-shocking
Wonder in a black slanting Ulster hill,
Or the prophetic astonishment in the tedious talking
Of an old fool, will awake for us and bring
You and me to the yard gate to watch the whins
And the bog-holes, cart-tracks, old stables where Time begins.

O after Christmas we'll have no need to go searching
For the difference that sets an old phrase burning –
We'll hear it in the whispered argument of a churning
Or in the streets where the village boys are lurching.
And we'll hear it among simple, decent men, too,
Who barrow dung in gardens under trees,
Wherever life pours ordinary plenty.
Won't we be rich, my love and I, and please
God we shall not ask for reason's payment,
The why of heart-breaking strangeness in dreeping hedges,
Nor analyse God's breath in common statement.
We have thrown into the dust-bin the clay-minted wages
Of pleasure, knowledge and the conscious hour –
And Christ comes with a January flower.

THE FUNCTIONAL WARD OF A CHEST HOSPITAL

It is clear that Kavanagh associated his notion of innocence and therefore an untrammelled awareness of love for the things of creation, from a primrose to a broken-down wall, with the presence of Christ: Jesus first as baby in the cradle, later as the adult Christ. This is a poem calling on the openness and clarity of imagination, rather than the closed and hide-bound workings of reason and the intelligence. In a poem written in 1943, 'Threshing Morning', this theme is taken up again. Echoes of Dylan Thomas and his delight in the things of creation about him in his childhood come into this piece: 'on an apple-ripe September morning … '. The poem recalls such a morning when he went 'with a pitchfork on my shoulder / Less for use than for devilment'. So, a morning of joy and laughter, gossip with a little work 'thrown in to ballast / The fantasy-soaring mind'. Though even when the morning was developing, Kavanagh was wondering if ever he could find such freedom again. 'And then I came to the haggard gate, / And I knew as I entered that I had come / Through fields that were part of no earthly estate.' In a poem called 'Peace', also written about this time, he writes:

> Out of that childhood country what fools climb
> To fight with tyrants Love and Life and Time?

In a poem written later, in 1951, it appears that Kavanagh has rediscovered innocence. The heroine of this discovery is 'love', though, as was the case with George Herbert in his poem 'Love', it was not intended, overtly at least, to be God, or Christ, but a form of transcendence and acceptance. He calls the poem 'Innocence' and it begins: 'They laughed at one I loved – The triangular hill that hung / Under the Big Forth.' He sees other people limiting his place in the world, 'But I knew that love's doorway to life / Is the same doorway everywhere.' For a time, he admits, he was ashamed of his love but is now back in that world, and is of 'no mortal age':

> I know nothing of women,
> Nothing of cities,
> I cannot die
> Unless I walk outside these whitethorn hedges.

Conscious of how people mocked his innocence, he worked to get rid of it; then returned, more firm and challenging, to himself and 'the world'. It is a poem that tells the truth that Christ himself told when he said, 'To save your life in this world you must lose it.' To love creation with real and ongoing intensity you must accept the earth on its own terms, and that includes suffering and death.

Kavanagh's ongoing criticism of Dublin society, and the 'acceptable' poetry of the time, was based on his idea that such 'love' and imaginative commitment to the world around had been lost. 'Now I must search till I have found my God … ', he writes in 'God in Women'. 'Surely my God is feminine, for Heaven / Is the generous impulse, is contented / With feeding praise to the good.' In another poem, 'Having Confessed', he writes: 'God cannot catch us / Unless we stay in the unconscious room / Of our hearts.' Then, showing how he has anticipated the contemporary movement in prayer, the work of 'emptying oneself' through a form of centring prayer and 'mindfulness', so that one might be filled with God, 'We must be nothing, / Nothing that God may make us something'. And 'God must be allowed to surprise us.' Kavanagh has come almost full circle, though it is not clear whether this actually worked in his own life. He stayed in Dublin, with only occasional visits back to Monaghan, but worked to find, in Dublin, spaces where he could sit and allow the wonders of creation to enter his soul.

Shortly after writing the poem 'The Hospital', Kavanagh wrote a poem in response to his hopes as expressed in that piece. 'October' was written in late 1957; there is renewed confidence in the 'innocence' he has won and he can again flaunt his love of creation.

THE FUNCTIONAL WARD OF A CHEST HOSPITAL

October

O leafy yellowness you create for me
A world that was and now is poised above time,
I do not need to puzzle out Eternity
As I walk this arboreal street on the edge of a town.
The breeze too, even the temperature
And pattern of movement, is precisely the same
As broke my heart for youth passing. Now I am sure
Of something. Something will be mine wherever I am.
I want to throw myself on the public street without caring
For anything but the prayering that the earth offers.
It is October over all my life and the light is staring
As it caught me once in a plantation by the fox coverts.
A man is ploughing ground for winter wheat
And my nineteen years weigh heavily on my feet.

    This delight, confidence and the techniques of the sonnet form that he had been developing as experience, defiance and thinking developed together, produced one of his finest poems; it takes to heart all his work towards renewing and reinvigorating his childhood innocence and faith in the value of loving the earth. Here he found his first love, peace and belonging, and if that faith is still a childhood faith, even a childish one, in our terms, it is still a sustaining and a liberating faith, playing the truest note of all of the music he has created and performed in his rich and caustic living.

    With 'Canal Bank Walk', Seamus Heaney suggests: 'We might say now the world is more pervious to his vision than he is pervious to the world. When he writes about places now, they are luminous spaces within his mind' (*Finders Keepers: Selected Prose 1971–2001*: Faber, London, 2002). Kavanagh has succeeded in turning inwards to the real spirit within through his own form of meditation: the writing of poems. In this poem he is pleading for passivity but in such a way that he will have mastered himself, poetry *and* the world. The poem recalls, too, that happy immersion in the everyday and common things he touches on in 'The Hospital': 'the inexhaustible adventure of a gravelled yard', or in such a very early poem as 'My Room', where 'my room is a musty attic, / But its little window / Lets in the stars'. And there is the ending of 'The Ploughman': 'I find a star-lovely art / In a dark sod. / Joy that is timeless! O heart / That knows God.' If, perhaps, he did not really 'know God' at that time, then he knows God now, because he has brought it down to reality, to do God's will, and in doing this he has 'found God'. This God is now settled in a bird's nest, as he is everywhere in the form of Christ, the Word. And it is my belief that Kavanagh has trumped both Yeats and Wordsworth in the redemption of what he has considered lost out of his childhood, both in his own life and in his poems. He discovered that the God he had first found as a baby in a cradle has become, through much interior argument and indeed overt anger and complaint, the Cosmic Christ; but he did not give him the name, nor did he have the language, as the Catholic Church would have cast cold water on the notion, and Irish faith and culture were far from prepared for it.

Canal Bank Walk

Leafy-with-love banks and the green waters of the canal
Pouring redemption for me, that I do
The will of God, wallow in the habitual, the banal,
Grow with nature as before I grew.
The bright stick trapped, the breeze adding a third
Party to the couple kissing on an old seat,
And a bird gathering materials for the nest for the Word
Eloquently new and abandoned to its delirious beat.
O unworn world enrapture me, encapture me in a web
Of fabulous grass and eternal voices by a beech,

THE FUNCTIONAL WARD OF A CHEST HOSPITAL

> Feed the gaping need of my senses, give me ad lib
> To pray unselfconsciously with overflowing speech,
> For this soul needs to be honoured with a new dress woven
> From green and blue things and arguments that cannot be proven.

The wonder of this odds and sods man, Patrick Kavanagh out of Monaghan, is that somewhere deep down inside him he intuited the cosmic Christ. Without doubt this began in his relating his Monaghan ploughman experience and his sense of freedom, innocence and at-homeness, with the freedom, innocence and homeliness of the Christmas Child. After many years of searching for something more complex, he eventually returned to that sense of innocence and freedom. And it was that same innocent Word, the Christ in the world, that brought him back to an awareness of being at home in his life. Those of us who have known the work of Teilhard de Chardin and his bringing together of evolution and Christianity know that he saw Christ as the future fullness of the whole evolutionary process. We say, 'Christ has died, Christ is risen, Christ will come again', and it is the awareness of that little word 'is' that sets the story alight; Christ did not simply leave the earth after his death as if his return would come some time in the future; Christ *is* risen; he is the one who is, and the one who is coming to be; he is the 'centrating principle', as Teilhard wrote, he is the 'pleroma' and he is the 'Omega point', creation, both individually and collectively, finding in Christ the end and fulfilment. But more than that, Christ is the mover of evolution, from within. Ilia Delio writes in *The Emergent Christ*: 'The ultimate mover of the entire cosmogenesis is something simultaneously *within* the sequence of beings as tendency, desire, and purpose, and *in front of* the advancing wave of development, beckoning it, as its ideal culmination'; that 'something' is Christ. We have the language for this; Kavanagh did not. But Kavanagh had the soul and language of poetry, and wrote several poems that find their fire in cosmogenesis, and in Christogenesis.

22

THE EMERGENT CHRIST

Ilia Delio

Ilia Delio OSF is a Franciscan Sister of Washington, DC, and a theologian specialising in the area of science and religion, with interests in evolution, physics and neuroscience and the importance of these for theology. Her writing and her talks have had great influence in spreading the awareness of evolution and Christianity and their symbiotic relationship. Her understanding, and bringing forward of, the work of Teilhard de Chardin and others is of huge value for our time. She has published many books; here I concentrate on her book, *The Emergent Christ* (Orbis Books, New York, 2011). She currently holds the Josephine C. Connelly Endowed Chair in Theology at Villanova University.

All of creation, with humanity at its crest, is in evolution, and is developing in a system of convergence and complexity. Up to our time, theology and ecclesiology made no attempt to open up to the essential discoveries of the last two centuries. With de Chardin, Delio holds that our awareness of God as love is essential so that we can understand that Christ is the source and end of the evolutionary process. The Alpha and the Omega, the source and the goal, is Christ. If this is so, then faith in God of necessity demands change in our awareness of Christian faith and the details of our response. The whole of the material creation must take its place alongside spirit in this evolutionary process. God must be seen as confluent with cosmogenesis.

'Christ is the symbol of creation's future in God, a future of newness in love, and our hope that love alone will endure' (p.5). God, in Christ, is no longer just the 'prime mover' of creation, pushing it forward, as it were, but has to be seen as drawing creation forward towards its end. In the incarnation, Christ made clear that divinity and humanity make one whole, 'in the unity of person, without change, division, separation, or confusion' (p.6). The true meaning of the word 'catholic', in this way of looking at the world, is catholicity; this means inclusivity and implies an outlook on life that is accepting of the whole of creation, not just the rules and rites of a particular faith. The Genesis story is renewed with the awareness of the 'Big Bang', how all the constituents that have come together to form the present, and that will continue into the future, were already there at the beginning of the universe. The story by which we live now becomes a much more dynamic story, this universe, this creation, biological life on earth: all demonstrating the emergence of complexity in life forms where, at critical moments, qualitative differences can be observed in the evolution of our created world.

Delio talks about being whole: being a whole part of a larger whole. 'The universe is bound together in communion, each thing with all the rest ... We live in interwoven layers of bondedness' (p.27). Aristotle thought of relationship as a quality of being; now relationship is seen as the very core of being; 'To be is to be related' (p.27). So, 'as human beings and societies we seem separate, but in our roots we are part of an indivisible whole and share in the same cosmic process' (p.29). Evolution suggests the universe is moving to a state of wholeness; it is moving forward so we must see change as integral to evolution, and therefore to the Creator. This is, in some ways, another definition of God's love. Christ came amongst us, into the process of evolution, to offer and implant in us, and in the whole of creation, the impulse of love. So the incarnation and the creation are one process of God's self-giving and self-communication. 'God is the future plenum of all that can be, and yet God is dynamically interior to creation, gradually bringing all things to their full being by a single creative act spanning all time' (p.47). Christ, and therefore the Trinitarian power and love, is within the process of creation because of the Incarnation: 'The ultimate mover of the entire cosmogenesis is something that is simultaneously within the sequence of beings as tendency, desire, and purpose, and *in front* of the advancing wave of development, beckoning it, as its ideal culmination' (p.49).

All of this may be seen, not as necessarily revolutionary in itself, but as a clarification of our origins, our development and our end. Teilhard wrote, in *Christianity and Evolution*: 'The universal Christ could not appear at the end of time at the peak of the world if he had not previously entered it during its development, through the medium of birth, in the form of an element. If it is indeed true that it is through Christ Omega that the universe-in-movement holds together, then it is from his concrete historical life, Jesus of Nazareth, that Christ-Omega derives his whole consistence, as a hard experiential fact. The two terms are intrinsically one whole, and they cannot vary in a truly total Christ except simultaneously'. So it becomes obvious that Christ, in his incarnation, is not an intrusion into an already evolving universe, but he is the true reason and the true goal of that evolutionary impulse.

Teilhard knew that divine love was at the heart of creation, and that heart was the love incarnate in the Christ who is coming to be. Christ is the *withoutness* and the *withinness* of matter in evolution. Because of Christ's incarnation, we can develop a new awareness of love as the ultimate force in the universe; he holds all of it together, he moves it forward towards greater complexity, and in this complexity is discovered a greater unity. 'The body of Jesus, like every human body, is made from cosmic dust birthed in the interior of ancient stars that long predated our planet and solar system' (p.55). This does away with the old notion of humanity having to repay a debt from the Garden of Eden. It clears away the mist and dust of the old notion of 'original sin', that we are all born inheriting the consequences and the guilt of sin, a notion originating with St Augustine and causing distress and negativity in Christian faith since Augustine's age. Sin is the refusal to accept responsibility for our connection to the universe 'What broke through in the person of Jesus was a new consciousness and relatedness to God that ushered in the world a new way of being God-centred, earth-centred, and in communion with one another' (p.62). To be 'catholic', then, is to take part in the process of developing unity, to participate in deepening relationships throughout the world; to be 'catholic' will then describe the whole universe in evolution. The old notion of 'seven days of creation', after which creation ceased, is also untenable. We are situated in an evolving world that is, as yet, far from complete. The Christ, in Jesus, shows what our humanity is to be.

The essence of resurrection is new life and a new future for the cosmos. 'What took place in Jesus Christ is intended for the whole cosmos, union and transformation in the divine embrace of love' (p.77). The resurrection recapitulates the cosmos: suffering and death anticipate new life. We know that without death, new life does not begin and evolution depends on death. Death is then seen as not being matter in dissolution, but its transformation into energy. 'If the life of Jesus is exemplary for all life in the cosmos, then what we say about Jesus must be true for all life in the cosmos' (p.81). Our life, then, and all of evolution may be seen as a drama, and we do not know how many acts remain before the curtain finally falls. So Christ is the one who is and the one who is coming to be. Teilhard wrote of Christ as the centrating principle, the pleroma and the Omega point. Christ, then, is 'the ultimate mover of the entire cosmogenesis … something simultaneously *within* the sequence of beings as tendency, desire, and purpose, and *in front* of the advancing wave of development, beckoning it, as its ideal culmination' (p.89). The new Christianity – far from being a clinging to what is perceived to be already there, in its flaws and glories – is now to be a daring adventure!

Our world appears to have become ever more fractured; it is the healing of Christ that will make all whole again, his mercy and compassion, his death on the cross bringing together all of creation in love. For all of this, its rich hope, its depth and breadth of meaning and of consequence, Christianity requires a new language and a new poetry. No longer have we a God who may be called static or apophatic; we have a God who does new things. We approach, through prayer, a greater intimacy with our

THE EMERGENT CHRIST

God through Christ. Through prayer, and the discovery of a more vitally open inner world, reason and action will yield more fully to the love of creation in Christ; 'We are called to love this created world as God loves it. We are to help transform this universe in Christ by seeing Christ in the universe and loving Christ in the heart of the universe' (p.137). To damage our world, the physical creation in which we are involved, is a sin. Hence, ecology takes on a more and more serious importance in our lives. We see Christ, too, in new ways, even beyond institutions, and in a more meaningful way with community. It is a world where we seek a oneness of heart with all others, a participation in our one earth, our whole cosmos. Christian faith is moving into a new depth of unifying love. It is not a lying down under dogmas and institutional priorities; the new Christian life is a fascinating and challenging journey forward.

23

OUR TATTERED FLAGS

Pádraig J. Daly (b.1943)

Pádraig J. Daly was born in Dungarvan, County Waterford, in 1943. He entered the Augustinian order and studied in Ireland and in Rome. He has worked as a priest in Dublin and in New Ross, County Wexford. He has published several collections of poetry, among them *Nowhere But in Praise* (Profile Press, Dublin, 1978), *A Celibate Affair* (Aquila, 1984), *Out of Silence* (Dedalus, Dublin, 1993), *The Voice of the Hare* (Dedalus, 1997) and *The Last Dreamers, New & Selected Poems* (Dedalus, 1999) and *The Other Sea* (Dedalus, 2003). 2007 saw the publication of a collection called *Clinging to the Myth*; in 2010 Daly published *Afterlife*, followed in 2015 by *God in Winter*. So there has been a steady stream of work from this priest poet, work that has moved on a downward-upward curve in terms of trust and hope, and on an upward curve in terms of language, form and imagery.

Daly offers perhaps the most sustained attempt at serious religious poetry in Ireland. He begins with an easy nostalgia for that innocent land we knew in our youth when Roman Catholic Ireland moved like a Titanic through untroubled waters. Daly's work, however, shifts quickly into the Augustinian concept that all our living is praise of God. In this sense he has offered his public a view of the earth that has always been ecologically aware and anticipated Pope Francis's encyclical, *Laudato Si'*. At the same time he realised that Luther, too, was an Augustinian, and Luther's spirit quickly enters Daly's work by subjecting his own life to examination. Embedded in the work is a willed and constant sense of loyalty to the faith this priest poet was born into. I chose a phrase from one of his poems to title a collection of essays of my own on faith and poetry; that phrase is 'in dogged loyalty', and it comes from a poem called 'The Last Dreamers'. Put the phrase, with that title, and another title of a Daly collection, 'Clinging to the Myth', together, and it is clear what this sense of holding on implies. It suggests, at times, that the dream of pilgrimage, of that voyage to a place apart, that voyage to a place within, has stalled; and that what is now needed is a willed loyalty to the early dream. The one deep and moving constancy that remains is that the absent, or hiding God, is still being addressed with sadness, anger or a withering hope.

The Last Dreamers

We began in bright certainty:
Your will was a master plan
Lying open before us.

Sunlight blessed us,
Fields of birds sang for us,
Rainfall was your kindness tangible.

But our dream was flawed;
And we hold it now,
Not in ecstasy but in dogged loyalty,

Waving our tattered flags after the war,
Helping the wounded across the desert.

This poem was published in the collection, *The Voice of the Hare*, in 1997. The poem says, 'Our dream was flawed'; bright certainty, a clear master plan, kindness tangible – all this was the dream, and all of it disintegrated when faced with real life. Wherein, then, lay the flaw? Perhaps in that assumed certainty, a stiff and persistent settling for dogma and ritual without a base of personal study and reading, a Church that demanded assent rather than thought and individual responsibility. Indeed, the insistently dogmatic voice of that Church has brought with it a sense of unease to those priests, those Catholics, who have tried to see Christ as a living presence in our own time. As Gabriel Daly has pointed out in his richly reasoned book, *The Church: Always in Need of Reform*, it is one thing to silence all opposing or dissenting voices – it is another to abrogate all orthodoxy to oneself. 'Truth is established by discussion and argument, not by the proclamations of authority; yet Rome has refused to conduct a caring discussion about some matters that are in legitimate dispute in the contemporary church. In many respects the Roman Catholic Church's curial administration has remained firmly lodged in nineteenth-century attitudes' (p.101). A priest's life can be difficult: the demands of parish and pastoral care combined with the personal commitment to the order creates a deep dependence on God through prayer and grace. If that sense of God's presence is tainted, then the life becomes more and more difficult. If the 'magisterium' of the Church does not even allow discussion of some pastoral issues, non-essential to the basis of faith, then the priest will feel even more isolated.

In Daly's work, the interior-desert imagery and the drudgery of living before an absent God make their first startling appearance in Irish poetry. The language becomes sparer as the life becomes more difficult. The immediacy and closeness of the experience of God's apparent absence is conveyed quickly and with the accuracy of anguish. Many of Daly's poems, then, turn for reassurance to his love and awareness of the wonders of creation, this being, too, a very Augustinian emphasis.

> Man cannot evade You:
> Every wary mouse,
> The ant that builds and climbs,

THE OUTLAW CHRIST

Each small limpet on a rock,
The waters sucked noisily
Through stones on the shore,

The sleek and watery cormorant
Compel him
To shout You out ...

And nowhere but in praise
Can quark or atom
Or any fraction else of mass

Find peace.

('Augustine: Letter to God', from *Nowhere But in Praise*, 1978)

There follows a series of poems hovering around the Merton ideal of productive silence and retreat where the Christ may be found again, where out of this silence words may flow with greater sound and fury. The natural response is to withdraw, to hide, but in a priest eager to serve others, a further response is needed. There comes a period of anger against this absent God. Anger, frustration, emptiness; is silence, then, an adequate response? And where does the poet move from here? The poetry Daly wrote in this period of his journey survives because of its music and the accuracy of its observation, not because of its content, which resorts so often simply to statement. The voice is unique; the lines move with a sense of breathing, slowly capturing a mood of awed certainty; the language is quite simply honed to perfection, 'sleek and watery cormorant', 'or any fraction else of mass ... '. In many ways, here we have an early George Herbert, relishing the world about him, and relishing it in terms of the music of poetry and the urgent and willed lifting of the heart towards God. Here it is the priest speaking, conscious of God, conscious too of the grace and promise that faith in a loving God can bring. Only when the deeply personal note is allowed in are we aware of any possible darkness in this picture. Already one might sense, in this poetry, in this pilgrimage, the great need for a more permeable faith, an acceptance of the human failure to allow God entry apart from the doctrines already imbibed.

Sagart I

In many ways you're like an old man. Perhaps
You walk alone more than most people twice your age.
You notice each change of weather, the drift
Of smoke to sky. There is a certain decorum
You follow in your dress, the way you comb your hair.

You have many acquaintances, few friends;
Besides your unreplying God you have no confidant.
Nevertheless you lift your hat to all. Old ladies
Especially will seek you out, sometimes a sinner.
You are guest at many celebrations, a must at birth or death.

Sometimes you wonder whether this is how God intended it.

In 1984, Pádraig Daly published his collection *A Celibate Affair*. The title itself ought to alert the reader to something strange and new in the book. Daly begins by taking a much closer look at the Jesus who up to now had been simply a matter of praising, a question of obedience. A new slowness and maturity begin to enter the poems. It may well be that the isolation and loneliness that formed the mood for the earlier poems had taken a stronger hold on the maturing priest who began to feel that the Christ, too, had led a similar, almost 'outcast' life. In an earlier poem, 'Problem', he had written, 'But I am blind still to the Jew / My life traipses after'. This trudging after Jesus, this sense of tagging along, needs to be clarified and strengthened if one is to stay close to one's priestly vocation, or even to a faith in Christ. In one of the poems of this collection, there grows a sense that Daly has now turned again to Christ and found an empathy and fellowship that is greatly needed in Christ's own isolation and his dream. This, it appears to me, is a profound meeting with Christ, a figure that is testing his own calling in a desert landscape and drawing some small strength out of that early dream of support and kindliness. The poem 'Encounter' (*A Celibate Affair*) has taken us a long way from the ease of the notion of praise to a harsher view of the interior spirit.

This is the figure of Jesus testing his own calling in the desert, drawing up, out of the depths of his belief, some original, promising motive for his fasting, his choosing the desert rather than the green paths.

Encounter

Monotony of sun
On sand and scrub,
A place of wild beasts
And long shadows;

At last he comes
To green and olive groves,
Vineyards,
Houses climbing beyond walls
Along a hillside.

Here the tempter waits,
Full of candour,
Offering for easy sale
All the green kingdoms of the world.

And he,
Though gaunt from fasting,
Needing rest,

Some perfect star
Seen a lifetime back
Determining him,

Passes slowly by.

An awareness of the depths of human misery (and a priest working in a city parish, in a deprived area of that city, is very aware of human misery) taints one's view of the beauty of natural things. The poetry, while maintaining its linguistic music and accuracy, and the line lengths of breathing and mood, with a definite mastery, is beginning to touch hurtful depths. Even his sense of the benevolence of God, that belief in a loving God, is sorely tested in the face of human suffering. How, then, address the Christ – in whom one still believes – when one's soul is bleeding with a sense that life is unjust; that there is too much unmerited pain in the ordinary lives of ordinary people? In 1997, the collection *The Voice of the Hare* shows a very different man, priest and poet from the early work.

Complaint

I will tell you, Sir, about a woman of yours,
Who suddenly had all her trust removed
And turned to the wall and died.

I remember how she would sing of your love,
Rejoice in your tiniest favour;
The scented jonquils,

THE OUTLAW CHRIST

> The flowering currant bush,
> The wet clay
> Spoke to her unerringly of benevolence.
>
> I remind you, Sir, of how, brought low,
> She cowered like a tinker's dog,
> Her hope gone, her skin loose around her bones.
>
> Where were you, Sir, when she called out to you?
> And where was the love that height nor depth
> Nor any mortal thing can overcome?
>
> Does it please you, Sir, that your people's voice
> Is the voice of the hare torn between the hounds?

Perhaps this is the lowest point to which this particular poet has sunk, in terms of his own capacity for joy, hope and faith. But it is a high point in his work, the most convincing poetry, the most piercing imagery and language. Here Daly has touched on the same cold flame that drove the poems of the later R.S. Thomas, this sense of an absent – worse, an uncaring God. And where can he go from here? We have moved a very great distance indeed from the hymn of praise that the creation is supposed to lift to its creator. Worse, this God begins to be seen as not really involved in human living: 'We cry out; / But if he hears, / He moves away from our voices'. Countering this sense of foreboding are figures like Thomas Merton and St Thérèse; the latter is, of course, the saint of small things, of isolation, of a dogged loyalty to her beliefs;

> And in her room at night,
> She shivered at the thought of God growing strange
> And a death as final as the death of stars.

The way God, Christ, is addressed in 'Complaint' as Sir, a word repeated in anger, distances the priest/pastor, yet even anger towards an absent God is preserving some relationship with that God. If the priest frames his faith in such terrible questions, how can he then speak with comfort to his people? A poem called 'Sorrow' has these lines:

> I watch one I have grown to love,
> Beautiful as the wind, languish;
> And I flounder in the grief around her …
>
> Your people mutter bitterly against you;
> How can I carry them?

There is, here, a version of what we know as the dark night of the soul. And we have learned that the only way to get through such a darkness (and this reminds me of Gerard Manley Hopkins and his time in Dublin) is to hold on, grimly, to faith, to know that belief is a question of grace and of will, not of sense and intellect.

The List

> The list of those who loved us
> And are gone
> Grows longer.
>
> Where can we find the will
> To let ourselves be loved,
> To love again?
>
> Like trees that show a Winter carapace,
> Like bulbs and seeds at rest,
> We bide till light returns.

This poem is in Daly's 2003 collection, *The Other Sea*. What a wonderful last three lines: trees that 'show a Winter carapace', and that word 'bide', its impact, its straining towards hope. Poems of memory and nostalgia take their place in this collection, but what appears of most importance is that echo of R.S. Thomas; that acceptance that perhaps our God exists, but he has taken himself away from us and cannot be found, not even intuited, yet must be accepted. Our God, our Christ, abides, but in 'unfathomable light'. One may travel a great journey with Pádraig J. Daly, a journey that shifts from the outer world of lovely things to a dark interior world where grey mists prevail. Those mists persist. But so does that doggedness in belief that he set out with. In a later poem that loyalty resurfaces, though now the thought patterns are more complex, and the language more concerned; the power of his observation and the vigour of the language have brought about a new vision of the impossible glory of a triune God. Before such mystery, Daly has learned, humanity is 'foolish'. Now it is God who must draw us rather than we trying to draw ourselves to a God we have not fully fathomed. And this, being drawn forward by God, is the response to an evolutionary world, the awareness of a life moving towards a purpose.

Trinity

The sea by itself is water merely:
Its miracle is in its beating against the shore,
Spreading out across flat sands,

Shifting shingle and stone,
Flowing over piers and jetties,
Halting before rock

And falling backward on itself to try again,
Leaping high in the storm,
Quietly attacking the very base of land.

OUR TATTERED FLAGS

And God and God and God are love merely
Until they find foolish us
To take love's overflow.

This poem, too, is in *The Other Sea*. Perhaps the last three lines are willed lines, but then faith, after going through all the doubts and dismays a genuinely caring life goes through, comes down to an act of will, a choice, a decision to opt for what may well be the only hope that gives meaning to our lives: the Trinity. And, closer, the Christ. We are left with loyalty, a dogged loyalty, but that loyalty, hard-earned, is perhaps the most true approach to religious faith, a loyalty urged and lived by people like Simone Weil. But the poetry is achieved, moving with a flow and certainty to those last lines, building up an image and sound pattern that earn the music of that last statement. The long 'e' sound of that first line is echoed in the third last line by the repetition of the word God and is re-echoed in the vowel of 'love'; and note those sound patterns that lead to the very final word, 'overflow': 'flat sands', the 's' music of the fourth line, the short and halted sixth line with its long and back-flowing seventh, and that forceful line that leads into the final triplet. And there are the exciting words that hit the mark so well, 'the very base of land', 'foolish us', 'love's overflow.'

Daly has 'come through' and the spirit rises again, though with a new knowledge and a new down-to-earthness. Christ is the answer, and the incarnation, Daly holds, is when 'God touched the world glancingly'. The priest, the man, the poet, is now 'clinging to the myth' and from that collection, published in 2007, comes this short poem (*Clinging to the Myth*, Dedalus Press):

Touch

We have never known miracles,
Yet believe that once in Galilee
God touched the world glancingly;

And nothing moved.
Yet all that saves us from despair
Resides there.

It is in Christ, in the incarnation, the showing-forth of who and what God is, that Daly has found full insight into faith. A poem he offered to me for the special issue of *Poetry Ireland Review* that I edited in 2012 is a clear and grace-filled summing up of a life. It is not the end of the journey, but we know that the rest of this soul's journey is more grounded, more secure, and the long clinging on, the dogged loyalty, has won favour. But to what does he now hold, to what does he cling? When I asked Pádraig J. Daly to write a new poem in response to the question Christ posed: 'Who do you say that I am?', he was inspired to write what I see as a life's summary, the summary of a journey, and a clarification of the centrality of Christ to that life. The poem is called:

Incarnation

1.
We would have done it otherwise:

We would have kept the fluttering messengers,
The journey in haste,
The wondrous birth.

Pity is important;
So we would have allowed him pain
And pity.

We would have kept the feasting,
The sinner companions,
The softness of God.

OUR TATTERED FLAGS

But what need was there
For the garden agony, the nails through the palms,
The roars from the cross?

2.
Feeling as men and women feel,
Quaking before pain
As men and women quake,

He entrusts Himself to the High Father
As men and women trust themselves
To human constancy;

And, trusting still that luminous love,
He edges on
To the blind halt of death.

3.
That all of this – sun, water's rush,
Men and women moving, haloed, through the streets –
Came from nothing, nowhere, nobody,
I cannot credit; so believe.

It is afterwards I baulk:
Mind-melting-Otherness?
Or Otherness-Made-Flesh,
Softly among us?

4.
And, being man,

THE OUTLAW CHRIST

Did he think, as men and women thought,
That Jonah dwelt three days within the whale,
Immune to belly juices?

That devils lived flamboyantly inside the sick
And, when his heart was moved to heal,
Left them, yelping?

That the world soon,
With hail and lightning bolt,
Must end?

How did he foresee
The horror of his dying,
The direful future of Jerusalem?

And how much grasp unknowable God,
Bending in his flesh
To pitch among us?

5.
(Jn 15: 9–11)

With human arms
Grappling each of myriad us to human heart,
There stilling us,

The love that flows from Father-God,
And all God's joy,
Holds each of us, through Him,

In an embrace,
Where every doltish one of us
Is marvellous and singular,

Where there is no longer need
For talk or explanation, gestures of regret;
Just simple surrender to our God's delight.

It is the Christ, then, that accompanies humanity on its journey, a journey out of simple acceptance through aridity and doubt, through anger and almost revolts, to a more serene and grounded awareness of who and what God is. That awareness comes through the poetry and life of Pádraig J. Daly and the Christ who remains doggedly loyalty to his faithful. We are held, then, by Christ 'In an embrace, / Where every doltish one of us / Is marvellous and singular.' And to this love we cling, beyond argument, reason and the rules of religion: 'Just simple surrender to our God's delight'.

During my semester in Loyola University, Chicago, I was in contact with Pádraig J. Daly and used some of his work in my teaching. Here is a response from one of the students:

THE 'GOING OF GOD' IN PADRAIG J. DALY'S 'COMPLAINT'
Jon Nilson (see Appendix)

'We feel God in the coming and going of God,' says Christian Wiman in *My Bright Abyss. Meditation of a Modern Believer*, ' − or no, the coming and going of consciousness (God is constant). We are left with these fugitive instants of apprehension in both senses of that word, which is one reason why poetry, which is designed not simply to arrest these instants but to integrate them into life, can be such a powerful aid to faith.'

Poetry, then, can truly bring faith to life. Yet is it an 'instant' of faith or of rebellion that Pádraig J. Daly arrests and integrates in his poem 'Complaint'? Who would dare to speak to God like this? In the Hebrew Bible Job comes close, but then backs down when God speaks: 'Will the one who contends with the Almighty correct him? Let him who accuses God answer him!' 'I am unworthy,' says Job, 'How can I reply to you? I put my hand over my mouth.. Therefore I despise myself and repent in dust and ashes' (Job 40:1–4; 42:6).

In 'Complaint', though, there is no bowing, backing down, or repenting like Job's. Instead, the poem is suffused with sarcasm, bitterness, and belligerence.

'*I will tell you, Sir:*' But, presumably, God does not need to be told about anyone or anything. Still, 'I will tell you' because the poet is so angry that he needs to tell God about this woman. And he refuses to address God as 'Father' (as Jesus had urged us to do) or even as 'Lord.' Instead, he uses that contemptuous 'Sir' over and over.

'*About a woman of yours:*' Suddenly she is robbed of any sense of God's love and dies in an agony of fear, 'cowering like a tinker's dog.' Since she was God's own, did not God have a special obligation to watch over and protect her? Aquinas and Karl Rahner, among others, argue that God does not intervene or interrupt the worldly order of cause and effect, but works in and through natural causes. So how can God be blamed for the removal and plight of this woman? Yet there are intra-psychic events, 'fugitive instants of apprehension,' flashes of insight or inspiration that feel as if they could come only from God. No wonder the poet is outraged to witness God's gift suddenly ripped away from her.

'*The wet clay / spoke to her unerringly of benevolence.*' So complete was her trust in God's love that even an element so ordinary and unremarkable as the clay under her feet gave her joy.

'*Where were you, Sir, when she called out to you? / And where was the love that height nor depth / Nor any mortal thing can overcome?*' The first line of this stanza echoes the feeling of Psalm 74, which cries out, 'Why do you hold back your hand, your right hand?' (Ps 74:11a). The poet will not leave it there because he knows of a stronger claim about divine care that goes way beyond the psalm. Paul declares, 'For I am sure that neither death nor life, nor angels nor rulers, nor things present nor things to come, nor powers, nor height nor depth, nor anything else in all creation, will be able to separate us from the love of God in Christ Jesus our Lord' (Rom 8:38–39). To which the poet responds, in effect, 'If this is so, where were you in her hour of most need?'

Finally, we come to the cold, controlled fury of the last stanza. Here the poet compares God to a wantonly cruel hunter who likes 'hare coursing.' This sport involves releasing a rabbit that flees in terror, only to be chased down and ripped apart by dogs specially bred and trained for this kind of 'amusement.' Perhaps the poet is alluding to the chapter entitled 'Rebellion' in Dostoyevsky's *The Brothers Karamazov*, where Ivan the atheist tells a story to his brother Alyosha. A peasant boy carelessly threw a stone that injured a wealthy landowner's favourite dog. On a frigid morning, the landowner ordered the child stripped naked and then sicced his wolfhounds on the boy. He was torn to pieces before his mother's eyes. Now if the suffering of innocent children is somehow necessary in God's world, says Ivan, then I respectfully return my admission ticket. I want no part of it. Alyosha whispers, 'That is rebellion.'

However, there is no hint that the poet too will return his ticket on account of the woman. 'Complaint' is not rebellion. It is the experience of the going of God, not simply of the going of consciousness, *pace* Wiman. The poem is sarcastic and bitter, but it is still a prayer, an utterly honest prayer born of a terrible crisis in the relationship between the poet and God. Who would dare to speak to God like this? Only one who is still sure that God will not respond to him in kind. Even our fury belongs to faith.

24

THE ZONE OF TIMELESSNESS

James Harpur (b.1956)

James Harpur was born in England in 1956 to an Irish father and a British mother, and now lives near Clonakilty in County Cork. He studied Classics and English at Cambridge University (pleased to be where George Herbert had studied), then taught English on the island of Crete. Harpur's most recent collection is *Angels and Harvesters* (Anvil Press, now distributed by Carcanet UK). He is the poetry editor of the *Temenos Academy Review*, founded by Kathleen Raine.

Harpur's richly wrought poems touch on spiritual subjects, and his work as a whole is an ongoing search into truths that may deepen and transcend the actual. His study is, simply, the human condition, but in terms of spiritual yearning and experience. His work on the lives of philosophers and contemplatives has led his own work into profound and moving poetry.

His collection, *Angels and Harvesters*, published in 2012, moved the poetry closer to the poet's own being, and it was this regarding of personal experience touched on by an intelligence deeply informed by the history of humankind's search for faith that prompted me to ask him to write a poem for the *Poetry Ireland Review* I was editing; this poem might attempt to answer the question that Christ himself proposed to his disciples: Who do you say that I am? I asked for a personal response to the person of Christ and the poem that Harpur wrote is a beautiful, richly achieved and in-depth approach to such an answer.

The best one can do with the poem is read it and tell it. For purposes of clarity I have here divided it into sections, some of which I will reproduce, others summarise. The poem starts in Wiltshire, England, aware of creation in its spectacular beauty. Perhaps there, something will 'ignite' and a life may catch the fire of love and awareness. Perhaps the writer may meet Christ. There is an impatience in him, at this early stage, that will not allow the presence of Christ to be known. It is a question, amongst most of humankind, of being impermeable, of allowing the noises and cares of the world to block out the presence of the spiritual and transcendent; the labour is to allow oneself to be permeable, to listen, to open to the presence of Christ within. The poem, then, becomes a pilgrimage in search of Christ, a deeply personal meditation on the journey and its many stages, in the hope that a resolution may be found. It begins:

The White Silhouette
for John F. Deane

> 'There went a whisper round the decks one morning, 'We have a mysterious passenger on board.' ... Often I thought of that rumour after we reached Jerusalem ... When I saw the man all in white by the Golden Gate carrying in all weather his lighted lamp, I always thought, 'There is a mysterious pilgrim in Jerusalem."
> – Stephen Graham, from *With The Russian Pilgrims to Jerusalem* (1913)

I thought we would meet in a holy place
Like the church in the hamlet of Bishopstone
Empty on a Wiltshire summer's day
The trees full of rooks and hung in green
And the stream in the meadows a rush
Of darkling silver beneath the bridge
Where I saw my first kingfisher flash
Its needle, leaving its turquoise stitch
In my memory; and I would sit

THE ZONE OF TIMELESSNESS

In the church and close my eyes
And wait in vain for something to ignite
And wonder whether this was my life
Wasting away in my mother's home.
Sometimes I'd bring Herbert's *Temple*
And read the quiet order of his poems
And picture him, as once he was glimpsed,
Hugging the floor in his church at Bemerton
Asking love to bid him welcome.
I sat with an upright praying disposition
Preoccupied in self-combing
Too callow and spiritually impatient
To notice if you had slipped in
As a tourist to inspect the choir or font
And buy a picture postcard and sign
The book with 'lovely atmosphere';
Or as a walker taking refuge from rain
Or a woman primping flowers by the altar.

We start, then, in a place where creation offers itself in its beauty and its inspiration. If, the poet thinks, he takes awareness of the wonders of creation with him into the church, closes his eyes and waits for revelation, that might be a wonderful beginning. The poetry of George Herbert is with him at times, and the plea that Herbert's work had been made to God in order to be offered love in return. What occurs is no sudden Saul/Paul moment of enlightenment and encounter, but the beginnings of self-knowledge, an awareness that he had been, in fact, too self-preoccupied, urgent for revelation, is the easy way out. It is a finely caught moment of truth and humility.

Harpur taught in Crete and travelled in Greece, finding himself on the island of the Revelation, Patmos, where John is reputed to have had his visions. He thought that Christ might have been that pilgrim with camera and rucksack, whom he might have encountered here, but he did not see him, images from John's Book of the Apocalypse holding his mind instead. Here, too, is a location filled with meaning and associated with revelation and wonder in the cave where the myth holds that John received the angels with the gift of the Book of Revelation, the 'Apocalypse'. Here might be a place where a modern pilgrim may turn out to be the Christ, but if the Christ had passed by, the poet has missed him, being again too taken up with the wonders of place and the magical accidents of Revelation.

> Or somewhere like the island of Patmos
> Out of season and the tourist flow,
> The sea leaching blue from the skies.
> In the cave of St. John, pointillist gold
> On tips of candles and highlights of icons,
> You might have visited that day in September
> When I was there, absorbing the coolness,
> Imagining John on the Day of the Lord
> Prostrate on the ground as if before a throne
> And you not dressed in a 'robe and gold sash'
> Nor with hair 'as white as wool or snow'
> But as a pilgrim with camera and rucksack
> Respectful, curious, guide-book in hand
> Appreciating the grain of raw stone
> Catching my eye and pausing for a second
> As if I were a schoolfriend from years ago.
> I never saw you, if you were there,
> For I was too blinded by the new Jerusalem
> Flashing out jasper, topaz, sapphire
> Descending from heaven like a huge regal crown.

THE ZONE OF TIMELESSNESS

Closer to home, the poet visits a well-known landmark in the centre of Ireland, a place beautifully caught in this section of the poem. Once again there is a locus of wonder, creation in its natural beauty all around him, and a relic of the cross in the abbey church. The poet recalls a time he watched a bride, on a frosty day in March, wait to enter the church – 'Like a swan gliding in its snowdress'; and he was too distracted by these beautiful things of earth to notice the stranger move away in his car from the scene, a stranger who may well have been the Christ he was seeking.

> Or somewhere like Holycross in Tipperary,
> The abbey at the meeting of road and river,
> You might have stopped to break a journey
> As I often do, and seen me there in the nave
> Ambling down the sloping floor
> Towards the relic-splinter of the Cross
> Or sitting outside on the banks of the Suir
> On a bench on a swathe of tended grass
> Perhaps that day when, heading north,
> I paused by the car park to watch
> A bride, fragile, and frozen by the door
> Her bridesmaids huddled in the cold of March
> Waiting and waiting to make her entrance
> Into the sudden shine of turning faces
> Like a swan gliding in its snowdress
> From an arch of the bridge in a state of grace.
> I was too mesmerised by her destiny
> To see you start your car, drive off,
> And raise your hand as you passed me by
> On the way to Cashel, Fermoy and the south.

THE OUTLAW CHRIST

Once, when he was absorbed in self-pity, being ill at home, he 'turned to meditation' and had a moment of seeming revelation, the self emptied out and a light opening; but, he says, he 'closed the door of my heart, afraid' that the world he knew might be taken from him. 'Too scared,' he says, so that he would look for Christ in public, where there would be others and he might feel safe. This, too, is so accurate and such a well-described sense we all may have of the demands the Christ might make if, in fact, we reach him and meet him face to face. We feel safe in our bodies and in our own half certainties; how can we then shift out of time into the demands of timelessness and abandon the safety nets of learned prayers and rituals?

> But there was that time I was so certain
> That I had finally found you;
> Sick at home, I turned to meditation
> And prayer to overcome self-pity
> For weeks accumulating quietude
> Till that morning when seconds were emptied out
> My thoughts cleansed, my self destroyed
> Within an uncanny infusing light
> That seemed to deepen and unfold
> More layers of radiance and lay me wide open
> So you could cross the threshold
> Or I could cross, at any moment.
> But I closed the door of my heart, afraid,
> Who knows, that I might have met you
> Afraid I would pass to the other side
> And never return to all that I knew;
> I thought I could always re-open myself
> And greet you properly, well prepared.
> I never did. I feared that sudden shift

THE ZONE OF TIMELESSNESS

Into the zone of timelessness; too scared
I looked for you in public, for safety,
I kneeled in churches, gave the sign
Of peace in St. James's Piccadilly,
I recited prayers, took bread and wine
And I concentrated so hard, but failed
To believe they were your blood and body;
I heard staccato prayers, like nails
Banged in, as if to board up windows.

In Greece once more, and the Christ appearing to come closer, dreamlike, a glimmer, night beautiful and the stars radiant; and the sense of the Christ as master of this universe. But it is not in dreams or near-visions that the Christ is to be found; on waking, the poet finds himself as puzzled as Belshazzar, governor of Babylon, who, during a feast, saw writings on the wall but could not interpret them; it was the prophet Daniel who interpreted the writing for him, and the words foretold the destruction of Babylon.

Sometimes I'd sense you as a glimmer
As in that dream I once had out of the blue
When you stood at night on a Greek island shore;
Your face was hidden, but it was you;
The stars pinned in place the layers of darkness
Then came the comets, perhaps a dozen,
Their tails fanned out with diminishing sparks;
Slowly they twisted and turned – your hands
Moving in concert, as if you were guiding them,
As if they were on strings, like Chinese kites.
The comets slowed and stopped, and changed
Into letters of Hebrew, emblazoning the night.

THE OUTLAW CHRIST

> And I knew if I could grasp those words,
> Your silent message across the stars,
> I'd know my destiny on earth.
> Instead I woke, as puzzled as Belshazzar.

After such travels, such misses and near misses, such hesitations and withdrawals, the poet gave up the active search, feeling weary and disillusioned, thinking perhaps that 'hope prevents the thing it hopes for'. Then the poem shifts gear, and we are now beautifully prepared by the accuracy and beauty of the writing, for the switch: the words 'And yet … '

> I do not search for you any more
> I don't know whom to seek, or where;
> Too weary, disillusioned, I'm not sure
> What I think or if I really care
> That much; my last hope – that my resignation
> Might be a sign of the Via Negativa,
> A stage of my self-abnegation –
> That hope prevents the thing it hopes for.
>
> And yet
>
> I still write to you, poem after poem,
> Trying to shape the perfect pattern
> Of words and the mystery of their rhythm,
> An earthly music audible in heaven –
> Each poem is a coloured flare
> A distress signal, an outflowing
> Of myself, a camouflaged prayer
> Dispatched towards the Cloud of Unknowing
> And all I have to do is stay
> Where I am, ready to be rescued

THE ZONE OF TIMELESSNESS

Not move, speak or think but wait
For the brightening of the Cloud
For your white silhouette to break
Free from it and come nearer, nearer,
Till I see your essence and I can ask
Where in the world you were
Throughout my days – and only then
Will I grasp why I never found you
Because you were too close to home
Because I thought I'd have to die
To see you there, right there, removing
The lineaments of your disguise –
My careworn wrinkled skin
My jaded incarnation of your eyes –
My face becoming your face
My eyes your eyes
I you us I you us
Iesus.

Frank O'Connor's translation of an early Irish poem is relevant here:

To go to Rome
Is little profit, endless pain;
The Master that you seek in Rome
You find at home, or seek in vain.

    Harpur's interior pilgrimage is so deftly delineated, and so deeply thought through, the details and the honesty of the responses to those details so convincing that the poem is, perhaps, one of the best to take on this difficult, demanding theme. It is also the movement of the poem that concentrates the spirit of the reader, the fluency of the lines and language, the steady progression, the music of the whole and the delightful accuracy of expression and imagery. And, after it all, a heartening lift to those who do try to pursue the Christ through their daily lives. The poem is the title poem of a wonderful collection, *The White Silhouette* (Carcanet, London, 2018).

ON *WHITE SILHOUETTE*, JAMES HARPUR
Angelo Canta (See Appendix)

James Harpur, born in Britain in 1956, appreciates the extent to which Christianity must remain a touchstone for contemporary poets in the West. In a 2011 interview with *Poetry Ireland Review*, Harpur notes that while he is 'deeply wary of institutional hierarchies and structures,' he contends that Christianity is so irrevocably embedded into Western culture that it touches everything from art and literature to the very 'air we breathe.' Over the course of his career, Harpur has taught English on the island of Crete, spent time as a resident writer at Exeter Cathedral, and published *The Gospel of Joseph of Arimathea* – an exploration of the human Christ through interviews with his disciples. All of this sets the stage for Harpur's 'The White Silhouette'. One of his rare explicitly Christocentric poems, 'The White Silhouette', embodies Harpur's pilgrimage toward Christ in his life. He presents all too familiar frustrations of a heart earnestly seeking an encounter with the Divine.

Before 'The White Silhouette' begins, Harpur includes an excerpt from Stephen Graham's *With the Russian Pilgrims to Jerusalem* that sets the tone for the poem. The mysterious passenger on board Graham's boat serves as a reference to the story of Jonah. As a prophet, God instructed Jonah to travel to the infamously sinful city of Nineveh and preach conversion. Jonah, fearful of his mission, embarks on a long journey away from Nineveh, only to eventually find himself there. With this biblical

THE ZONE OF TIMELESSNESS

allusion, Harpur draws a parallel between himself and Jonah. He is the prophet who travels far from his intended destination only to find himself exactly where God intended. Graham's mysterious passenger is also Christ for Harpur. As the poem progresses, Harpur alludes to images of Christ in the ordinary, often ignored, people of his mundane life.

Harpur, writing directly to Christ, begins with three missed attempts to find Jesus in traditionally holy places. In the idyllic church in Bishopstone, Harpur impatiently waits for Jesus to come as George Herbert's *Love*. He sits there, eyes closed, concentrated and frustrated, waiting for Love to bid him welcome. Here, Harpur presents the image of self-absorption. He is wrapped up too much in his own picture of Christ to notice that perhaps Christ comes as the tourist and passer-by. Next, Harpur moves to the ancient pilgrimage place of Patmos in Greece. This is the traditional location of St John's apocalyptic visions as recorded in the Book of Revelation. Here, Harpur juxtaposes the 'pointillist gold' of the holy site with the mundane appearance of Christ as a 'pilgrim with camera and rucksack.' The pilgrim Christ even turns to Harpur with a look of distant recognition. Yet Harpur is too distracted by the ornaments of the church like the jewels of the New Jerusalem to notice the ordinary Christ. Finally, Harpur writes about Holycross in Tipperary, a medieval place of pilgrimage. Here, he finds himself caught up in the beautiful moments of a bride and her bridesmaids huddled by a church door just before entering. He is too caught up in this moment to notice Christ starting his car in the parking lot and waving goodbye. All three of these instances demonstrate how distracting traditional religious places can be for Harpur. This resonates with the pilgrim-reader who has experienced frustration and distraction in similar holy sites. Yet, Harpur poetically paints these moments not as a total absence of the Divine, but as missed encounters. Christ is there in all three places, but not as he is traditionally imagined.

'The White Silhouette''s next stanza offers a true encounter with Christ and a fear-filled movement away from conversion. Unlike the exotic, holy places of the previous stanzas, Harpur is at home, sick in his bed. Turning to meditation, Harpur finally finds Christ, like Julian of Norwich and her *Shewings*. This encounter with Jesus results in a total self-emptying. In a moment of kenotic surrender of ego, Harpur finds Christ as a light that opens him to divine reality. And yet, the encounter is only an opportunity for conversion. He is caught up in fear of leaving his old, comfortable understanding to enter into the new unknown. His repetition of the word 'cross' juxtaposes Christ's Cross with Harpur's own unwillingness to cross the threshold. Instead, he closes the door for a false, yet comforting future when he is more prepared to receive Jesus. Harpur also expresses his fear of total vulnerability in that encounter. He runs to the safety of public expressions of faith like services at St James' Piccadilly. However, these rote instances of prayer are inauthentic for Harpur. As mentioned in the *Poetry Ireland* interview, he is weary of religion and instead must find Christ outside the church.

Harpur concludes the poem with a fleeting engagement with the cosmic Christ, a resignation to stop searching, and a final, lasting encounter. As in a dream, he imagines Christ as the cosmic Lord, conducting the stars in heaven to move as he pleases. Yet, this Christ is inaccessible to him. He is enraptured by it, but in the end is frustrated and confused. The imagery of Christ moving the stars to form a Hebrew phrase relates to Harpur's movement away from Jesus in the tradition. He cannot understand the Hebrew phrase and feels, like many, that he cannot relate to the Christ who comes forth from the Judaeo-Christian tradition. The next stanza solidifies his resignation. Harpur's disillusionment and confusion lead him to a kind of *Via Negativa* theology that seeks to show what God is not, rather than speak positively about what God is. Even in this resignation, we get the sense that Harpur is still on his pilgrimage. Perhaps this is the moment, as in Jonah's story, when he resigns himself to go to the place to which he was always called. The final stanza affirms this point. He still writes to Christ in his uncertainty with poems like 'camouflaged prayer[s].' However, here Harpur understands that he must allow Christ to come to him rather than go out searching for some image of Christ. Staying still and waiting patiently for the White Silhouette to draw nearer and nearer reveals to Harpur that he was always unable to find Christ because he did not look inward. He closes the poem with the beautiful picture of Christ drawing so near that Harpur is finally able to see Jesus in his own face.

25

THAT BODY WHEREOF I AM A MEMBER

John Donne again

It is perhaps time to look again at John Donne's most famous prose piece, the 'Devotion' number XVII, titled 'Now, This Bell Tolling Softly for Another, Says to Me: Thou Must Die'. The meditation was written around the same time as the poem 'Hymn to God My God, in My Sickness', in 1630, when he was severely ill and expecting death at any moment. In the third and fourth stanzas of the poem, Donne speaks of lying on his back like a map flattened out; if such a map is rolled around a globe, then west meets east and his meeting with Christ in death is filled with promise, 'So death doth touch the Resurrection'. The developing imagery joins the whole world into one, and Donne's ever-present thinking how humanity should see itself as moving through the world and accepting the development of our world fits into place. His move from Roman Catholicism to the Reformed Church he clearly saw as a form of evolution alongside the development of thought and spirituality, and he never seriously thought of it as defection. *The Meditation on the Bell* draws his thinking beautifully together:

> Perchance he for whom this bell tolls may be so ill, as that he knows not it tolls for him; and perchance I may think myself so much better than I am, as that they who are about me, and see my state, may have caused it to toll for me, and I know not that. The church is Catholic, universal, so are all her actions; all that she does belongs to all. When she baptizes a child, that action concerns me; for that child is thereby connected to that body which is my head

too, and ingrafted into that body whereof I am a member. And when she buries a man, that action concerns me: all mankind is of one author, and is one volume; when one man dies, one chapter is not torn out of the book, but translated into a better language; and every chapter must be so translated; God employs several translators; some pieces are translated by age, some by sickness, some by war, some by justice; but God's hand is in every translation, and his hand shall bind up all our scattered leaves again for that library where every book shall lie open to one another. As therefore the bell that rings to a sermon calls not upon the preacher only, but upon the congregation to come, so this bell calls us all; but how much more me, who am brought so near the door by this sickness. There was a contention as far as a suit (in which both piety and dignity, religion and estimation, were mingled), which of the religious orders should ring to prayers first in the morning; and it was determined, that they should ring first that rose earliest. If we understand aright the dignity of this bell that tolls for our evening prayer, we would be glad to make it ours by rising early, in that application, that it might be ours as well as his, whose indeed it is. The bell doth toll for him that thinks it doth; and though it intermit again, yet from that minute that that occasion wrought upon him, he is united to God. Who casts not up his eye to the sun when it rises? but who takes off his eye from a comet when that breaks out? Who bends not his ear to any bell which upon any occasion rings? but who can remove it from that bell which is passing a piece of himself out of this world? No man is an island, entire of itself; every man is a piece of the continent, a part of the main. If a clod be washed away by the sea, Europe is the less, as well as if a promontory were, as well as if a manor of thy friend's or of thine own were: any man's death diminishes me, because I am involved in mankind.

In his meditation on these thoughts he goes on to write, speaking of the sound of that bell: 'I hear that which makes all sounds music, and all music perfect; I hear thy Son himself saying, 'Let not your hearts be troubled'; only I hear this change, that whereas thy Son says there, 'I go to prepare a place for you,' this man in this sound says, I send to prepare you for a place, for a grave.' And in a 'prayer' following on this meditation, he prays: 'When thy Son cried out upon the cross, 'My God, my God, why hast thou forsaken me?' he spake not so much in his own person, as in the person of the church, and of his afflicted members, who in deep distresses might fear thy forsaking'.

In *Field of Compassion* (Sorin Books, Indiana 2010), Judy Cannato tells a story culled from the British biologist Rupert Sheldrake; in Southampton, 1920s, the blue tit could be seen tearing cardboard tops off milk bottles delivered to the doorsteps of homes; they sipped the cream off the top. This was observed in 1921 and other bird-watchers began reporting that this habit seemed to be picked up by blue tits all over the country so that by 1947 the habit had spread to Sweden, Holland, Denmark and Germany. During the war, such milk deliveries were stopped throughout Holland and only resumed about 1948. The birds, several generations later, almost immediately took up the habit of pecking away the tops of the bottles and sipping the cream. She tells other similar stories and goes on to develop the theory of 'morphogenic fields', suggesting that such learned habits slip into the common memory of species and are carried forward from generation to generation.

This particular story of the working of the universe, is as Cannato writes, 'a story that tells us that the universe is a single evolutionary process, dynamic and organic, and that all life is fundamentally connected'. Every individual is a morphogenic field in himself/herself and each group to which one belongs is a morphogenic field. In the 1960s, Arthur Koestler coined the word 'holon', meaning that each thing is a whole part: 'Nothing is whole apart from everything else, and nothing is a part separate from other wholes'. A whole person is part of a whole community. Cannato writes: 'According to Sheldrake, there is a non-energetic exchange of information that takes place between morphogenic fields. It is nonlocal in nature, meaning that morphic resonance involves a sort of 'action at a distance' both in space and time. Contact with a morphogenic field does not depend on physical proximity, in other words; its energy can be experienced and its influence felt over any spatial separation.' It has been obvious to my own generation that our children and grandchildren have somehow picked up skills with information technology that we certainly did not teach them; they appear to start learning from a higher level than we have attained.

The thinking about morphogenic fields insists that they are grounded in the physical world. They are related to matter, just as gravitational and electro-magnetic fields are. They are interacting with and organising our actual world. So there is a mutuality of exchange, and each holon, each field, is related to the others. John Donne's thinking could not possibly have moved this far, but his words and ideas do, indeed, anticipate such a unification of the universe.

In a poem from his 1984 collection, *Station Island* (Faber & Faber), 'A Kite for Michael and Christopher', Seamus Heaney urges his sons to take the string that holds the kite into their own hands and 'feel the strumming, rooted, long-tailed pull of grief'. A new generation is being introduced to an awareness of life as a struggle, and the father adds that they should now stand in front of him and 'take the strain'.

It is the generation theme, sons stepping in to take over from the father, becoming acquainted, as they must, with grief in life. The fall of the kite that will make the line between flier and kite useless already touches on the loss that one generation feels for the one gone before. In the collection published in 2010, *Human Chain*, elegy predominates. The early poems in the book touch on the generations before his own, his mother, his father. John Donne, faced with a powerful awareness of mortality, said, 'No man is an island'. And yet, in a sense, every human being is an island, as in a holon, a whole-part, a whole person in a whole society, and faced with an awareness of mortality, may feel such an isolation (an island-ness) all the more – islands, whole in themselves, and part of the great world, islands of the sea.

In 2006, Heaney had suffered a serious stroke and, while being taken by ambulance to hospital, thinks of loss: 'When we might, O my love, have quoted Donne / On love on hold, body and soul apart'. And he goes on in the next section of that poem to dwell on that islanding word, 'Apart: the very word is like a bell … '. The following poem returns Heaney to an earlier theme, that of the healing by Jesus of the paralytic, and the people who had lowered him down through the roof to place him before the healer. But this time he focuses on the helpers: 'Their shoulders numb, the ache and stoop deeplocked / In their backs … ' .

This consciousness of self and helpers leads Heaney to the rich title poem of this collection, 'Human Chain', which speaks of working alongside others at a difficult task. The poem begins with a common sight: aid workers forming a chain to pass out goods and food donated by charities to starving people. The sight of soldiers trying to keep order amongst the 'mob', firing over their heads, brings the notion of death into the poem. Heaney associates the TV footage with a memory of his younger years in the farm at home when he had to 'brace' himself to take part in another form of human chain; this emphasised the details of how he grasped, held, lifted and swung a heavy sack up onto a trailer. The emphasis is on the joy of releasing the weight, the 'unburdening', the reward for breaking one's back. The 'letting go' is what is relished, each time different. The poem twists suddenly at the end, towards an awareness of the final letting go, which is a once and for all time letting go, and will happen just once for every human being in the chain of life.

In the final poem of this collection that moves from recollecting the past in their generations, the poet shifts his view to the future generations, thus extending that human chain. He also reverts to the original poem of kite flying, that to his own sons; this time, 'A Kite for Aibhín' is a kite-poem for one of his grandchildren. Now 'I take my stand again …

back in that field to launch our long-tailed comet'. The kite flies high, 'Climbing and carrying, carrying farther, higher / The longing in the breast and planted feet / And gazing face and heart of the kite flier'; but inevitably the string breaks, the flier is left bereft and the kite 'separate, elate – the kite takes off, itself alone, a windfall'. This is one generation aware of its own passing; the child, like the kite, will move away into its own air and space, but the earlier generation, though now 'separate', is also 'elate' and sees the new arrival as a 'windfall'.

The whole collection, Heaney's final collection during his lifetime, is deeply enriched and ennobled by the concept of John Donne's 'no man is an island' meditation. It moves brilliantly out of and through the concept of the solitary individual and into the notion of the part an individual plays in the whole human endeavour. Christians would refer to it as 'the mystical body'. But after Teilhard de Chardin and developments in the idea of evolutionary humanity moving towards cosmogenesis and Christogenesis, towards an Omega which is Christ, the human chain concept has grown ever richer and more optimistic. Interestingly, John Donne had written, in that meditation, 'I hear thy Son himself saying, "Let not your hearts be troubled"'; at the funeral Mass in Dublin for Seamus, his son Michael told the smitten congregation that his last words were 'in a text message he wrote to my mother just minutes before he passed away, in his beloved Latin, and they read: "Noli timere" – "don't be afraid." "Let not your hearts be troubled".'

To speak of the world in evolution, in 'cosmogenesis', in the word Teilhard de Chardin used, then all of creation, human and non-human, becomes a struggling mass working towards unity. In the case of humanity, the sense of a 'human chain', a 'communion of saints' and of sinners, has been made clearer and more urgent in the face of such an evolutionary process. Ilia Delio quotes de Chardin: 'The universal Christ could not appear at the end of time at the peak of the world if he had not previously entered it during its development, through the medium of birth, in the form of an element. If it is indeed true that it is through Christ Omega that the universe-in-movement holds together, then it is from his concrete historical life, Jesus of Nazareth, that Christ-Omega derives his whole consistence, as a hard experiential fact. The two terms are intrinsically one whole, and they cannot vary in a truly total Christ except simultaneously.' And Delio adds: 'Christ is not an intrusion into an otherwise evolutionary universe, but its very reason and goal' (*The Emergent Christ*, p.49).

When it comes to the contemporary awareness of the actuality of evolution, and the notion of a directional evolution towards the fulfilment of Christ's incarnation, then the work of Ilia Delio, particularly *The Emergent Christ*, is extremely valuable. Keeping in mind Donne's 'No man is an island', alongside Heaney's 'Human Chain', with the Christian notion of the Communion of the Faithful, we can understand Delio's view that all of creation, humanity its crest, is in evolution, developing in a system of convergence and complexity; Christ is source and goal of such evolution. In this sense, too, the word 'catholic' needs to be freed from its closed-world sense; it really means being a whole-maker, uniting what is separate, evolving things towards greater unity. No man is an island. Delio writes: 'The universe is bound together in communion, each thing with all the rest … We live in interwoven layers of bondedness'. One of the conclusions of this way of thinking is that 'as human beings and societies we seem separate, but in our roots we are part of an indivisible whole and share in the same cosmic process'. All of this opens up a hope and a wonderful challenge to our times, to be aware of the purpose of our being, of our being together, of our bondedness in the love of God and Jesus Christ.

Sean Freyne, in *Jesus, a Jewish Galilean*, references Isaiah 11, a poem from verse 1 to verse 9, a poem celebrating a future ruler 'of the stock of Jesse', David's father.

> A shoot will come up from the stump of Jesse;
> from his roots a Branch will bear fruit.

THE OUTLAW CHRIST

The Spirit of the LORD will rest on him –
  the Spirit of wisdom and of understanding,
  the Spirit of counsel and of might,
  the Spirit of the knowledge and fear of the LORD –
and he will delight in the fear of the LORD.

He will not judge by what he sees with his eyes,
  or decide by what he hears with his ears;
but with righteousness he will judge the needy,
  with justice he will give decisions for the poor of the earth.
He will strike the earth with the rod of his mouth;
  with the breath of his lips he will slay the wicked.
Righteousness will be his belt
  and faithfulness the sash around his waist.

The wolf will live with the lamb,
  the leopard will lie down with the goat,
the calf and the lion and the yearling[a] together;
  and a little child will lead them.
The cow will feed with the bear,
  their young will lie down together,
  and the lion will eat straw like the ox.
The infant will play near the cobra's den,
  and the young child will put its hand into the viper's nest.
They will neither harm nor destroy
  on all my holy mountain,
for the earth will be filled with the knowledge of the LORD
  as the waters cover the sea.

Freyne comments: 'The spirit of Yahweh will endow this ideal ruler not with military prowess, but with the gifts of understanding and wisdom. Truth and peace will reign through the establishment of justice for the poor and the humble, while the powerful and greedy will be restrained. There is a subtle parallelism between the harmony that is established in the human world and the animal kingdom, as the powerful and the predatory will be transformed' (p.99). Freyne speaks of this poem as having 'cosmic overtones', thus crediting the Old Testament prophet with almost uncanny foresight into how the world will develop in Christian thinking. Delio sums it up well in her book; 'The good news that emerged in the life of Jesus was the news of God's healing love; the binding of wounds; the reconciling of relationships torn apart by anger, hurt, jealousy, or vengeance; the revelation that love is stronger than death and that forgiveness is the act of love that creates a new future. Jesus the Christ shows us what is possible for humanity. In Jesus is seen, in the context of the whole complex of events in which he participated, what God intends for all human beings. He represents the consummation of the evolutionary creative process that God has been effecting in and through the world' (p.63). It is not just humanity that is at the growing tip of this evolutionary process, but humanity in the world that's committed to the unity of being and the welfare of the cosmos itself.

In his wonderful book, *Jesus, An Historical Approximation*, José Pagola writes: 'Jesus spoke quite naturally of the reign of God as something that was already present, and at the same time as something still to come … God's reign is not a timed intervention, but an ongoing action of the Father which calls for responsible acceptance' (p.118).

And St Paul outlines the idea of the 'mystical body' of Christ in the first letter to the Corinthians: 'Just as a body, though one, has many parts, but all its many parts form one body, so it is with Christ. For we were all baptised by one Spirit so as to form one body – whether Jews or Gentiles, slave or free – and we were all given the one Spirit to drink. Even so the body is not made up of one part but of many … The eye cannot say to the hand, 'I don't need you!' And the head cannot say to the feet, 'I don't need you!' … But God has put the body together, giving greater honour to the parts that lacked it, so that there should be no division in the body, but that its parts should have equal concern for each other. If one part suffers, every part suffers with it; if one part is honoured, every part rejoices with it.'

To end with a quotation from Thomas Merton: 'In Louisville, at the corner of Fourth and Walnut, in the center of the shopping district, I was suddenly overwhelmed with the realization that I loved all those people, that they were mine and I theirs, that we could not be alien to one another even though we were total strangers. It was like waking from a dream of separateness, of spurious self-isolation in a special world, the world of renunciation and supposed holiness … This sense of liberation from an illusory difference was such a relief and such a joy to me that I almost laughed out loud … I have the immense joy of being man, a member of a race in which God Himself became incarnate. As if the sorrows and stupidities of the human condition could overwhelm me, now I realize what we all are. And if only everybody could realize this! But it cannot be explained. There is no way of telling people that they are all walking around shining like the sun' (*Conjectures of a Guilty Bystander*).

APPENDIX

As part of my participation in the Teilhard de Chardin Fellowship in the University of Loyola, Chicago, I met with several students who followed the course on poetry and Christ I offered. Some of them came up with critical responses and I have added them to the talks above. We spent some time discussing ways they might begin to write poems themselves; here I present some of their work in that area.

Teresa Vazquez was born in Chicago, Illinois, to a Mexican family of seven (two wonderful parents and five siblings). She graduated from Loyola University Chicago in May 2017 with a BA in English and a BSc in psychology. Hoping to publish her original work one day, she currently is helping to educate and counsel teenagers from low-income families so they can pursue a college degree.

Return to Vibrancy

The door squeaks open
announcing a presence creeping inside. Whiteness
paints the room into a dull corner
with sun breaking in ever so lightly,
shining on the flowers, violets colouring the space.

A voice whispers into existence,
hoarse and polite, dragging me
into a burning memory
of red chili sauce and a blue figure
sketching us around the dinner table

blessing us with a golden smile of gratitude
gently drawn on her lived-in skin.
The comforting hues of home call out ...
come back to me.

Mackenzie Hanlon was born in Youngstown, Ohio. She is a senior at Loyola University Chicago pursuing degrees in English and art history and studying Italian, Latin and French. She recently interned at Leslic Hindman Auctioneers in the department of books and manuscripts. She plans to continue her studies in art business at the graduate level and work for an international auction house or art advisory firm.

Broken

The rain fell densely, as if the universe knew
what was coming. The weather
foreshadowing the tears that would soon fall silently.

I sat next to my little sister as she smiled
as if it was a tormenting joke.
We clutched our mother's cold, trembling hands.

I watched the last moments of silence
as if they would be my salvation, my saving grace.
Mother told us about our father's

unforeseen heart attack earlier that day.
I silently begged her to stop speaking. If she didn't
say the words, it didn't have to be real.

I could not prevent my heart from learning
what my brain already knew.
Daddy was in heaven now, exactly how she said it.

APPENDIX

And then, something inside of me broke.
No matter how much time passes, no matter how hard I try,
that something will never be fixed.

Angelo Canta is originally from Quezon City, Philippines, and raised in New Jersey; he studied theology at Loyola University Chicago. He will be spending one year in New York City as an O'Hare Postgraduate Fellow with *America Magazine*, and will then continue in further theological studies.

The Path

The path sloped slowly to the Cliffside
where blue-grey boulders that colour the horizon,
worn by time, the storms, the wind, the rain,
beckoned me to sit awhile and pray.

I breathed deeply of the sweet, incensed air
and relished these stolen moments of solitude.
I could be as Christ was in the desert, on the shore,
marvelling at Creation, wandering

Galilean boulders and shorestones,
walking barefoot and alone.
Then, the crackling of dead-orange leaves
under heavy boots

broke into my blue-grey dreaming;
a woman in bright violet sweatsuit
was crossing the path ahead. I saw
only a blur of violet and red as this

surefooted hiker moved towards, then
around me, intent, and purposeful. I stirred
out of reverie to touch the world again,
graced now with presence and intent.

James Egan was born in in Evanston, Illinois in 1994. He recently graduated with a BA in philosophy from Loyola University Chicago, where he is currently pursuing a MA in philosophy. He hopes to continue studies in philosophy and eventually teach in a university.

Sanctuary

You sat in a room
panelled with dark wood;

lanterns hung down from a white ceiling,
there was a fireplace of rough cut beige stones

with a grey slab jutting out.
At a table in the corner

you watched the rain through the window,
watched it pour down the glass and cast

shivering shadows on your table,
you looked out at the winds that shook the trees,

while the storm spattered the mud
where puddles formed.

Remember that within there was only
quiet, stillness and calm

and the gentle light of lanterns
sheltering you from storms.

Jon Nilson (PhD, University of Notre Dame, 1975) is Professor Emeritus of Theology at Loyola University Chicago. He served on the Anglican-Roman Catholic Consultation in the United States from 1984 to 2007 and was President of the Catholic Theological Society of America in 2002–3. Along with numerous articles and reviews, his most recent book is *Hearing Past the Pain. Why White Catholic Theologians Need Black Theology*.

Recall

Here, in the shelter of an upstairs room
a swivel chair of polished steel
and green leather padding
sits heavy by a desk, surrounded
by black wooden shelves,
weighted with books.

Here, all is still; then

Her voice, as she comes up the stairs:
'Ants are running riot all over the basement floor!'

Ant traps – and paint brushes, pliers, a trowel, a rake –
all these and more
come with the room upstairs.

In them, too, is a gravity
and there is grace.

THE OUTLAW CHRIST

I add some further texts that touch on the Cosmic, on the Christic, on our hopes:

Joseph Mary Plunkett, one of the signatories of the Irish Proclamation of Independence, was part of the Easter Rising in Dublin in 1916; he was born in 1887 and was executed on 4 May 1916, in Kilmainham Gaol, in Dublin. His most famous poem, 'I See His Blood' was written in 1915.

I See His Blood

I see his blood upon the rose
And in the stars the glory of his eyes,
His body gleams amid eternal snows,
His tears fall from the skies.

I see his face in every flower;
The thunder and the singing of the birds
Are but his voice and carven by his power
Rocks are his written words.

All pathways by his feet are trod,
His strong heart stirs the ever-beating sea,
His crown of thorns is twined with every thorn,
His cross is every tree.

from Proverbs: 8:22

Yahweh created me when his purpose first unfolded,
before the oldest of his works.
Form everlasting I was firmly set,
from the beginning, before earth came into being.
The deep was not, when I was born,
there were no springs to gush with water.

APPENDIX

Before the mountains were settled,
before the hills, I came to birth;
before he made the earth, the countryside,
or the first grains of the world's dust.
When he fixed the heavens firm, I was there,
when he drew a ring on the surface of the deep,
when he thickened the clouds above,
when he fixed fast the springs of the deep,
when he assigned the sea its boundaries
– and the waters will not invade the shore –
when he laid down the foundations of the earth,
I was by his side, a master craftsman,
delighting him day after day,
ever at play in his presence,
at play everywhere in his world,
delighting to be with the sons of men.

This, from Teilhard de Chardin: *Mass over the World*: 'Glorious Lord Christ ... power as implacable as the world and as warm as life; you whose forehead is of the whiteness of snow, whose eyes are of fire, and whose feet are brighter than molten gold; you whose hands imprison the stars; you who are the first and the last, the living and the dead and the risen again; you who gather into your exuberant unity every beauty, every affinity, every energy, every mode of existence; it is you to whom my being cried out with a desire as vast as the universe, 'In truth you are my Lord and my God'.'

Acts 4: Peter before the rulers: 'This Jesus is "the stone that was rejected by you, the builders; it has become the cornerstone". For in this city, both Herod and Pontius Pilate, with the Gentiles and the peoples of Israel, gathered together against your holy servant Jesus, whom you anointed.'

Matthew: Jesus had to flee to Egypt to escape Herod's slaughtering aims. Chapter 4, verse 12 can be too easily skipped over: 'When Jesus heard that John had been put in prison, he withdrew to Galilee': showing how aware he was of the danger he was in already, being associated with John the Baptist, and beginning to work outside the accepted norms.

Ephesians 1: Praise be to the God and Father of our Lord Jesus Christ, who has blessed us in the heavenly realms with every spiritual blessing in Christ. For he chose us in him before the creation of the world to be holy and blameless in his sight. In love he predestined us for adoption to sonship through Jesus Christ, in accordance with his pleasure and will – to the praise of his glorious grace, which he has freely given us in the One he loves. In him we have redemption through his blood, the forgiveness of sins, in accordance with the riches of God's grace that he lavished on us. With all wisdom and understanding, he made known to us the mystery of his will according to his good pleasure, which he purposed in Christ, to be put into effect when the times reach their fulfilment – to bring unity to all things in heaven and on earth under Christ.

In him we were also chosen, having been predestined according to the plan of him who works out everything in conformity with the purpose of his will, in order that we, who were the first to put our hope in Christ, might be for the praise of his glory. And you also were included in Christ when you heard the message of truth, the gospel of your salvation. When you believed, you were marked in him with a seal, the promised Holy Spirit, who is a deposit guaranteeing our inheritance until the redemption of those who are God's possession – to the praise of his glory.

The Cosmic Christ

Where, then, from here? The concept of the Cosmic Christ is a comparatively new one in the faith journey, and one that is intimately bound up with ecology and the whole belated awareness of our relationship to the planet and to a Christ beyond Christianity.

APPENDIX

We believe that 'the Kingdom of God' is within us; it exists in hiddenness. St Paul, in 1 Corinthians 11:24 ff, writes of Jesus at the 'last supper': 'Until the Lord comes, therefore, every time you eat this bread and drink this cup, you are proclaiming his death, and so anyone who eats the body or drinks the cup of the Lord unworthily will be behaving unworthily towards the body and blood of the Lord'. The death of Christ, then, is a representative death for the salvation of all people. The beginning of the first letter of John is as follows: 'Something which has existed since the beginning, that we have heard, and we have seen with our own eyes; that we have watched and touched with our hands: the Word, who is life – this is our subject. That life was made visible, we saw it and we are giving our testimony, telling you of the eternal life which was with the Father and has been made visible to us. What we have seen and heard we are telling you so that you too may be in union with us, as we are in union with the Father and with his Son Jesus Christ.' Here we touch on the corporeality of salvation in the Incarnation where Christ is all in all.

From this it is an inevitable step to the study of the Eucharistic prayer, the centre and essence of the celebration of the Mass. In *The Sign of Jonas*, Thomas Merton writes of his ordination to the priesthood and his wonder at the celebration of the Mass; 'Now there is much more. Instead of *myself* and *my* Christ and my love and my prayer, there is the might of a prayer stronger than thunder and milder than the flight of doves rising up from the Priest who is the Centre of the soul of every priest, shaking the foundations of the universe and lifting up – me, Host, altar, sanctuary, people, church, abbey, forest, cities, continents, seas, and worlds to God and plunging everything into Him ... The greatest gift that can come to anyone is to share in the infinite act by which God's love is poured out upon all men ... It is at Mass that I am deepest in solitude and at the same time mean most to the rest of the universe.'

The Eucharistic prayer of the Mass, then, is more than this, today's celebration of the death and resurrection of Christ; it is the celebration and the meaning of all of creation, in all time, in all space, and in all eternity. And that is why, after the great doxology: 'Through Him and with Him and in Him, O God, almighty Father, in the unity of the Holy Spirit, all glory and honor is yours, forever and ever', we cry out with faith, joy and hope: Amen! Yes, we cry, Yes, Amen!

As Celia Deane-Drummond says in her book *Eco-Theology*, 'Christ came as an expression of God's love for all of creation … not simply as a way of dealing with human sinfulness.' She quotes Colossians and comments: 'Jesus Christ is the one through whom and for whom the whole creation was made'. Romans 8:18–25: 'I consider that the sufferings of this present time are not worth comparing with the glory about to be revealed to us. For the creation waits with eager longing for the revealing of the children of God; for the creation was subjected to futility, not of its own will but by the will of the one who subjected it, in hope that the creation itself will be set free from its bondage to decay and will obtain the freedom of the glory of the children of God. We know that the whole creation has been groaning in labour pains until now; and not only the creation, but we ourselves, who have the first fruits of the Spirit, groan inwardly while we wait for adoption, the redemption of our bodies.'

Logion 77 of the Gospel of Thomas reads:

> I am the light over all things.
> I am all.
> From me all things have come
> And all things have reached me.
> Split a piece of wood.
> I am there.
> Lift up the stone
> And you will find me there.

It has been of great interest and relevance that Pope Francis brought forward his encyclical *Laudato Si'*; and here are a few phrases from that encyclical, pointing to the force of the arguments for essential ecological awareness in the context of a faith in the Cosmic Christ – speaking of the earth as 'our common home'; 'It is our humble conviction that the divine and the human meet in the slightest detail in the seamless garment of God's creation, in the last speck of dust of our planet' (9). 'The ultimate purpose of other creatures is not to be found in us. Rather, all creatures are moving forward with us and through us towards a common point of arrival, which is God, in that transcendent fullness when the risen Christ embraces and illumines all things' (83), and 'The entire material universe speaks of God's love, his boundless affection for us.' This is the wonderful and hope-giving mystery of the Cosmic Christ: 'In the Christian understanding of the world, the destiny of all creation is bound up with the mystery of Christ, present from the beginning' (99). The encyclical specifically honours the once disregarded work of Teilhard de Chardin, whose writings are now, at last, taking their deserved and vital place in our contemporary thinking and our faith.

Here I offer a poem of Patrick Kavanagh's that, in its way, encapsulates this awareness; it is a poem with a deceptive but wonderfully relevant title:

Miss Universe

> I learned, I learned – when one might be inclined
> To think, too late, you cannot recover your losses –
> I learned something of the nature of God's mind,
> Not the abstract Creator but He who caresses
> The daily and nightly earth; He who refuses
> To take failure for an answer till again and again is worn.
> Love is waiting for you, waiting for the violence that
>   she chooses
> From the tepidity of the common round beyond exhaustion
>   or scorn.
> What was once is still and there is no need for remorse;

> There are no recriminations in Heaven. O the sensual throb
> Of the explosive body, the tumultuous thighs!
> Adown a summer lane comes Miss Universe,
> She whom no lecher's art can rob
> Though she is not the virgin who was wise.

And again, John, Chapter 1: 'In the beginning was the Word, and the Word was with God, and the Word was God. He was with God in the beginning. Through him all things were made; without him nothing was made that has been made. In him was life, and that life was the light of all mankind. The light shines in the darkness, and the darkness has not overcome it.'

Ephesians 1

'Praise be to the God and Father of our Lord Jesus Christ, who has blessed us in the heavenly realms with every spiritual blessing in Christ. For he chose us in him before the creation of the world to be holy and blameless in his sight. In love he predestined us for adoption to sonship through Jesus Christ, in accordance with his pleasure and will – to the praise of his glorious grace, which he has freely given us in the One he loves. In him we have redemption through his blood, the forgiveness of sins, in accordance with the riches of God's grace that he lavished on us. With all wisdom and understanding, he made known to us the mystery of his will according to his good pleasure, which he purposed in Christ, to be put into effect when the times reach their fulfilment – to bring unity to all things in heaven and on earth under Christ.'

Fr Richard Rohr in conversation with Msgr Walter Nolan (to be found on YouTube):

> They mention the 'Christ beyond Christianity', that Jesus existed in time but as Christ He existed for all eternity, the Christ exists as

soon as God decides to come forth, to show himself, the 'big bang'. So the Christ, there for all eternity, appears at a moment in time, in the incarnation. Up to now our focus has been on the historical Jesus, and that's fine, but the Cosmic Christ opens up a much more magnificent and immense sense of the whole of creation. Salvation is not just a concept for humans, it's a global thing. In Genesis each 'day' of creation is actually devoted to creatures other than humans. We see God in everything, the revelation is the presence of God through all creation. We are, then, to build bridges and bonds instead of putting up boundaries. There is 'cosmic allurement', beauty, truth, goodness, to bring us to grow this cosmic unity; this is God seducing us into a more magnificent creation.

The end of it in the letter of Paul to the Philippians, chapter 2:

> Therefore if you have any encouragement from being united with Christ, if any comfort from his love, if any common sharing in the Spirit, if any tenderness and compassion, then make my joy complete by being like-minded, having the same love, being one in spirit and of one mind. Do nothing out of selfish ambition or vain conceit. Rather, in humility value others above yourselves, not looking to your own interests but each of you to the interests of the others. In your relationships with one another, have the same mindset as Christ Jesus:
> Who, being in very nature God, did not consider equality with God something to be used to his own advantage; rather, he made himself nothing by taking the very nature of a servant, being made in human likeness. And being found in appearance as a man, he humbled himself by becoming obedient to death – even death on a cross! Therefore God exalted him to the highest place and gave him the name that is above every name, that at the name of Jesus

every knee should bow, in heaven and on earth and under the earth, and every tongue acknowledge that Jesus Christ is Lord, to the glory of God the Father.

And this, from Teilhard from *La messe sure le monde*:

Glorious Lord Christ ... power as implacable as the world and as warm as life; you whose forehead is of the whiteness of snow, whose eyes are of fire, and whose feet are brighter than molten gold; you whose hands imprison the stars; you who are the first and the last, the living and the dead and the risen again; you who gather into your exuberant unity every beauty, every affinity, every energy, every mode of existence; it is you to whom my being cried out with a desire as vast as the universe, 'In truth you are my Lord and my God'.

SELECT BIBLIOGRAPHY

Armstrong, Karen, *St Paul: The Misunderstood Apostle*. London: Atlantic Books, 2015.

Barron, Robert, *Exploring Catholic Theology*. Ada, MI: Baker Academic, 2015.

Judy Cannato, *Field of Compassion*, Notre Dame, IN: Sorin Books, 2010.

de Chardin, Teilhard. *La messe sur le monde*. Various, published originally in 1923.

Daly, Gabriel. *The Church: Always in Need of Reform*. Dublin: Dominican Publications, 2015.

Daly, Pádraig J. *Nowhere But in Praise*. Dublin: Profile Press, 1978.

– *A Celibate Affair*, Aquila, 1984.

– *The Voice of the Hare*. Dublin: Dedalus Press, 1997.

– *The Other Sea*. Dublin: Dedalus Press, 2003.

– *Clinging to the Myth*. Dublin: Dedalus Press, 2007.

– *God in Winter*. Dublin: Dedalus Press, 2015.

Deane-Drummond, Celia. *Eco-Theology*. London: Darton, Longman & Todd, 2008.

Delio, Ilia. T*he Emergent Christ*, New York, NY: Orbis Books, 2011.

Donne, John. *Selections from Divine Poems, Sermons, Devotions, and prayers*. Mahwah, NJ: Paulist Press, 1990.

Drury, John. *Music at Midnight: The Life and Poetry of George Herbert*. London: Allen Lane, 2013.

Freyne, Seán. *Jesus, a Jewish Galilean*. New York, NY: T&T Clark, 2004.

Harpur, James. *Angels and Harvesters*. London: Anvil Press, 2012.

– *The White Silhouette*. London: Carcanet, 2018.

Heaney, Seamus: *Station Island*. London: Faber & Faber, 1984.

– *Human Chain*. London: Faber & Faber, 2010.

Kasper, Cardinal Walter. *Mercy*. New York, NY: Paulist Press, 2013.

– *Jesus the Christ*. London: Burns & Oates, 1976.

King, Ursula. *Spirit of Fire: The Life and Vision of Teilhard de Chardin*. New York, NY: Orbis Books, 2015.

Mariani, Paul. *Gerard Manley Hopins: A Life*. New York, NY: Viking, 2008.

Merton, Thomas. *New Seeds of Contemplation*. New York, NY: New Directions 1962.

Pagola, José A. *Jesus, an Historical Approximation*. Miami, FL: Convivium Press, 2009.

Poetry Ireland Review, issue no. 112, 2012.

Salmon, James SJ, and Farina, John. *The Legacy of Pierre Teilhard de Chardin*. Mahwah, NJ: Paulist Press, 2011.

Stubbs, John. *Donne, The Reformed Soul*. London: Penguin Books, 2006.

Thomas, R.S. *Selected Poems of George Herbert's Verse*, London: Faber & Faber, 1967.

Weil, Simone. *Gravity and Grace* (tr. Gustave Thibon). London: Routledge, 1987.

Wiman, Christian. *My Bright Abyss: Meditation of a Modern Believer*. New York, NY: FSG, 2013.

Want to keep reading?

Columba Books has a whole range of books to inspire your faith and spirituality.

As the leading independent publisher of religious and theological books in Ireland, we publish across a broad range of areas including pastoral resources, spirituality, theology, the arts and history.

All our books are available through
www.columbabooks.com
and you can find us on Twitter, Facebook and Instagram to discover more of our fantastic range of books. You can sign up to our newletter through the website for the latest news about events, sales and to keep up to date with our new releases.

columbabooks

@ColumbaBooks

columba_books

columba
BOOKS